Effective Motivation Through Performance Appraisal

Effective Motivation Through Performance Appraisal

DIMENSIONAL APPRAISAL STRATEGIES

ROBERT E. LEFTON, PH.D.
V. R. BUZZOTTA, PH.D.
MANUEL SHERBERG
DEAN L. KARRAKER

A WILEY-INTERSCIENCE PUBLICATION

JOHN WILEY & SONS, New York • Chichester • Brisbane • Toronto

Published by John Wiley & Sons, Inc.

Library of Congress Cataloging in Publication Data:

Main entry under title:

Effective motivation through performance appraisal.

"A Wiley-Interscience publication."
Includes index.
1. Employees, Rating of.   2.   Employee motivation.
3. Performance standards.   I.   Lefton, Robert Eugene,
1931-

HF5549.5.R3E35   658.31'25   77-22948
ISBN 0-471-02994-7

Printed in the United States of America

10 9 8 7 6 5 4 3

Acknowledgments

It would be impossible to acknowledge all the people whose work in inter-personal psychology, group dynamics, motivation theory, and psycho-therapy laid the groundwork for the Dimensional Models, just as it would be impossible to mention the many researchers in communication, learning theory, organization development, and systems analysis whose insights were so useful throughout the book. But we must mention Louis Allen, S. E. Asch, Robert F. Bales, Chester Barnard, Alex Bavelas, Warren Bennis, John Dollard, Amitai Etzioni, Leon Festinger, Mason Haire, Frederick Herzberg, Karen Horney, Carl Hovland, Paul Lazarsfeld, Timothy Leary, Harold Leavitt, Rensis Likert, Robert F. Mager, A. H. Maslow, David McClelland, Douglas McGregor, Jacob Moreno, Gardner Murphy, Henry Murray, Peter Pipe, and Muzafer Sherif. Each of them has significantly influenced our thinking.

We gratefully acknowledge our intellectual debt to all those listed above. In addition, it's our pleasure to acknowledge two special debts: one, to Ronald M. Schwartz, Ph.D., Manager of Executive Development of Merrill Lynch, Pierce, Fenner and Smith, who provided both intellectual stimu-lation and sustained encouragement; the other, to Merrill Lynch, Pierce, Fenner and Smith for providing the conducive environment in which many of the ideas in this book took form.

ROBERT E. LEFTON
V. R. BUZZOTTA
MANUEL SHERBERG
DEAN L. KARRAKER

St. Louis, Missouri
June 1977

Contents

Note to the Reader

Two matters relating to the language used in this book should be cleared up at the outset:

1. English, unhappily, is not a neuter language. This creates difficult problems for writers who want to address, and write about, both sexes. Throughout this book, we've tried a number of devices for desexing the prose. We've written many of the sections in the second person, thereby avoiding constant use of "he" and "she" and other masculine and feminine pronouns. We've varied the sex of pronouns in other sections, sometimes talking about "he" and "him," other times about "she" and "her." And we've used examples about both men and women. Nevertheless, if the book still seems male-oriented, that's because of a bias in English usage, not in the authors. We've worked with too many competent managers of both sexes not to have the strongest respect for both women and men in management. We've tried to convey that respect in this book.

2. In earlier drafts of this book we wrestled with the problem of what to call the person who does a performance appraisal and what to call the person who's appraised. We discarded "manager" because, in many cases, both people in an appraisal are managers. We decided against "supervisor" for the same reason. "Appraiser" and "appraisee" were rejected because the eye can too easily confuse one with the other. Finally, we settled upon the usage in this version of the book: "superior" for the person who does the appraising, "subordinate" for the person who's appraised. We think our choice is a good one because it clearly denotes who has the authority in an appraisal—who's boss. We're aware, nevertheless, that some readers may be put off by the word "superior" because it smacks of elitism and exclusiveness. We can only

say that, as we use it, the word does not imply that the superior is in any way "better" than the "subordinate," or that the "subordinate" is in any way "inferior" to the "superior." The word denotes functional authority and responsibility, nothing more.

R.E.L.
V.R.B.
M.S.
D.L.K.

Effective Motivation Through Performance Appraisal

1

Performance Appraisal

WHAT IT'S ALL ABOUT

Appraisal is as old as civilization. The earliest people for whom we have written records, the Sumerians, who flourished in the lush Tigris and Euphrates Valley some 6000 years ago, almost surely did frequent appraisals. Why? Because they needed to know the value of the things they traded: the metals, the hides, the tools—and only skilled appraisers could determine those values. It's unlikely that the Sumerians ever did performance appraisals, but there's no doubt that they did appraisals of the things that mattered most to them: the material objects on which their prosperity depended.

The prosperity of our own society also depends upon material objects, but, even more, it depends upon people. So we've added a whole new category of appraisal to the appraisals done by the Sumerians: *performance* appraisal. And we've extended the whole idea of what appraisal is all about.

When the Sumerians appraised an object, all they wanted to know was how much it was worth. If an axe, for example, was appraised as well made and durable, it had a high exchange value; if it was appraised as poorly made and not likely to last, it had a low exchange value. That's all there was to it. But in appraising *performance* we've added a whole new concept: value can be *increased*. The idea behind performance appraisal is not merely to find out what someone's performance is worth; the idea is to find ways to make it worth more.

Performance appraisals are something fairly new in history, although the reason *why* they're done is as old as the Sumerians. Like them, we do appraisals because our prosperity depends upon what's appraised. In our case, nothing is more vital to continued prosperity than helping people contribute more on the job. In the organizations that make up our complex and fast-changing economy, nothing counts more than what people do at work. Helping them do it better is what performance appraisal is all about.

WHAT THIS BOOK IS ABOUT

This book is about *performance appraisal* and how to do it. Let's begin by defining the key term:

Performance appraisal is (1) a formal discussion between a superior and a subordinate (2) for the purpose of discovering how and why the subordinate is presently performing on the job and (3) how the subordinate can perform more effectively in the future (4) so that the subordinate, the superior, and the organization all benefit.

Let's look closer at each of the four parts of this definition:

1. Performance appraisal is a formal discussion. It's not done on the spur of the moment. It's not a casual get-together. It's planned. It occurs at specified times and follows a prescribed format.

2. One purpose of performance appraisal is to discover how a subordinate is presently doing on the job—and why. We say "discover" because usually neither the superior nor the subordinate has all the answers at the beginning of the appraisal. The answers have to be searched for. As we'll see, the search is often long and hard.

3. The appraisal not only looks at the recent past (how has the subordinate been doing on the job, and why?) and the present (how is he doing on the job, and why?) but also at the near future (how can he do better?). Thus, it offers both a diagnosis (how effective is performance, and why?) and a prescription (how can it be made more effective?).

4. The final purpose of performance appraisal is to produce benefit for the subordinate and the superior and the organization. What kind of benefit? That depends on the subordinate, the superior, and the organization. For some *subordinates,* an appraisal may lead to more money, or a promotion, or greater job satisfaction; for others, it may simply help them hold on to their jobs. For some *superiors,* an appraisal may help increase out-

put, or cut down on problems, or develop a managerial record that leads to promotion. For some *organizations,* an appraisal may help to increase sales or production or growth; for others, it may reduce demoralization or sabotage. There's no one definition of "benefit," but every appraisal should produce clearcut benefits for all three: the subordinate, the superior, and the organization.

How Appraisal Pays Off

There's no one definition of benefit, but all the benefits of performance appraisal have one thing in common: they're dynamic. *Dynamic* means *producing continuous advances,* and that's exactly what effective appraisal does: it produces continuous advances, progress, forward movement, both for the organization and its people. The final purpose of performance appraisal is to develop people who are steadily growing, enlarging their skills, learning new and better ways to do things. An organization in which effective performance appraisal is the rule rarely stands still or moves backward because effective appraisal develops people who move forward, and forward-moving people make forward-moving organizations.

Something Must Be Wrong

Effective appraisal is dynamic; it produces continuous advances. But, in the real world, unhappily, performance appraisal is seldom dynamic. Consider these facts:

- Subordinates frequently say: "I don't know where I stand around here. Sure, we have performance appraisals, but they never tell you anything you don't already know. Even after an appraisal, I still have to guess at what the score is."
- In some organizations, subordinates complain: "We don't have performance appraisals. Oh, sure, when I do something wrong I hear about it. But I never get an overall picture of how I'm doing." Or: "There's no such thing as performance appraisal around here. Once in a while, I get a pat on the back from the boss, but that's all." Or: "I don't hear much from the boss, good or bad. He just leaves me alone. Performance appraisal? Never heard of it."
- Some organizations spend lots of money developing elaborate performance appraisal forms—long, detailed documents designed to help superiors do effective appraisals. Yet, even in these organizations, the cry is often heard: "We don't know where we stand."

Something must be wrong. Effective, dynamic performance appraisal is the exception, not the rule. In many organizations, performance appraisal is nonexistent, random, or useless. Why? There are at least three reasons:

1. Effective performance appraisal involves *confrontation*. It requires facing up to disagreement and conflict. Many superiors have trouble managing confrontation. Others don't even try to manage it; they simply squelch any views that differ from their own. Many subordinates also have trouble confronting harsh facts in an appraisal; they prefer not to learn how competent or incompetent they are. The appraisal may make them feel threatened, embarrassed, angry, tense, resentful, hurt—and they may *manifest* these feelings. They may argue, disagree, plead, shout, sneer, withdraw, sulk, or belittle what the superior says. They may even launch a verbal attack on the boss ("If I'm doing a lousy job, it's all your fault . . . you never explain anything so I can understand it . . . you're never around to help out when I need you . . ."). Performance appraisals can be heavy going; they're often unnerving, or at least unsettling. Many superiors feel that they're just not up to this kind of thing.

2. Effective performance appraisal *takes time*—lots of it. It cannot be done in 10 or 15 minutes; first-rate appraisals frequently last several hours. Many superiors simply aren't willing to spend that much time, so they don't do performance appraisal, or they do "quickie" versions—slapdash appraisals that may do more harm than good.

3. Effective performance appraisal requires *skills*—plenty of them. We won't list these skills here, since they're the subject of the rest of the book. But we will say that effective appraisers are *made,* not born; they're effective because they've *learned* how to be. Many superiors admit that they don't do performance appraisal because they don't know how. They're probably right. All too many appraisals are messed up by "appraisers" who know little or nothing about appraising.

WHAT IS PERFORMANCE?

As we use the word, *performance* is two things: (1) it's the *results* that people get on the job, and (2) it's whatever they *do* that affects those results. Performance is the outcome of actions on the job and it's also the actions that produce that outcome. Put another way, performance is the effects that people get on the job, and it's also the things they do that cause those effects. Performance involves inputs (the actions people put into the job) and outputs (the consequences of those actions). Some examples follow:

The manager of an oil refinery is almost completely shut away from his staff. As one engineer puts it, "It's downright spooky. I don't see the man more than a few minutes every week. He sits behind a closed door all day and doesn't see anybody. If you ask his secretary for an appointment, she tells you he's busy and you'll have to come back. The worst of it is you can't get anything done around here because you can't get the boss to make a decision. This place just runs itself." Lately, however, the place hasn't been "running itself" very effectively. Several people have been seriously hurt in work-related accidents; a committee of industrial engineers has presented some ideas to the refinery manager for preventing further accidents, but the manager hasn't responded. Now, exasperated by the delay, a number of people in the plant are talking about filing a complaint with a federal agency. That's *performance.*

The vice-president in charge of creative services at an advertising agency has hired three copywriters in the past year. Each of them quit after several months because the v.p. persistently belittled their writing skills ("You call this jargon advertising copy? Why, this stuff wouldn't sell drinking fountains in the Sahara") and rewrote all their copy ("When you've been around here as long as I have, then maybe you'll get to do it your way. Till then, you're going to do it my way"). A fourth copywriter is about to quit for the same reasons. That's *performance.*

The director of marketing for a manufacturer of men's clothing drinks heavily each evening, and comes to work each morning with a hangover. He spends the first two or three hours of each day at the office "getting in shape" (drinking coffee, taking aspirin, reading the newspaper). If the phone rings during this period, he instructs his secretary to "tell them I'm in a meeting." He doesn't really start *work* until after lunch. As a result, several major marketing projects have been delayed recently, and the general sales manager is complaining that "those people over in marketing have dropped the ball." That's *performance.*

These examples illustrate four points:

1. Performance is always tied to *results*—the on-the-job outcome of what people do.
2. Performance is also tied to *behavior*—the things people do that produce the results.
3. Behavior can be either *active* or *passive*—do-something (as in our second and third examples) or do-nothing (as in our first example). Either way, it can affect job results.

4.   Most of the behavior discussed in a performance appraisal will be *on*-the-job behavior. But not necessarily all. *Off*-the-job behavior (as in our third example) belongs in the appraisal if—and only if—it affects the results obtained *on* the job.

WHAT PERFORMANCE IS NOT

People do lots of things on the job that don't affect results. And people display many characteristics on the job that don't influence the outcome. *None* of these things comes under the heading of *performance*. The key question is always: What *difference* does it make? If someone does something on the job that makes no difference in results, then that behavior shouldn't be discussed in a performance appraisal.

Let's look at two situations, and then ask: "What difference do they make?"

Susan Cummings is head furniture buyer for a large department store. She's considered one of the most knowledgeable "furniture people" in the country. As a buyer for a competing store says: "Susan's a real pro. She's got a sure instinct for what to buy and how much. She rarely makes a bad buying decision." Susan has decorated the wall of her office with prints of modern paintings, all very abstract, "far-out" works that she's collected over the years. These prints annoy the vice-president in charge of merchandising, for whom she works. "A department store is a business," he says, "and I think a business should have a businesslike image. Those kookie modern prints may be okay on a living room wall, but they don't belong in a business setting. I'd much rather see Susan decorate her office with some solid, traditional stuff . . . some good representational pictures that wouldn't offend anybody. These abstract things don't belong in a business office."

Jeff Stone is Assistant Director of Research for a middle-sized manufacturer of chemicals. He does most of his work alone, isolated from other people in the company as he pores over research reports, plans research projects, and evaluates the work done by other chemists in the company. He's considered one of the best "brains" in the industry; as one competitor puts it: "That guy can sniff a new development five years before it actually happens. I'd hire him in a minute if I could get him." Jeff has one characteristic, however, that exasperates his boss: he's a sloppy, disheveled dresser. He wears creaseless, baggy pants, frayed shirts, and, quite often, tennis shoes. Worst of all, from the boss's point of view, Jeff rarely bothers to tuck in his shirttail. "The guy's a mess," complains the supervisor, "and I can't get him to change. Every time I talk to him about his appearance, he promises to improve, but he never does. It's disgraceful for a man in his position to look like that."

Let's examine these examples:

· What difference do Susan Cummings' paintings make when it comes to results? Probably none. There's no evidence that her office decorations affect her work. Therefore, they should *not* be a topic in her performance appraisal, even though they annoy her boss.
· What difference does Jeff Stone's attire make when it comes to results? Absolutely none. Since he works isolated from others, his unkempt appearance doesn't affect his work. Therefore, it should *not* be a topic in his performance appraisal, even though it bothers his boss.

The best general rule is this: restrict performance appraisal to behavior that *matters*. Trivial, inconsequential behavior—chewing gum while working on balance sheets, wearing a bow tie to work each day, whistling in the halls, etcetera—doesn't belong in a performance appraisal.

PERFORMANCE APPRAISAL AND OTHER KINDS OF FEEDBACK TO SUBORDINATES

Performance appraisal is only one way to let subordinates know how they're doing on the job. In fact, there are at least three ways in which superiors can keep people posted on their progress. We can range these on a continuum as shown in Figure 1.

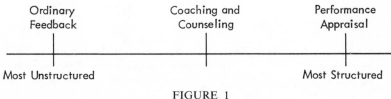

FIGURE 1

1. *Ordinary feedback.*

This is the day-in, day-out commentary that every superior offers his subordinates. Ordinary feedback ranges from the briefest comments ("Good job," "Keep it up," "Nice going," "I'm proud of you") to slightly more detailed evaluations ("You're working too fast; slow down or you're going to mess things up," "If you keep on talking to people that way, you're going to have trouble on your hands," "That was a pretty good sales meeting, but I think it ran too long; I noticed the guys getting fidgety at the end"). Two things should be noted: (a) ordinary feedback *is* developmental, even though it may not seem so; most subordinates take these comments seriously and many base future action on them; (b) ordinary feedback is usually pretty casual; many of the comments are unplanned or spontaneous.

2. *Coaching and counseling.*

The "curbstone conference" between a sales manager and a salesperson is a good example of coaching and counseling. In a typical curbstone conference, the sales manager and the salesperson analyze a sales call *immediately after the manager observes it.* The surroundings may be informal (the salesperson's automobile, a customer's reception area), but the discussion itself (if it's done right) is fairly structured. The manager has a number of points that he wants to cover (how effectively did the salesperson open the presentation? how effectively did he present his product? and so forth) and he covers them in an orderly, systematic way. The typical discussion may last 5 to 15 minutes, depending upon circumstances and the amount of ground to be covered. The purpose is always the same: to analyze the sales call, to determine why it turned out as it did, and to determine what should be done differently on future calls. A curbstone conference (and all coaching and counseling) is a systematic analysis of how a task was performed, so that similar tasks can be performed more effectively in the future. (Our example is from sales, but any superior in any field should do periodic coaching and counseling.)

3. *Performance appraisal.*

An appraisal differs from ordinary feedback and coaching and counseling in five important ways: (a) More preparation goes into performance appraisal. Both superior and subordinate should gather and analyze plenty of data before the appraisal. (b) Performance appraisal covers a lot more ground; it focuses on a subordinate's *whole* performance for a period of several months. Ordinary feedback and coaching and counseling, on the other hand, zero in on one specific task. (This doesn't mean that the superior *never* refers to other parts of the subordinate's performance, but the main concern is with one observed task. Performance appraisal is much more inclusive.) (c) As a rule, performance appraisal takes longer, since it covers more ground. (d) Performance appraisal usually takes place in the superior's office; coaching and counseling and ordinary feedback usually take place wherever the superior and subordinate happen to be.

(e) Performance appraisal is the most structured of the three methods. It follows a carefully organized format.

PERFORMANCE APPRAISAL, MANAGEMENT BY OBJECTIVES, CAREER COUNSELING, AND COMPENSATION REVIEW

Performance appraisal is often lumped together with management by objectives, career counseling, and compensation review. These are, however, separate activities. Let's look at the differences among them.

1.   This book is about performance appraisal. Performance appraisal focuses on the recent past and the relatively near future. It asks: How has this subordinate performed in the past several months (since his last performance appraisal)? Why? What does this tell us about how he ought to perform in the next several months (until his next performance appraisal)? The time between appraisals usually varies from six months to a year.

2.   This book is *not* about the formal system called "management by objectives" (MBO). Different people define "management by objectives" differently, but a definition that comes pretty close to covering most others is this: Management by objectives is a system for achieving organizational objectives by assigning specific, measurable, interlocking goals to specific individuals in the organization. Thus, MBO is a formal system for making sure that an organization gets steered in the direction it's supposed to go.

Superficially, it might seem that the managers of every organization try to steer it in the direction of its objectives. But, in fact, in many organizations many managers aren't even sure what the objectives are, nor is there any system for steering toward those objectives.

What distinguishes a formal MBO program is that (1) every manager in the organization knows precisely what the organization's objectives are, what his own objectives are, and how the two sets of objectives fit together, and (2) there's a carefully thought-out, precisely articulated system that all managers follow to achieve the objectives. In other words, an organization with an MBO program is like a ship on which every officer knows which port the ship is supposed to reach, and manages one operation that's part of a system for reaching that port. If the ship runs into trouble, responsibility can be quickly pinpointed, and steps can be quickly taken to correct the matter and get back on course because (a) there's no confusion about where the ship should be headed, and (b) there's a method of getting there. All of this sounds pretty fundamental, and most managers pay lip service to the idea, but remarkably few organizations have thoroughgoing MBO programs. Maybe the trouble is that the concept sounds so simple that many managers don't take it seriously enough to do much about it.

In organizations that do have formal MBO programs the goals set for each individual through MBO are among the goals discussed in performance appraisal. But MBO is not performance appraisal. MBO is a much broader, more inclusive system. It sets interlocking goals at every level of the organization; performance appraisal concentrates on the goals and achievements of single individuals. In organizations with MBO programs, the performance appraisal system is (or should be) part of the larger system, but organizations without formal MBO programs can still operate effective performance appraisal systems. Performance appraisal is a way of finding out if each person in the organization has reached his own goals (which should tie in with the organization's) and what he should do to reach his new goals (which should also tie in with the organization's).

Maybe we can make the distinction between MBO and performance appraisal clearer by going back to our ship analogy. Suppose a ship is scheduled to sail from New York City to a port in Madagascar. Before it embarks, the captain summons his officers and tells them their destination, their route, their schedule, and what each of them must do to make sure the ship reaches Madagascar on time. In effect, the ship has an MBO program: a formal system for steering in the direction of its goal. Now, suppose that on the second day out, as the ship, on schedule, steams toward the South Atlantic, the captain checks with the engineering officer to find out how things are going. The captain learns that one engine is malfunctioning. He and the officer discuss what to do; they decide to cut all engines in order to repair the defective engine, and they agree on what action must be taken tomorrow to make up for the time lost in repairs. This discussion is the equivalent of a performance appraisal. It "fits" into the "MBO program" by checking out one part of the system that must be followed if the ship is to reach port on schedule. Performance appraisal is always concerned with the performance of one person; MBO is concerned with all aspects of an organization-wide system.

3. This book is *not* about career counseling. Career counseling is done from a longer perspective. It focuses on career goals, on long-range individual objectives. It asks questions like: What are this subordinate's long-term ambitions? What does she want out of her working life? Does her potential match her ambition? If not, how can she be guided toward more realistic aspirations? How can she best utilize her potential so as to achieve her ambition?

Not all organizations do career counseling for all employees. Policies vary. Some counsel all employees above a certain level. Others counsel only those designated as "fast track." Still others don't do it at all, at least not formally.

Career counseling and performance appraisal are, of course, related. Career counseling deals with long-range goals; the surest way to reach these is by achieving a series of *intermediate* job goals. These intermediate goals, steps along the way to the ultimate goal, are the subject of performance appraisal. Each successive appraisal is a paving stone in the road to a subordinate's final career goal. But the two sets of goals shouldn't be confused. The objectives of career counseling are separate from the objectives of performance appraisal.

4.   This book is *not* about compensation review. Compensation review deals with one question: Is this subordinate going to stay at his present income or is he going to get more money (or fringe benefits)?

What happens in a compensation review depends partly upon the subordinate's job performance. But only partly. Obviously, someone whose performance has been "lousy" is unlikely to get a salary increase. But performance is rarely the *only* consideration. Other factors affect compensation; for instance, the financial condition of the organization, salary-range policies, the availability of other people to do the same job, what other organizations in the same area are paying for the same position, the wages paid by competitors, the condition of the economy, and so on. This book does not deal with this subject.

Performance appraisal, management by objectives, career counseling, and compensation review are separate activities, each with its own purposes and methods (even though some organizations may lump appraisal, objective setting, compensation review, and career counseling together in one session). Still and all, while separate, the four activities *are* related. Let's see how:

1.   Ideally, individual performance should not be appraised in a vacuum. A person's performance should be measured against his goals, and his goals should fit into the overall aims and purposes of the organization. Ideally, then, an individual's performance should be appraised within a context provided by an MBO program. After all, the fact that everyone in an organization is performing effectively and achieving his goals doesn't mean very much unless all the separate goals lead in one direction. In the last analysis, the really significant question is not "Are the individual's job goals being met?" but "Are the organization's goals being met?" However, a *yes* answer to the second question requires a *yes* answer to the first. The only reasonably sure way to get *yes* answers to both is to have a sound MBO program *and* a sound performance appraisal system.

2.   Ideally, career counseling and compensation review should *flow out of* performance appraisal. The data for deciding whether someone qualifies for promotion or deserves more money should come from that person's performance appraisal. So appraisal ought to *precede* career counseling and compensation review.

3.   The skills needed to do effective appraisal are also needed to do effective career counseling. *Both* activities should be a dialogue, a give-and-take, between superior and subordinate. In most organizations, however, when it comes to compensation review, monologue replaces dialogue. For various reasons (company policy, precedent, etc.), the amount of the subordinate's compensation is often decided ahead of time. The superior can *tell* the subordinate what his new compensation will be, but the decision is rarely negotiable. Even so, it's important to explain the reasons for the decision, and to give the subordinate a chance to voice his feelings about it.

4.   Practices vary, but it's probably accurate to say that *ideally* performance appraisal, career counseling, compensation review, and the setting of MBO goals should be done at *separate* times. There are two good reasons for this: (a) it's hard for people to absorb too much at one time, and a discussion of all four matters is probably "too much"; (b) if the subordinate knows that performance *and* compensation are going to be discussed, she's likely to be more defensive and less candid about her performance than she should be.

"HOW TO" VERSUS "WHAT"

This is a how-to book. It tells how to do effective performance appraisal. It is not concerned with "what" the appraisal is *about*. Our focus is on process, not content, on the way the various topics in the appraisal are handled, not on the topics themselves. The "what" will differ from job to job and organization to organization. Many organizations have their own appraisal systems that prescribe what should be discussed in an appraisal. Our recommendations do not conflict with these prescriptions. In fact, our recommendations, if carried out, will help insure that the prescribed topics are handled effectively.

In a sense, this book is like a manual on safe driving. Safe-driving manuals help drivers drive without getting into trouble, *no matter what they're driving:* the same safe-driving guidelines apply to drivers of private automobiles, taxis, trucks, small cars, big cars, limousines, and so on. This book is designed to help you do appraisal without getting into trouble, *no matter what content or system your organization prescribes.* The same appraisal guidelines apply to appraisers of line people, staff people, production people, administrative people, sales people, and on and on. They apply whether the topic is marketing, manufacturing, accounting, researching, or any other kind of performance. The "what" may change; the "how to" stays the same.

SUMMARY

Let's recap this chapter:

1.   Performance appraisal can be defined by four characteristics: (a) it's formal; (b) it tries to discover how a subordinate is doing on the job, and why; (c) it tries to determine how the subordinate can do better in the future; (d) it tries to produce benefit for the subordinate, the superior, and the organization.

2.   Performance appraisal is *effective* when it's dynamic: when it produces continuous improvements. When it's done right, performance appraisal leads to better work.

3.   Effective performance appraisal is rare in many organizations, for at least three reasons: (a) it usually involves confrontation, something many superiors prefer to avoid; (b) it takes more time than many superiors are willing to give; (c) it requires skills that many superiors lack.

4.   *Performance* is what people do on the job that affects results, and it's also the results themselves. On-the-job behavior that has no effect on results should not be the subject of a performance appraisal.

5.   Performance appraisal is only one way to let subordinates know how they're doing on the job. Others are ordinary feedback and coaching and counseling, both of which are less structured than performance appraisal—and both of which are concerned with only part of performance, while appraisal is concerned with overall performance.

6.   While related to one another, performance appraisal, management by objectives, career counseling, and compensation review are different activities. MBO is a formal system by which all of an organization's managers help steer it in the direction of its goals. Performance appraisal zeros in on an individual's accomplishments in the recent past and on how he can do better in the near future. Career counseling focuses on long-range individual objectives. Compensation review focuses on individual salary and fringe benefits. Ideally, each should be done separately.

7.   This book is about how to do effective appraisal. Its guidelines will work in any organization and with any kind of content.

A LOOK AHEAD

By now, you're probably thinking: "Okay . . . enough of the preliminaries. Let's get down to cases. Tell me how to do better performance appraisal."

Unfortunately, we're not quite ready for that. If we were to get into the "how-to" part of this book immediately, you'd have every right to ask: "What justifies *this* system? What makes these guidelines so special? Why wouldn't some other guidelines . . . guidelines that require less time and effort . . . work just as well? Why should I take all this stuff on faith?"

You shouldn't, and we won't ask you to. Instead, before we explain "how-to," we're going to explain "why." We're going to justify our recommendations by describing what's likely to happen if they're not followed. Before we can expect you to buy our guidelines, we have to demonstrate that they'll deliver more benefit to you than other guidelines. To do that, we have to let you compare the various ways in which performance appraisal is usually done, so that you can see the pluses and minuses of each. Only then, when the various methods are stacked up against one another, will *our* system justify itself.

So, in the next three chapters, we're going to look at the following:

1. *The four basic ways of managing people.*

It's important to understand these because your basic, everyday way of managing has strong impact on how you come across in performance appraisal.

2. *The four basic ways of appraising performance.*

It's important to understand these because, as we'll see, each way produces different results, and one of the four ways is more likely to produce *top* results.

3. *How you appraise performance.*

We'll try to give you some insight into the way you do appraisals, so you can begin to see whether you're using the optimal approach or some other, less effective approach. If you're using one of the less effective approaches, then the guidelines we'll recommend will mean all the more to you.

4. *How subordinates react in appraisals.*

It's important to understand what happens on the other side of the desk, if you want to understand why you encounter problems in appraisal. Once you understand that, our guidelines for overcoming those problems will make sense to you.

Let's get started.

2

Four Ways of Managing

We closed our last chapter by saying that what a superior does day-by-day has a strong impact upon what happens when he does performance appraisal. A couple of examples will clarify this.

Imagine a superior who treats his people like puppets, insists that they do things his way, and rarely shows any regard for what they think. Naturally, some of his subordinates feel resentful, spiteful, and antagonistic. These feelings don't disappear when they get their performance appraised. No matter what the superior does during the appraisal, the results he gets are conditioned by the animosity he's generated day-by-day. Even if his appraisal skills are "textbook" models (which is unlikely), he can't *undo* months or years of mishandling his people. Performance appraisal doesn't happen in a vacuum; it happens in a context of existing attitudes.

Imagine a superior who's generally remote from her subordinates, a hard-to-talk-to "loner" who steers clear of everybody. Her chilly behavior convinces her people that she's indifferent to them. If, during an appraisal, she were to try to demonstrate concern and interest, her behavior would ring false. Her subordinates' reactions would range from "She's a phony" to "I'd better watch out . . . something's fishy around here."

The fact is this: your subordinates *anticipate* how you're going to act in a performance appraisal; their anticipations are based on their experience, on their daily encounters with you. These anticipations influence *their* behavior during the appraisal. You can't wave these anticipations away. The only way to change them is by changing your *everyday* behavior.

Before we look at the details of performance appraisal, then, we'd better look at the daily behavior of superiors. Once we do, our prescriptions will make more sense.

THE DIMENSIONAL MODEL OF MANAGERIAL BEHAVIOR*

One good way to look at the behavior of superiors is by using *dimensions* that "measure" how much *dominance* or *submission* and how much *hostility* or *warmth* a superior displays on the job.

Let's define the four italicized words:

Dominance. Dominance means *exercising control,* taking charge and being in charge. Dominant behavior guides and leads. It tries to get on top of situations, to master them, to control them.

Submission. Submission means *following the lead of others,* acquiescing, going along. Submissive behavior looks to others for guidance. It assents to direction from other people.

Hostility. Hostility means a *lack of regard for others and a cautious, skeptical approach to them.* Hostile behavior shows little sensitivity or responsiveness to the ideas, needs, and feelings of others. It also exhibits doubt about their motives and abilities; it is wary and sometimes distrustful.

Warmth. Warmth means *regard for others and a basic trust in them.* Warm behavior is sensitive and responsive to other people's feelings, needs, ideas. It approaches people openly and with confidence.

These dimensions can be pictured as two lines:

Dominance ————————————— Submission

Hostility ————————————— Warmth

* A much fuller treatment of the Dimensional Model can be found in the authors' *Dimensional Management Strategies* (Psychological Associates, St. Louis: 1970).

In picturing the dimensions as lines, it's important to stress three points:

1. *Neither line has specific endpoints.*

We can't really talk about behavior in terms of "the ultimate" or "the most." If we were able to speak of "ultimate" hostility, for instance, as a specific degree of hostility (as we can speak of the freezing point of water as a specific degree of temperature), we could then represent that degree of behavior as an endpoint on the line. Or, if we were able to pinpoint "ultimate" warmth (as we can pinpoint the boiling point of water), we could plot that point as the other end of the line. But we can't quantify behavior in this way. We can't identify the "most" extreme degree of dominance, say, or the "maximum" degree of submission. So, even though the lines drawn above do have ends, the dimensions are really *open*-ended.

2. *The more extreme someone's behavior is, the farther from the middle of the line that behavior should be pictured.*

Exceedingly hostile behavior should be depicted quite distant from the middle of the dimension, *slightly* hostile behavior should be plotted much closer to the center, and so on. A few possibilities are shown in Figure 2.

3. *Don't be misled by the idea of "graphing" behavior.*

Depicting behavior on a line is useful, but it doesn't mean behavior can always be described by a single point. As behavior shifts in intensity, it can only be plotted by a series of points. These points are often in the same part of the line, but not always. Even when we use a point to describe be-

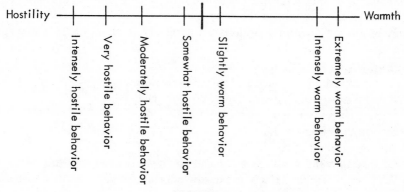

FIGURE 2

havior at a given moment, the point is only a general indicator of behavior; it cannot be a precise description. Behavior is far too complex to be reduced to a point on a line.

We can use our two dimensions to describe four basic kinds—or strategies—of superior behavior. This doesn't mean that all superiors behave in four and only four ways. Not by a long shot. There are as many distinctive superior behaviors as there are superiors; no two are identical. But these behaviors can be grouped according to their most significant common characteristics (dominance, submission, hostility, warmth).

Let's describe—"caricature" might be a better word—these four basic ways of managing people. To do this, we've drawn a chart, Figure 3—or *quadrant model*—that will help us keep our eyes on *both* dimensions (dominance-submission and hostility-warmth) at the same time. In studying the chart, keep in mind that all of us *actually* display all four patterns of behavior at varying times.

Let's look closer at these four alternative ways to manage people. From now on, we'll call the four quadrants Q1, Q2, Q3, and Q4.

Q1 (Dominant-Hostile) Management

This is keep-them-running-scared management (or keep-them-in-line management). When a superior chooses this alternative, he makes decisions by himself; delegates as little as he can; exercises tight, demanding control; maintains close supervision; uses one-way (I tell-you do) communication; and motivates by threat, coercion, fear. This approach typically produces negative commitment (resentment, sullenness), discourages creativity, stimulates high turnover, stifles personal growth, suppresses disagreement, and generates fear and tension. The end-result is *high* output in the *short* run, but only *average* output in the *long* run.

Here are some common notions that typically go along with Q1 management:

- Give people half a chance and they'll mess things up.
- If you want something done right, do it yourself.
- When I want your opinion, I'll ask for it.
- Leave the thinking to me.
- Do it my way or else.
- Do this right and you'll get a reward: you'll get to keep your job.
- What matters is results, no matter how you get them.
- Nice guys don't win ball games.

Dominance

Quadrant 1

Basic attitude. People work best when they're somewhat scared. If you want results, make your people feel insecure, build on their fears, and keep them moving.

Control. Very tight. Exerts close supervision.

Involvement. Discourages ideas from subordinates. Convinced that they rarely have any worthwhile suggestions.

Decisions. Makes decisions alone. Expects subordinates to carry them out without questioning.

Conflict. Suppresses dissent. Insists on own position and views.

Quadrant 4

Basic attitude. People work best when they see how their work can help them achieve their own goals. They're most likely to get good results when they're actively and intelligently involved in their jobs.

Control. When possible, exerts control by generating understanding of, and commitment to, job goals.

Involvement. Encourages independent thinking; believes subordinates can be a source of innovation and improvement.

Decisions. Bases decisions, when possible and advisable, on candid exchange of views with subordinates.

Conflict. Faces up to conflict, and seeks its reasons before resolving it.

Hostility ———————————————————————— Warmth

Quadrant 2

Basic attitude. People are lackadaisical about work. Not much can be done to motivate them; they'll work when they want to.

Control. Keeps people in line by reminding them of what *his* boss expects ("The man upstairs won't like it if you . . .").

Involvement. Minimal. Doesn't seek out or encourage suggestions from subordinates.

Decisions. Waits to see what the boss wants, then makes decision on that basis.

Conflict. Ignores dissent, hoping it will go away in time.

Quadrant 3

Basic attitude. People work best in a cheerful, harmonious environment. If you want results, make sure your subordinates are happy.

Control. Expects hard, loyal work to follow automatically if people have good personal relationships with the boss.

Involvement. Encourages suggestions. Tries to follow through on popular ones and avoids those that are unpopular.

Decisions. Tries to make decisions that subordinates will accept readily and be happy with.

Conflict. Settles disagreements by compromise and appeasement.

Submission

FIGURE 3. The Dimensional Model of Superior Behavior.

Q2 (Submissive-Hostile) Management

This is don't-rock-the-boat management (or why-bother? management). When a superior selects this option, she serves as a pipeline for decisions made by people above her; stays in control by "borrowing" clout from her boss and using it to insure that her subordinates don't make waves; either delegates too little or too much; provides little direction; procrastinates; uses no-way communication ("Don't bug me and I won't bug you"); and makes little or no effort to motivate. This approach typically generates very little commitment or creativity, keeps turnover low, produces haphazard personal growth, ignores disagreement, and generates apathy, passivity, and a "who cares?" attitude. The end-result is *mediocre* output.

Here are some characteristic Q2 notions:

- Let's do it the way we've always done it.
- Managers who get good results are just lucky.
- Don't rock the boat.
- Why take a chance?
- Keep a low profile.
- I don't want to be a hero. I just want to hold on to what I've got.
- Play it safe.
- If you wait a while, things usually take care of themselves.
- Let's wait and see what everybody else does.

Q3 (Submissive-Warm) Management

This is let's-be-pals management (or take-it-easy-on-them management). The superior who adopts this alternative sets vague, easily achievable goals; delegates in a loose, unpredictable way; maintains loose, undemanding controls; provides little real direction (but much conversation); makes "popular" decisions; uses partial communication (focuses on the silver lining but ignores the cloud); and motivates by sociability and affection. This approach typically produces high social morale, but not much commitment to business goals; moderate creativity (new ideas are approved but not followed through); low turnover; haphazard growth; compromises; and an easygoing, unbusinesslike climate. The end-result is *mediocre* output.

Here are some typical Q3 notions:

- This department is just one big, happy family.
- I don't think of myself as the boss. I'm just another one of the gang.
- Nice guys win ball games.
- I try to be a pal to my people.
- Always look at the bright side. Why dwell on problems?
- What really matters is positive thinking.

- My door is always open.
- High morale is 90% of the ball game.
- A pat on the back goes a long way.

Q4 (Dominant-Warm) Management

This is get-the-best-out-of-them management (or let's-produce-maximum-benefit-for-everybody-involved management). The superior who chooses this option gets his people strategically involved in decisions; delegates in a planned, purposeful way; ties subordinate needs to company goals; encourages analysis and critique of what's going on; practices two-way communication (candid and complete disclosure from both directions); and motivates through involvement, understanding, and commitment. This approach typically produces positive commitment (a willingness to stretch), high creativity, low-to-average turnover, optimal growth, resolution of disagreements, and an open, involved, task-oriented climate. The end-result is *consistently high* output.

Here are a few ideas usually associated with Q4 management:

- I don't manage people, I manage individuals.
- Any manager who thinks he can do it all on his own is kidding himself.
- Don't turn your back on disagreements, welcome them. Differences generate ideas.
- I want to hear what *you* think.
- Don't be afraid to make a mistake. But learn from it so you don't repeat it.
- You can't expect a guy to do his best if he doesn't understand what's in it for him.
- I have some ideas about what should be done, but I want to hear yours.
- I don't have all the answers.

Shifts in Behavior

As we said a few pages back, superiors in the real world display all four patterns of behavior at varying times. To see why, we have to distinguish between *primary* strategies, *secondary* strategies, and *mask* strategies.

1. *Primary strategy.*

Most superiors lean more toward one of the quadrants of behavior than the other three. The one you lean toward is the one that seems most "natural" or "comfortable," the one you've learned to use over the years. This habitual behavior, the on-the-job behavior that you use most consistently, is your *primary strategy.*

2. *Secondary strategy.*

Superiors may, without thinking, automatically shift to secondary strategies when frustrated. When your primary behavior fails to produce the result you want, you may become frustrated. *Frustration* is the dissatisfaction you feel when you're thwarted—blocked from achieving a goal. To overcome this dissatisfaction, you try to surmount the obstacle. This may cause a shift in your behavior. Much like a knee-jerk reflex, this shift will be automatic and unintentional. These unplanned, unconscious responses to frustration are called *secondary strategies*. Unlike primary strategies, secondary strategies are usually short-lived.

Most secondary strategies are either Q1 (attack behavior) or Q2 (withdrawal behavior). As a rule, when we respond reflexively to frustration, we either lash out (Q1) or retreat (Q2).

3. *Mask strategies.*

Superiors may deliberately shift to mask strategies. A *mask strategy* is a premeditated response to external pressures. When you "don a mask," you make an intentional effort to disguise or hide your primary behavior.

A superior who's using Q1 behavior, for instance, may find that a subordinate is so intimidated by her threats that he's virtually unable to talk; to overcome this, she may put on a Q3 mask ("I'm a pleasant, easygoing person; you don't have to be afraid of me"). A mask strategy, like a secondary strategy, is temporary; once the mask has served its purpose, the superior reverts to her primary strategy.

Mask strategies are most likely to be Q3 (genial behavior) or Q4 (reasonable behavior). The idea is that "You can catch more flies with honey (warmth) than with vinegar."

To sum up: superiors don't behave only one way all the time. Their behavior reflexively shifts from primary to secondary when they're sufficiently frustrated; it shifts to mask behavior when they want to consciously disguise their basic feelings or motives. But there are still other reasons why superior behavior varies. Let's look at them next.

Additional Reasons Why Behavior Varies

1. *Behavior varies within quadrants.*

Even when a superior's behavior remains in one quadrant, it shifts in *intensity*. Behavior is sometimes more intense, sometimes less. Just as it can move from one quadrant to another, it can move to different points *within* a quadrant.

2. *Position and power affect behavior.*

The rule here is simple: A superior's behavior may vary as the position and power of the *other* person—the person he's interacting with—vary. To understand what happens in any transaction, it always helps to ask: "Who's got the clout?" Who's *superior* to whom? Here are three possibilities:

- When interacting with his subordinates, a superior's behavior might be Q1 (curt, demanding, dogmatic).
- When interacting with his fellow managers, the same superior's behavior might be Q3 (easygoing, affable, good-natured).
- When interacting with his boss, the same superior's behavior might be Q2 (tight-lipped, cautious, compliant).

As a rule (and there *are* exceptions) a superior's behavior will become more manipulative and more guarded as the power of the other person increases. Behavior, in other words, is frequently political. (It's even possible that a superior will "take it easy" on a subordinate during a performance appraisal if he thinks the subordinate is a "comer" who has powerful "connections" in the organization.)

3. *The impact of the other person affects behavior.*

Aspects of the other person's strategy (besides his power position) may cause the superior to change his own strategy. For example, if a superior's boss is behaving in a soft, eager-to-compromise way (Q3), the superior may take advantage of the situation by behaving in a hard, unyielding Q1 way ("He wants peace at any price, so let me see how high I can set the price"). He may do much the same thing if his boss is evasive and unassertive (Q2). "It's obvious," the superior might think, "that he doesn't have much stomach for this discussion. Let me see if I can exploit the situation."

These examples (and we could produce dozens of others) show that any behavior is likely to change in ways that are partly determined by the *other* person's behavior.

4. *The situation may force a change.*

A superior who's angry with a subordinate may "chew him out" if he's alone with the subordinate. But if his *own boss* is around, and if his boss disapproves of bawling out employees, the superior may gently rebuke the subordinate, nothing more. Behavior is always related to situations, and situations vary. (A superior may even pull his punches during an appraisal if he's afraid that word will get back to his boss that he's being too rough on people. The boss doesn't have to be *physically* present to provoke this kind of concern.)

5. *Instructions from above influence behavior.*

Instructions from higher management usually affect a superior's behavior. If the people "upstairs" say, "Take it easy . . . we don't want to get our work force riled up and start a strike," the impact is almost sure to be different than if they say, "We don't care how you do it as long as you get a 5% increase in production."

6. *The superior's experience and self-confidence influence his behavior.*

A superior who feels "green" or inadequate may use Q1 tactics as a cover-up ("I don't dare let these people see that I don't feel up to the job . . . so I'd better come on strong."). When he acquires more self-assurance, he may shift to Q4 behavior. Or a superior who feels green and inadequate may try to hide her uncertainty by using Q2 tactics: keeping to herself, seldom talking to subordinates, and so on. She may also adopt Q3 tactics ("If I can't get them to respect me, at least I can get them to like me"). Know-how and self-assurance affect behavior.

7. *What are the stakes?*

A superior's behavior in any task will be influenced by *how important* it is to him. For example, a superior who's usually relaxed and easygoing may become autocratic and demanding on a project that could bring him a pro-motion. As he puts it: "I'd better tighten up. There's a lot riding on this one." (This can happen in performance appraisal too. If a lot is "riding" on the outcome, the superior may become untypically demanding.)

8. *Emotional stakes.*

For reasons on and off the job, a superior may feel gloomy or "blue," and, as a result, display behavior that he wouldn't ordinarily display (like closeting himself in his office for several hours and talking to no one—Q2 behavior—until he "snaps out of it"). Or he may feel "like a million bucks" and show his high spirits with Q3 behavior. Moods and dispositions readily affect behavior.

9.   *Economics.*

A superior's behavior (like anyone else's) is obviously affected by her financial situation and economic outlook. In a tight job market, for instance, she may "cool it" ("Why rock the boat and get myself into a jam?"). A superior whose personal bills are mounting many push her people harder than usual ("If we get just a little more volume out of this district, I'll get a bonus"). Economics and behavior are inseparable.

To summarize: superiors almost always display varied behavior. So pigeonholing yourself or anyone else is unrealistic. Instead of labeling people ("He's a Q1, she's a Q2") observe and categorize *behavior*. Recognize when shifts occur and what they're all about. Stereotyping *people* is useless; labeling people's *behavior* (and bearing in mind that that behavior is complex) is useful.

Does It Make a Difference?

Does your on-the-job behavior really matter? Since you have a number of behavioral options, is any one option best—that is, does it produce *superior results?*

Yes. By and large, over the long haul, *Q4 behavior,* when appropriately applied, increases your chances of getting superior results. That's a sweeping generalization, and it should be backed up. We provide supporting evidence throughout this book.

SUMMARY

Let's recap this chapter.

1.   Your everyday behavior as a superior strongly influences the results you get in a performance appraisal. So, before discussing appraisal, it makes good sense to understand the way superiors behave day-in and day-out.

2.   Everyday superior behavior can be explained by using two dimensions of behavior: dominance-submission and hostility-warmth. *Dominance* is the exercise of control, taking charge. *Submission* is following the lead of others, going along. *Hostility* is lack of regard for others and a cautious, skeptical approach to them. *Warmth* is regard for others and a basic trust in them.

3.   When combined in the Dimensional Model of Superior Behavior, the two dimensions give us four basic patterns of behavior, four optional ways in which a superior can interact with others on the job.

4.   Q1 behavior (dominant-hostile) "keeps them running scared." Based on the idea that people do their best work when they feel insecure or threatened, Q1 behavior is bossy, insistent, coercive.

5.   Q2 behavior (submissive-hostile) is careful not to rock the boat. Based on the idea that people can't really be motivated much anyway, Q2 behavior is distant, unresponsive, and intent upon staying out of the line of fire.

6.   Q3 behavior (submissive-warm) takes it easy on people. Based on the idea that people work best in happy, relaxed settings, Q3 behavior is friendly, undemanding, quick to compromise differences.

7.   Q4 behavior (dominant-warm) tries to produce maximum benefit for the organization, the subordinate, and the superior. Based on the idea that people do their best work when they're seriously involved in the joint pursuit of the organization's goals and their own, Q4 behavior is challenging, businesslike, toughminded.

8.   Superiors display all four patterns of behavior at various times. A superior's most repetitive behavior is his primary strategy; the behavior he unintentionally shifts into when sufficiently frustrated is his secondary strategy; the behavior with which he deliberately tries to foster a different image of himself is his mask strategy.

9.   Any superior's behavior varies from time to time and situation to situation, so labeling people should be avoided; on the other hand, labeling their behavior, as it occurs, helps a great deal.

10.   When it comes to getting consistently good results over a long period, Q4 behavior usually pays off best.

A LOOK AHEAD

The four basic patterns of superior behavior extend to performance appraisal as well as to other management functions. There's a Q1 way to do performance appraisal, a Q2 way, and so on. In our next chapter, we look at these approaches, and give you a chance to determine which approach you usually use. Then, in the chapter following, we describe the ways subordinates behave in appraisals, and you get a chance to determine which are typical of your subordinates. Then we'll be ready to present how to do Q4 performance appraisal.

3

Four Ways of
Appraising Performance

We've just described four different ways to manage people. Each of these can be used in any interaction between a superior and a subordinate. In this chapter we're going to see how these behaviors are likely to show up in appraisals. To do this, we'll use the quadrant model we introduced in our last chapter.

The Dimensional Model of Superior Appraisal Behavior (see Figure 4) is based on the five basic steps that ought to be included in any performance appraisal. These steps are the foundation on which an appraisal stands or falls.

1. *Arousing interest and testing readiness to participate.*

The first thing to do in any appraisal is to make sure your subordinate is *ready* to participate, that he's *willing* to proceed.

2. *Increasing readiness to participate and promoting self-evaluation by the subordinate.*

If your subordinate *isn't* mentally disposed to take a constructive part in the appraisal, you must get him to that point. And you must also get him to present his *own* evaluation of his performance.

3.   *Presenting your evaluation.*

Once your subordinate's self-evaluation is out in the open, you must give him *your* evaluation of his performance so that the two can be compared and reconciled.

4.   *Venting emotions and resolving disagreements.*

You must reduce interfering emotions; you must try to resolve any disagreements about the two evaluations.

5.   *Working out the final resolution.*

Finally, the two of you must develop improvement goals for the future and work out plans for reaching them. Then you must make sure the subordinate is committed to the goals and plans.

We consider each of these steps in detail later. Right now, let's get a general idea of the four basic ways in which each step can be handled (or mishandled) (Figure 4).

Let's look further at each approach. Remember: (a) our descriptions are "caricatures"; real-world behavior is usually less extreme; (2) real-world superiors are usually a "mix" of these behaviors.

THE Q1 APPROACH TO PERFORMANCE APPRAISAL

This is a closed-minded, "let me tell you" approach. The underlying idea is: most people aren't capable of evaluating their own performance, so it's up to me, the boss, to do it for them. The appraisal moves one way: *from* superior *to* subordinate. Here are the major characteristics of Q1 appraisal:

1.   It's coercive. The superior imposes his ideas. Or, more accurately, he *tries* to impose them. The subordinate may openly resist by arguing, contradicting, and disagreeing, or passively resist by pretending to "buy" the superior's views. A superior who adopts the Q1 approach always tries to force his views on the subordinate.

2.   If this doesn't work, the superior threatens ("Do it my way or else . . .").

3.   Even if the superior doesn't openly threaten, there's usually an implied threat in what he says. Subordinates usually "get the message" without having it spelled out.

4.   The threats vary from situation to situation and from company to company. A subordinate who doesn't play the game, who doesn't go along,

Q4

Arousing interest. Starts out in appropriately sociable, business-like way. Arouses interest by tying appraisal to subordinate's needs. Individualizes approach to suit subordinate's behavior. Gets subordinate involved.

Increasing readiness. Accurately assesses subordinate's willingness to proceed.; increases it if low. Promotes realistic self-evaluation by subordinate.

Presenting your evaluation. Responds to subordinate's self-evaluation, then presents own assessment openly and candidly. Presents clear, realistic picture.

Venting and disagreements. Encourages venting of interfering emotions and open expression of disagreement. Tries to resolve differences through candid give-and-take.

Final resolution. Develops challenging goals that are mutually agreed on. Goals are designed to pay off for subordinate, for superior, and for organization. Generates full understanding and high commitment.

Warmth

Q1

Arousing interest. Starts out gruffly ("Let's get on with it"). Expects subordinate to accept advice without backtalk. Little interest in subordinate's response.

Increasing readiness. Unaware of, or unconcerned about, subordinate's receptivity. Doesn't really try to get subordinate to make full evaluation of own performance. More concerned with putting over own ideas.

Presenting your evaluation. Presents ideas even if subordinate isn't tuned in. Swamps subordinate with facts and comments. Implies "I'm right." Sweeps aside disagreement.

Venting and disagreements. Squelches differences and emotions. Fights fire with fire. Implies "Don't argue with me."

Final resolution. Imposes own goals and plans with little regard for subordinate's reaction or commitment. Implies "Do it my way or else."

Hostility

Q3

Arousing interest. Comes across as overly sociable and unbusinesslike. Takes "this is between pals" approach. Takes a long time getting down to business.

Increasing readiness. Assumes that friendliness and reassurance will make subordinate eager to proceed. Doesn't test out this notion. Encourages over-positive self-evaluation by subordinate.

Presenting your evaluation. Presents unrealistically positive picture. Plays down troublesome issues.

Venting and disagreements. Doesn't really vent interfering emotions; instead, pacifies them. Compromises and appeases to settle any disagreements.

Final resolution. Concludes by agreeing to easy goals designed to promote harmony. Produces superficial understanding and misdirected commitment.

Q2

Arousing interest. Seems guarded and uncomfortable ("Let's get this over with"). Does little to arouse interest or test receptivity. Just plods ahead mechanically.

Increasing readiness. Shows little concern about subordinate's readiness to proceed. Asks few or no questions. Doesn't actively seek subordinate's self-evaluation, although latter may volunteer some comments.

Presenting your evaluation. Presents ideas superficially, with little conviction. Tries to be noncommittal.

Venting and disagreements. Doesn't encourage expression of interfering emotions. Avoids disagreements. Tries to stay neutral.

Final resolution. Concludes appraisal on vague note. Emphasizes continuance of status quo. Produces little understanding and weak commitment.

Submission

FIGURE 4. The Dimensional Model of Superior Appraisal Behavior.

may face the threat of getting fired, passed over for promotion, passed over for a salary increase, demoted, bawled out, humiliated, and so forth.

5.   The appraisal concentrates on what's wrong. What's *right* is minimized or ignored. There's little praise but much blame, often accompanied by scolding, nagging, preaching, and chewing out.

6.   The appraisal is lopsided. The superior focuses entirely on the subordinate. He never asks: "Is it possible that *I'm* doing something wrong? Could circumstances beyond the subordinate's control have contributed to the problem?"

7.   The appraisal is a show of strength. The superior dominates the session from start to finish. Both his words and his manner communicate power, rank, influence.

8.   In the end, power prevails. Unless the subordinate is willing to quit, he usually gives in. He winds up knowing what his superior thinks about his performance, and what he's supposed to do differently from now on. But he's usually not very committed to any "agreement" reached by him and his boss. The superior gets capitulation rather than commitment. He generates little self-discovery by the subordinate, little development, and little growth.

THE Q2 APPROACH TO PERFORMANCE APPRAISAL

This is a routine, mechanical, "let's not create more problems than we've already got" approach. The underlying idea is: people are what they are, so discussing their performance with them can't make much difference in how they do their jobs in the future. The communication is no-way; very little solid information flows in either direction. Here are the major characteristics of Q2 appraisal:

1.   It's passive. Generally, superiors who adopt this approach don't believe appraisal makes much difference anyway. However, since the organization insists on periodic appraisals, they go through the motions. Candid, searching analysis is avoided. "Why look for trouble?" the superior asks.

2.   It may include some threats if the superior's *boss* is "putting the heat" on her. If her *boss* has laid down the law ("Get those people in line . . . fast") the superior will use the appraisal to convey the boss's demands ("Believe me, there's a lot of unhappiness upstairs. If you don't shape up, we're all gonna be in trouble"). This is passive behavior; the superior serves as a pipeline for someone *else's* ideas.

3.   A Q2 appraisal is usually brief and superficial, lasting only as long as necessary to go through the motions.

4.   The appraisal is a show of *apathy*. The superior's words and man-

ner show clearly that she doesn't believe in what she's doing. She's appraising because she must, because it's expected of her, not because she thinks it will do any good.

5.   The subordinate usually comes out of Q2 appraisal confused or unsure about how she's doing or what she can do to improve. Little or no self-discovery happens; little or no groundwork is laid out for future development. As a result, the subordinate may feel cheated or let down ("I was hoping for a real appraisal and all I got was a fast shuffle").

THE Q3 APPROACH TO PERFORMANCE APPRAISAL

This is an easygoing, "I know you've been doing the best you can" approach. The underlying idea is: people will improve if the appraisal is positive, nonthreatening, and doesn't make harsh demands; the organization will eventually benefit. The communication is *selectively* two-way; pleasant information flows freely in both directions, while unpleasant information is minimized or suppressed ("Accentuate the positive; eliminate the negative"). Here are the major characteristics of Q3 appraisal:

1.   It "takes it easy" on the subordinate. The superior provides alibis, rationalizations, outs ("I know all the problems you've been having . . . and I know they're not your fault").

2.   It exaggerates positives and plays down negatives. Good performance is upgraded to terrific performance; poor performance is upgraded to "not bad" (or isn't mentioned at all).

3.   It uses many superlatives ("fantastic," "outstanding," "great," "sensational").

4.   It uses evasive language to avoid saying the unpleasant. Instead of saying "Joe, we both know you've been doing a poor job of selling this past quarter," the superior dilutes the remark by saying, "Joe, we both know you've been in a hitting slump lately" or "Joe, it looks like you haven't scored too many points this past quarter."

5.   Q3 appraisal is marked by a lack of tension. There's little argument; at the first sign of disagreement, the superior backs off, or jokes, or works hard to pacify the situation. Voices are rarely raised, unpleasant topics are skirted. The atmosphere is relaxed.

6.   The subordinate usually comes away convinced that his performance has been better than it really has been, and equally convinced that he needs to make few, if any, significant changes. Little self-discovery takes place. While he may feel pretty good immediately after the appraisal, he may also, upon reflection, feel cheated ("Come to think of it, the boss never really *said* anything").

THE Q4 APPROACH TO PERFORMANCE APPRAISAL

This is a businesslike "let's find out how things are really going and what should be done about it" approach. The underlying idea is: most people can get a straightforward view of their performance if they take part in a thorough, systematic analysis with their superiors. Q4 appraisal is *two-way*: relevant information flows candidly in both directions. Here are the major characteristics of Q4 appraisal:

1. It's candid. The idea is to get *real* insight into how the subordinate is doing. There is no evasion, game-playing, or make-believe by the superior, and she tries to see that there is none by the subordinate.

2. It's balanced. Instead of zeroing in mainly on strengths (as in Q3 appraisal) or on weakness (as in Q1), Q4 appraisal zeros in on *both,* in whatever proportion reflects the *real* picture.

3. It strives for understanding. Instead of making superficial statements ("You're doing a terrible job") and letting it go at that (as in Q1 appraisal), the superior tries to get the subordinate to see why she's not performing effectively and what difference it makes.

4. It's a mutual activity. Both superior *and* subordinate are involved in searching for information that will produce an objective evaluation. Both take an active part in asking questions and providing answers. Q4 appraisal is never a one-person show.

5. It strives for commitment. Instead of pressuring the subordinate to accept new goals, the superior tries to get her to "buy" the goals, to feel a sense of ownership in them. She does this by helping the subordinate see "what's in it for her."

6. Since "what's in it for her" differs from subordinate to subordinate, Q4 appraisal is highly individualized. It's tailored to fit the subordinate who is being appraised. It's the most flexible of all the approaches we've considered.

7. Q4 appraisal tries to maximize self-discovery. The idea is to get the subordinate to analyze her *own* performance, with guidance and help from the superior.

8. The subordinate usually ends up with a better understanding of both her strengths and weaknesses, a detailed plan for improvement, and a solid commitment to carrying it out. As a result, improved performance is a realistic possibility.

Since most of this book deals with Q4 appraisal, we won't expand on these points now. We discuss all of them later.

A LOOK AT YOURSELF

By now, you're probably wondering: "What kind of performance appraisal do *I* usually do?" The questionnaire on the following pages will help answer that question and, at the same time, deepen your insight into the differences between Q1, Q2, Q3, and Q4 appraisal. Here's how the questionnaire works:

1. The five basic steps in performance appraisal that we used in the Dimensional Model are listed. Below each are four short paragraphs describing, respectively, the Q1, Q2, Q3, and Q4 way of handling that part of an appraisal.

2. Read each cluster of four paragraphs. As you do, compare them with your *own* behavior when you conduct appraisals. (If you've never done a formal performance appraisal, complete the questionnaire anyway. Just ask yourself: "How do these statements compare to the way I'd *probably* behave?"). Remember, the statements are extreme, while your behavior is probably less than extreme, so your behavior may *not* coincide *exactly* with any of the statements.

3. After reading each cluster of four paragraphs, distribute 100 points among them so that the points reflect the degree to which the paragraphs describe *your* appraisal behavior. In other words, the number of points assigned to any paragraph should be proportionate to how descriptive that paragraph is of what you do in an appraisal. For example, if you feel that the first paragraph in a cluster describes your behavior "perfectly," and that the remaining three paragraphs don't apply to you at all, then distribute the points in this way: 100–0–0–0. This is extremely unlikely, however. In all probability, you'll see something of your own behavior in several or all of the paragraphs. If so, your point distribution might look like this: 10–30–30–30 *or* 25–25–10–40 *or* 60–0–10–30 *or whatever seems genuinely descriptive of your appraisal behavior.* Be sure to use *all* 100 points for each cluster of four paragraphs.

4. Don't assign the most points to the "ideal" answer unless it really describes your behavior. Pick the candid answer, even if you don't feel it compliments you. All you want at this point is to get a realistic portrait of how you conduct appraisals.

5. Remember, there are no "right" or "wrong" answers; there are only *more descriptive* and *less descriptive* answers.

6. This questionnaire is a useful summary of how you see your appraisal behavior at this time. You may want to rate yourself again after reading this book to find out whether your initial rating was somewhat too optimistic.

HOW I CONDUCT PERFORMANCE APPRAISALS

1. *Arousing interest and testing readiness to participate*

————**Q1.**   I don't start out by being sociable, because I don't believe in wasting time. I believe in getting on with it; to do that, an abrupt, no-nonsense approach works best. I make it plain, by word and manner, that even though my advice may be hard to take, I expect my subordinate to accept it; that's the only way he'll do better in the future. I'm not much concerned about whether he's ready to carry on with the appraisal; the appraisal must be done, whether he likes it or not. So I go ahead regardless of his attitude, and plunge into the heart of the matter: the evaluation.

————**Q2.**   I don't make any special effort to be sociable, because I'm not convinced that sociability between superior and subordinate is such a good thing; I think it's better, if you're the boss, to keep your distance. And I don't make much effort to arouse interest; after all, interested or not, we've both got to get through the appraisal since the organization requires it. So I just start in by telling my subordinate whatever I must; I don't ask for her reactions because it doesn't make sense to stir up problems and complaints. I just go by the book, trying to make as little trouble for myself as possible.

————**Q3.**   I work hard at being sociable and friendly. The idea is to make my subordinate feel relaxed and unthreatened. I reassure him that everything's going to be okay, I use compliments and small talk to establish rapport, and I try to offset his anxiety by explaining that the appraisal is simply a chat between two friends. I don't ask many questions because I realize he's tense, and questions can only increase tension. I find that if I express my good will and make it plain that nothing bad can come out of the appraisal, my subordinate is usually willing to proceed.

————**Q4.**   I begin in an appropriately sociable way, extending the usual courtesies and keeping in mind the particular social needs of my subordinate; some people require more pleasantries than others, but I don't overdo it. I try to arouse interest by explaining what the subordinate can expect out of the appraisal; I base this explanation on what I know about her needs and aspirations. Then I ask for her reaction to determine if she's willing to proceed. If not, we discuss the potential benefits of the appraisal some more; I try not to go ahead with the actual evaluation until the subordinate is really ready to play a constructive role. Otherwise, the evaluation isn't likely to make much of an impression. Throughout, I try to size up her behavior so that I can respond to whatever she's trying to tell me; if I don't, the whole appraisal is likely to be irrelevant.

2. *Increasing readiness to participate and getting the subordinate's self-evaluation*

_____**Q1.** I don't worry about my subordinate's readiness to participate, or whether she is taking in what I say. I don't think she has any real choice but to pay attention and accept my views. My aim is to get her to understand what I think, and I do that in whatever way works best: pushing my ideas hard, promising a lavish payoff, or, if necessary, using threats. I'm the boss and my ideas are supposed to prevail, so I see no reason to waste time on her views. I pass on my evaluation of her performance; if I detect doubt or skepticism, I simply restate my views in stronger terms or, maybe, ask a few questions designed to produce agreement. If she comments, I respond mainly to those remarks that strengthen my case. I don't intend to let the appraisal get out of control or to let my subordinate call the shots.

_____**Q2.** I'm not worried about whether my subordinate takes in what I say or not because it doesn't make much difference anyway. I can't do much to improve the performance of someone who doesn't want to improve, and someone who does will do so without my help. People are what they are, and I don't kid myself that I can make much difference in how they perform. I see no real value in getting my subordinate's self-evaluation, either; it won't change anything, and it may bring matters to the surface that are better left buried. So I don't ask for self-evaluation. I just tell him whatever I'm supposed to, and let it go at that.

_____**Q3.** I rely on friendliness and encouragement to increase my subordinate's readiness to take part in the appraisal. Anybody is bound to be a little tense going into an appraisal, and may therefore have trouble paying attention. I try to eliminate this anxiety by being reassuring, genial, and relaxed. Then I get my subordinate to do some self-evaluation. I encourage positive self-evaluation; berating or blaming yourself for a poor performance can only be demoralizing and demoralization can only lead to further problems. High morale is vital, and high morale comes when the subordinate sees that we're all human and we all make mistakes. There's no point crying over spilled milk. So, during her self-evaluation, I'm careful not to ask embarrassing or unsettling questions. I prefer to look at the bright side.

_____**Q4.** I pay a lot of attention to my subordinate's readiness to proceed with the appraisal; if he is not really ready to take a constructive part, the appraisal won't sink in. If I observe signs that he is not ready, I try to increase his readiness before proceeding. If emotions interfere with our continuing, I give him a chance to express those emotions; if silence and withdrawal stand in the way, I try to get him involved; if he doesn't seem ready to settle down to business, I try to focus his attention on the task at hand. Once he's really ready to proceed, I encourage realistic self-evaluation. I ask questions that focus on key issues and that help both of us understand what is being said. My purpose is to get my subordinate to make a candid, balanced, thorough self-evaluation.

3. *Presenting my own evaluation*

————**Q1.**   Whether or not my subordinate seems ready to listen, I go ahead with my evaluation. I use all the facts and logic I can muster, and I make a strong, airtight case. The best way to do this is to present my opinions without interruption; if my subordinate tries to inject questions, or objects to something I've said, I squelch the interruption and continue. After all, the purpose of the appraisal is to get my views across to him, so I have no intention of getting sidetracked or delayed. I don't bother much with trying to get his reactions; I'm smart enough to know that much of what I say is not welcome. Still and all, the things I say must be said, like them or not. So I say them in plain English and let it go at that.

————**Q2.**   As quickly as I can, I present my evaluation to my subordinate. There's no point in dragging it out, since we've both got other things we'd rather be doing, so I try to get the appraisal over with rapidly. I tell her whatever I'm expected or required to say, and I don't get worked up over it; after all, when all's said and done, the appraisal isn't going to change anything. That's why I try not to argue with my subordinate; the appraisal isn't worth arguing over. I try to maintain a neutral tone; if I must criticize her performance, I back up my criticisms by referring to organizational policies or external influences. That way, I come across as personally noncommittal, which is a good way to avoid rocking the boat and creating new problems.

————**Q3.**   When I get around to presenting my evaluation to my subordinate, I do it in a positive, forward-looking way. Nothing is gained by weeping over the past; the important thing is to create a supportive environment for the future. So, even if clouds darken my subordinate's performance, I look for the silver linings and focus on them. I don't blame or berate him for what's gone wrong, and I don't dwell on mistakes or problems. I admit that mistakes happen in any organization, that we're all human, and that I'm confident things will improve. My approach is general; I'm not especially concerned with the nit-picking details of performance—I'm concerned with my subordinate's frame of mind. I want to give him a confident, reassured, optimistic outlook; the best way to do that is to talk about the "big picture" in hopeful, genial terms.

————**Q4.**   Before starting the evaluation, I explain which parts of my subordinate's self-evaluation I agree or disagree with, and I check to make sure she's ready to listen to, and consider, my views. Then, openly and candidly, I explain how and why I disagree in certain areas. I try to document my views with solid data, and not to sound as if my views are carved in stone. In fact, I try hard to keep an open mind and to remember that her views may be closer to the truth than mine; this is something to be determined after examining all the evidence. In presenting my evaluation, I pause from time to time to check her understanding and reaction; the pace of the evaluation is businesslike but unhurried, so that we can stop at any point to discuss any issue. At the end, I summarize those matters about which we agree and disagree, bearing in mind that there's almost sure to be some disagreement.

4. *Venting emotions and resolving disagreements*

_____**Q1.** I don't see much reason to let my subordinate express any emotions, positive or negative. Positive emotions waste time; I've got more important things to do than sit around listening to how happy she feels. Negative emotions also waste time; after all, my evaluation is my evaluation, and I don't intend to change it or debate it. As long as I'm boss, my opinion must prevail, whether my subordinate is happy about it or not; my views are not negotiable. So I see to it that her feelings, positive or negative, don't get voiced; I squelch them or bury them under a pile of contrary evidence. I don't allow disagreements, either. If she takes exception to something I've said, I cut off the discussion or make the issue look trivial. One way or another, I see to it that my viewpoint wins out.

_____**Q2.** I do all I can to keep emotions from surfacing during the appraisal. Emotional people are hard to handle, and openly expressed emotions only make the appraisal tougher than it already is. If my subordinate does express feelings, positive or negative, I sometimes pretend I haven't heard; if you ignore emotions, they may go away. For the same reasons, I try to avoid disagreement and debate; I don't want to get embroiled in something that's almost sure to cause problems. So if my subordinate insists on disputing something I've said, I change the subject, or back down, or tell him "it doesn't matter anyway," or give a neutral answer to get myself off the hook. If I must stick to my position, I bolster it by referring to organizational policies or external forces, both of which are beyond my control.

_____**Q3.** I see little or no value in dwelling on negative emotions; they just detract from the positive climate I'm trying to create. So, if my subordinate expresses unhappy feelings, I soothe them over. I do this by giving strong reassurance, by compromising differences, and, if necessary, by backing off from my original position. On the other hand, I encourage positive emotions; they enhance the optimistic atmosphere I'm trying to foster. If my subordinate voices disagreement, I become conciliatory; I try to placate her by recommending a "look at the bright side," or I simply gloss over our differences. As far as I'm concerned, disagreements should be buried and forgotten during the appraisal so that we end on a note of harmony and goodwill.

_____**Q4.** I encourage open expression of emotions, positive and negative, by my subordinate. In the long run, this reduces tension and clears the air so that we can look at performance more objectively. It also tells me a lot about what he thinks and feels; knowing this, I can make sure I deal with his concerns so the appraisal is relevant and meaningful. I also encourage the open expression of differences; I want to know how and why he disagrees with my views, so that we can resolve our differences. I don't think it's possible to reach 100% agreement with every subordinate, but it is possible to settle many disagreements through searching discussion. I encourage such discussion in which we both present data to support our positions and question one another. In the end, if my position proves weak I modify or even change it. My concern is not to "look good" by being right, but to get the real truth about performance.

5. *Working out the final resolution*

_____**Q1.**   Since it's the boss's responsibility to set goals, that's what I do during the appraisal; I set forth my subordinate's new goals, and make it plain that I expect to see them achieved. As a rule, I set tough goals; nothing is gained by making things easy for people. I don't ask his opinion about the goals; the point I want to get across is that they're final and not something we can bargain about. By presenting them as nonnegotiable, I convey the message that they must be met or else. A goal is really an order, and I see no reason to disguise that fact. I use the same approach with action plans; I give the subordinate a plan of action and make it plain that I expect it to be followed. Deviations can only create problems.

_____**Q2.**   I conclude the appraisal by passing on any new goals and action plans that the organization has set for the subordinate. If there are no new goals and plans, I simply tell her to carry on pretty much as in the past. The important thing to remember is that goals aren't going to make much difference anyway, so there's no reason to get excited about them. People who are self-motivated will do what they're supposed to do, and people who aren't, won't; goals won't change anything one way or the other. About the only message I try to convey to my subordinate is that if she does what she's expected to, it will help keep everyone "off our backs."

_____**Q3.**   I conclude by setting goals that can be achieved without strain, and then giving a short pep talk. There's no point in setting goals that are too tough; if the goals aren't met, people will only get discouraged and demoralized. The pep talk is intended to conclude the appraisal on a high, optimistic note. In my talk, I stress the importance of team play, of doing a good job so as to engender goodwill throughout the organization and maintain the harmony that's so important to everybody. As far as action plans are concerned, I don't worry much about them; I don't want to put my subordinate in a straitjacket by getting too involved in details. It's better to hang loose and play things by ear.

_____**Q4.**   At the conclusion of the appraisal, my subordinate and I agree to the goals and action plans that we've developed together. I make sure that these are specific, challenging, and good for the future development of the subordinate and the organization. Then I ask her to suggest changes or improvements; if these make sense to both of us, we incorporate them into the goals and plans. Only when absolutely necessary do I impose my own goals and plans on the subordinate; whenever possible, I stick with those that we've worked out together. And I always check to make sure that the subordinate understands the benefits she'll gain from meeting the goals; I want to be sure the payoff is clear. Then I check, one last time, to make certain that we agree on what's been decided and that my subordinate is committed to pursuing it. Finally, we agree on a procedure for reviewing progress at a later date.

HOW I CONDUCT PERFORMANCE APPRAISALS

Score Sheet

First Rating	Q1	Q2	Q3	Q4
Step 1: Arouse Interest				
Step 2: Readiness & Subordinate Self-Evaluation				
Step 3: Own Evaluation				
Step 4: Venting & Disagreement				
Step 5: Resolution				
Sum equals				
	Q1	Q2	Q3	Q4

Subsequent Rating	Q1	Q2	Q3	Q4
Step 1: Arouse Interest				
Step 2: Readiness & Subordinate Self-Evaluation				
Step 3: Own Evaluation				
Step 4: Venting & Disagreement				
Step 5: Resolution				
Sum equals				
	Q1	Q2	Q3	Q4

CONCLUSION: THE CASE AGAINST Q1, Q2, AND Q3 APPRAISAL

We started this book with a four-part definition of performance appraisal:

Performance appraisal is (1) a formal discussion between a superior and a subordinate (2) for the purpose of discovering how and why the subordinate is presently performing on the job and (3) how the subordinate can perform more effectively in the future (4) so that the subordinate, the superior, and the organization all benefit.

In this chapter we've seen some of the reasons why all four elements are rarely present in one appraisal.

1.   In many appraisals, there is no "formal discussion." In fact, there may be practically no discussion of any kind, formal or informal. In a Q1 appraisal, the superior doesn't want a discussion; he wants an I-talk-you-listen session. A discussion involves contributions by at least *two* people; a Q1 appraisal is much closer to a lecture, or a sermon. A Q2 appraisal isn't much of a discussion either. In real discussion, two people are genuinely involved; they're absorbed in what they're doing. This is rarely the case with Q2 appraisal, which is a mechanical, going-through-the-motions affair. Even a Q3 appraisal is not a real discussion. It stays on the surface. Too many important matters are avoided, sugarcoated, and rationalized. In fact, those topics most likely to arouse real gut-feelings are the very topics most likely to be distorted or avoided. So, in the strict sense of the word, neither Q1, Q2, nor Q3 appraisal qualifies as "discussion."

2.   In many appraisals there is no real "discovery" either. "Discovery" means learning something you didn't know before. It means seeing new relationships, gaining new perspectives, new understanding. But in Q1, Q2, and Q3 appraisal, the superior doesn't *want* to learn something new. The nice thing about Q1 appraisal is that it lets the superior go right on believing what she's always believed: that her subordinates couldn't possibly do their jobs right if she didn't keep them under constant surveillance. The superior can't discover evidence of initiative or competence on the part of her subordinates, because she begins the appraisal with ready-made opinions and sticks with them. A superior can't discover much new in a Q2 or Q3 appraisal, either. A Q2 appraisal is a perfunctory, let's-get-it-over-with affair; it's too superficial to lead to discovery. And a Q3 appraisal is structured to *prevent* any awareness of harsh truths (pleasant truths are okay).

3.   In too many cases subordinates come away from an appraisal without the foggiest notion of how they can perform more effectively in the

future. What a subordinate learns in a Q1 appraisal is not necessarily how he can do *better,* but how he can keep his job. He learns what he must do to stay out of trouble, but he doesn't necessarily learn how he can *improve.* The basic message, "Do it my way," is not always the same as "Do it the best way." As a rule, subordinates learn even less from Q2 and Q3 appraisals than from Q1. This isn't surprising; in Q2 appraisal the superior doesn't try to teach his subordinates anything ("You can't teach people. Those who want to learn will, and those who don't, won't"). In Q3 appraisal, the superior is an ineffective teacher because good teaching depends upon generating dissatisfaction with the way things are, and the superior doesn't want to stir up dissatisfaction of any kind.

4.   The end-result is that many performance appraisals don't benefit either the subordinate or the organization. They may benefit the *superior,* but they don't do much for anyone else. For example, a superior may derive benefit from a Q1 appraisal because it gives him a chance to sound off, to flex his muscles, and "keep the troops in line"; this benefits him, but it's not likely to benefit either the subordinate (who may find the experience downright unpleasant) or the organization. A Q3 appraisal gives the superior a chance to promote harmony and show what a "nice person" she is; this benefits her, but it probably doesn't benefit her subordinate (who may be bored stiff) or the organization.

To summarize: performance appraisal that does what it's supposed to do (Q4 appraisal) is rare.

SUMMARY

1.   There are four basic approaches to performance appraisal; we call these Q1, Q2, Q3, and Q4.

2.   Q1 appraisal is a coercive, closed-minded, tell-and-do approach. Everything that happens is imposed by the boss: the evaluation, the goals, the action plans.

3.   Q2 appraisal is a routine, mechanical, let's-not-rock-the-boat approach. What happens isn't significant; mostly, the two people involved go through the motions, but don't achieve much.

4.   Q3 appraisal is an easygoing, optimistic, lets-look-at-the-bright-side approach. It's highly selective; the superior focuses on good news and minimizes or ignores bad news. The result is a distorted picture.

5.   Q4 appraisal is a businesslike let's-get-to-the-bottom-of-things-and-see-how-we-can-do-better approach. It involves both superior and subordinate in searching analysis and discussion based on solid evidence. The re-

sult is an accurate, balanced appraisal and a workable plan-of-action for the future.

6.   Of these four approaches, Q4 gives you the best chance of obtaining superior results.

A LOOK AHEAD

Up to now we've concentrated on what superiors do in a performance appraisal. But, obviously, we can't really understand appraisal unless we understand what the subordinate does as well. To help us get a complete picture of what goes on in an appraisal, we discuss subordinate behavior in our next chapter. That will pave the way for a closer look at how to do Q4 appraisal.

4

The Other Side
of the Desk

So far, we've talked about performance appraisal as if it happens mainly
on one side of the desk, the *superior's* side. But of course it doesn't. In
any appraisal, things constantly happen on the other side of the desk, the
subordinate's side. Unless we understand what happens on both sides, we
can't really understand the outcome.

THE INTERACTIONAL NATURE OF APPRAISAL

Interaction means action between people. In interaction a superior does
not act upon an inactive subordinate; a superior is not a sculptor shaping
a lump of clay. Instead, the superior acts upon the subordinate and the
subordinate *acts back* upon the superior who in turn reacts upon the subordinate and so on. Interaction (and appraisal *is* interaction) is *reciprocal*
action. (This is true even when the subordinate acts in a passive, unresponsive Q2 way. The very fact that the subordinate is passive and unresponsive causes the superior to *react* in a certain way. Passivity is considered a form of action because it triggers responses in others.)

It's important to remember that in performance appraisal you not only
act—you're acted *upon*. The responses and reactions of your subordinate
are as important in forming the total situation as your own actions. Inter-

action is give-and-take. Even apathy and silence from a subordinate *influence* you, and influence is a form of activity. In interaction what appears to be inactivity is really activity, although a very quiet and withdrawn kind.

SUBORDINATE BEHAVIORS

The model in Figure 5 introduces the four basic ways subordinates behave in appraisals. Keep in mind that in the real world subordinates, like supe-

Dominance

Q1
Tries to take control by disagreeing with superior, displaying negative emotions, or making strong, dogmatic statements. Takes an I've-got-my-mind-made-up attitude. Overstates own achievements. Resists boss's attempts to explore the record. Disputes boss. Reluctant to assume responsibility for mistakes or problems. Pushes own evaluation in spite of contrary evidence. Inflates own image. Doesn't explore superior's ideas. Doesn't listen carefully; plows ahead with own views. Stubborn, resistant, argumentative.

Q4
Appropriately friendly. Candid and attentive. If he disagrees, he gives reasons; listens thoughtfully to boss's responses. Seeks thorough discussion. Takes part willingly; is realistic and able to accept criticism. Takes responsibility for errors. Doesn't alibi or rationalize. Takes credit for achievements but doesn't inflate them. Works hard with superior to develop insight into past and future performance. Doesn't undermine boss, but insists on respect and a fair hearing. Asks sensible questions; expects straightforward answers. Businesslike, involved, growth-oriented.

Hostility ———————————————————— Warmth

Q2
Apathetic; unwilling to reveal own thoughts or get deeply involved. Quietly resists being drawn into discussion. Seems afraid that whatever he says will be used against him. Passively accepts boss's evaluation. Responds in cautious, noncommittal way. Maintains air of neutrality by saying little or stating views without conviction or refusing to ask questions. Rarely disagrees. Procrastinates; listens distrustfully. Remote, hard to read, uncommunicative.

Q3
Overly friendly and eager to please. Good-naturedly accepts boss's views without serious question. Voices ideas in a vague way; emphasizes positives, downplays negatives. Doesn't express underlying doubts. Wanders off subject. Seems uninterested in details; settles for generalities. Enthusiastically agrees, even if there's no evidence of real understanding. Asks only questions designed to produce happy answers. Doesn't seem to hear everything that's being said; screens out unpleasant facts. Genial, good-natured, accepting.

Submission

FIGURE 5.   The Dimensional Model of Subordinate Appraisal Behavior.

riors, mix and vary their behavior, and that they often display behaviors less extreme than those we've described. In an appraisal a subordinate may display several, or even all, of the behaviors. Real subordinate behavior is always more complex than our caricatures.

SUBORDINATES' APPRAISAL BEHAVIOR

Let's look closer at each approach.

Q1

The basic idea is: If you come on strong enough, you may actually prevail upon the boss to give you a more favorable appraisal than otherwise; the only way to get through an appraisal is to try to equalize the relationship between yourself and the boss by being hard-nosed, argumentative, and obstinate. The idea is to use strength to offset the boss's initial advantage. So the subordinate comes on strong at the outset, almost daring the superior to "put him down." He resists attempts to explore his opinions; he argues and contradicts ("How can you say a thing like that? I think you're being unfair . . . you're refusing to give me credit for a terrific performance. Everybody else around here knows what a fantastic job I've done"). He's dogmatic, opinionated, fixed in his ideas. The appraisal may turn into a struggle of wills in which the subordinate tries to force his own conclusions, or tries some "horse-trading," or refuses to concede points to the boss ("I still say you're being unfair. I don't know why you're picking on me. I'm the one guy in this whole place who deserves praise instead of blame"). The approach is stubborn and at times may border on the belligerent.

Q2

The basic idea is: The best way to get through an appraisal is to keep your mouth shut and "play it cool"; just endure whatever you have to endure, but don't make trouble for yourself by speaking out. So, from the beginning, the subordinate is quiet and noncommunicative, determined to "stay out of it." Concerned that anything she says might be used against her, she tries to say very little ("The less you say, the longer you stay"). At times it's difficult for the boss to know whether or not she's getting through because she hears so few responses from the subordinate. The responses the boss does get are noncommittal ("Okay"; "I guess so"; "Whatever you say"). The subordinate is fearful and uptight; she seems tense, as if anticipating the worst: a tongue-lashing, a chewing-out, what have you. And she seems determined to get it over with as quickly as possible; one reason for her silence is that it speeds things up ("Why prolong the ordeal?").

Q3

The basic idea is: Be pleasant and agreeable, and the appraisal will be fairly mild as a result; affable behavior generates affable responses, so the best way to temper the outcome of the appraisal is by being genial and accepting. Thus, from the beginning, the subordinate comes on in a good-natured, friendly way. He seems, at least on the surface, relaxed and unconcerned. He accepts whatever the boss says without argument or contradiction; if asked to explain his behavior, he usually has a rationalization ready. These rationalizations never *blame* anyone; the alibis always center around "circumstances" but never around specific individuals. The whole approach is amiable and talkative. The subordinate not only "agrees" with the superior, but agrees too wholeheartedly ("You're absolutely right"; "I'll buy that"; "You took the words right out of my mouth").

Q4

The basic idea is: An appraisal is a good opportunity to learn and grow, so avail yourself of it; the best way to do this is to collaborate in an open, inquiring, well-informed way. The subordinate is appropriately friendly (but not overly so), candid, and interested. She seems neither tense nor defensive. She readily answers questions, gives her own views, and explains her actions straightforwardly. She is open about her shortcomings, and doesn't grope for alibis. And she doesn't merely *respond* to her superior; she exerts initiative by questioning the boss, by asking for more information or better explanations. If she disagrees, she says so, without evasion but without a chip on her shoulder, either. She does what she can to establish candid, constructive give-and-take. She is active, realistic, involved, frank.

A LOOK AT YOUR OWN SUBORDINATES

A good way to understand how subordinates behave in performance appraisal is to look at your own. The questionnaire on the following pages will help you. It's designed much like the one in the last chapter, except that it focuses on *subordinate* behavior, and it enables you to examine the behavior of several subordinates, not just one. Here's how to use it:

1.   We've divided the questionnaire into four main sections. Under each are four paragraphs; these describe, respectively, the Q1, Q2, Q3, and Q4 strategies used by subordinates in appraisals.

2.   Alongside the paragraphs, four columns are provided. Select up to four subordinates whose performance you're responsible for appraising, and write their names at the head of each column. If you want to examine the behavior of more than four subordinates, simply use another sheet of paper for the extra columns. (If you've never done formal performance appraisal, select up to four employees whom you know well and then try to picture what their appraisal behavior would be like.)

3.   Distribute 100 points *per subordinate* among each group of four paragraphs, using the same guidelines you used on the questionnaire in the last chapter. In other words, for each subordinate, assign the 100 points in a way that reflects that subordinate's appraisal behavior. Make certain that your point assignments for each subordinate in each section of the questionnaire total 100.

4.   You may want to score these on completion. You'll find a score sheet at the end of the questionnaire. You may also want to rerate these same subordinates after reading the book; as you read further, your ratings may change.

**HOW MY SUBORDINATES BEHAVE IN
PERFORMANCE APPRAISAL**

Names of subordinates			

1. *Initial reaction*

Q1. Comes on strong. Challenges and defies. Starts out with self-inflating statements ("I guess this shouldn't take long. After all, I've been doing a darned good job") or with statements designed to throw me off balance ("Well, I guess you're going to rake me over the coals, aren't you?"). Seems smug and ready for an argument.

Q2. Quiet, tense, uncommunicative. Seems worried, suspicious. Volunteers nothing. If I say something that requires response, response is brief and noncommittal. Subordinate seems waiting for other shoe to drop.

Q3. Very friendly, outgoing, eager to please. Shows no urgency about settling down to business. Responses are good-natured and long-winded. Seems unhurried.

Q4. Appropriately friendly, candid, business-like. Wastes little time on irrelevancies. Seems eager to get down to business. Responses are forthright, direct, to-the-point. Early statements are neither defensive nor cocky.

Names of subordinates			

2. *Communication*

Q1. Overbearing, know-it-all. Makes extreme statements ("Here's the greatest idea you ever heard"; "Anybody who says that is completely screwy"; "That'll never work in a million years"). Exaggerates; uses many superlatives. Listens impatiently. Interrupts a lot. Sticks to views stubbornly; belittles others. Asks questions only to get own views confirmed or to put me on spot. Often inattentive, uninterested.

Q2. Aloof, unresponsive. Talks little; stays mainly on surface. Rarely discloses deep feelings or opinions. Rarely makes strong, committed statements. Hesitant and noncommittal. Seems wary, skeptical, eager to see appraisal end. Uses many gestures (nods, shrugs) or very short phrases ("Uh-huh"; "I guess so"; "Okay").

Q3. Talky, genial, meandering. Avoids or shrugs off unpleasant topics. Exaggerates a lot, so things sound better than they are. Rarely argues, and then does so in good-natured, apologetic way. Eager to agree. Rarely has bad word for anyone. When I talk, subordinate frequently injects approval ("Great"; "Fine"; "And how!"; "You bet!").

Q4. Candid, analytic, businesslike. Listens closely, asks for clarification, then gives own views fully. Backs them with data. Willingly changes mind if shown persuasive evidence. Disagrees without belligerence or stubbornness. Sticks to subject. Respectfully listens without interrupting or knocking my views.

Names of subordinates			

3. *Disagreements*

Q1. Pushes own views exclusively ("There's only one way to do it . . ."). If I insist on imposing a decision, subordinate accepts grudgingly ("Okay, but I still say . . ."). Isn't attentive to all my ideas; often argues or belittles ("Naw, I don't think that'll work").

Q2. Lets me make decisions. Shows no desire to be involved. If I urge involvement, subordinate tosses the ball back ("Whatever you say is okay with me"; "I'll go along with you"; "Just tell me what you want and I'll do it"). Lukewarm or indifferent. Doesn't argue or contradict.

Q3. Overenthusiastic in going along with my decisions ("That's sensational!"; "I don't know why *I* never thought of that"). Doesn't argue or contradict, but does chime in and agree ("Say, I really like that").

Q4. Constructively tries to be part of decision-making. Offers own ideas, discusses mine in depth, is willing to debate or contradict if that seems in order. Listens closely and respectfully before offering comments. Backs up views with data; asks plenty of questions.

Names of subordinates			

4.   *Resolution and goals*

Q1.   Doesn't always understand final goals or action plans because of sloppy listening and failure to ask searching questions. Agreement is half-hearted and smug ("Look, since you insist, I'll do it your way. But I still say my approach would work better").

Q2.   Usually understands final goals and action plans because follow-through is necessary for survival. Commitment may be low or nonexistent. Voices agreement, but unenthusiastically.

Q3.   May not fully understand final goals and action plans because of failure to listen carefully. Nevertheless, voices enthusiastic agreement and commitment, even though commitment may be false.

Q4.   Understands final goals and action plans. Is committed to them because convinced that they're reasonable or essential. Pledges commitment even if not fully convinced because of awareness that there's no better way ("I don't really like it, but I see why we have to do it. I'll support you all the way").

Score Sheet

Subordinate 1	Q1	Q2	Q3	Q4
1. Initial reaction				
2. Communication				
3. Disagreements				
4. Resolution				
Sum				

Subordinate 2	Q1	Q2	Q3	Q4
1. Initial reaction				
2. Communication				
3. Disagreements				
4. Resolution				
Sum				

Subordinate 3	Q1	Q2	Q3	Q4
1. Initial reaction				
2. Communication				
3. Disagreements				
4. Resolution				
Sum				

Subordinate 4	Q1	Q2	Q3	Q4
1. Initial reaction				
2. Communication				
3. Disagreements				
4. Resolution				
Sum				

WHY SUBORDINATES RESIST CHANGE

As we've said, what really matters in an appraisal is not what you alone do, or what your subordinate alone does, but what you do together—the *interaction*.

Once we examine the interaction, we can see why performance appraisal is such hard work. Almost always, an appraisal is supposed to produce some kind of *change* in the subordinate's way of doing things. But, as we've just seen, subordinates often behave in ways that make it very difficult to produce change. Why? There are at least three basic reasons.

1. *Most people have an emotional investment in their present way of doing things.*

Their self-image, their sense of who and what they are, is tied to their behavior on the job. So, when a subordinate takes, say, a Q1 approach and resists your ideas, insisting *his* way, the way he's been doing things all along, is best, he's not being stubborn for the sake of being stubborn. He's protecting his self-image by refusing to admit that he's doing anything wrong or that he needs to improve.

All of us have an emotional investment in the way we are, and, like all investors, we want to protect our investment. We've all spent a lot of time and energy and effort becoming what we are on the job, and most of us want to think that what we are is really okay. We've all got a sizable emotional investment in our present way of doing things; we're committed to ourselves as we presently are. Unless and until we become less complacent about our self-images, we're not likely to change. An appraisal should make the subordinate less complacent and more aware of the fact that there *is* room to improve.

2. *For many people, change is threatening.*

One nice thing about staying the way we are is that it makes life more predictable. As long as we behave as we always have, we can assume that people will respond to us as they always have. But the minute we start to do things differently, we introduce uncertainty into our lives. For many people, uncertainty is threatening; it suggests that something may happen that they won't be able to handle. So, *even if we are dissatisfied with ourselves,* we may choose to stay as we are rather than risk an uncertain future. The desire for certainty may win out over the desire to become something different and more effective. An appraisal should make the subordinate confident of her ability to manage change.

3.   *Change in hard work.*

Even if we want to change, and even if we aren't afraid to, we're still faced with the fact that change is demanding, whereas staying as we are is more or less easy. As long as we do things the way we've always done them, we can rely on habit, on familiar behavior. We don't have to think through everything we do, we don't have to be tense and watchful all the time. But this changes when we try to adopt new ways. Attempting new behavior, practicing it until it becomes habitual, is hard work. And very few people willingly undertake such hard work unless they're convinced that, in some personal way, *their efforts are going to pay off*. Without this conviction, most of us won't bother to change. An appraisal should make it plain to the subordinate that change is *worth* the effort.

SUMMARY

1.   There are four basic ways subordinates behave in performance appraisal: Q1, Q2, Q3, Q4.

2.   Q1 subordinate behavior is based on the idea that the best defense is a strong offense; come on strong during the appraisal and you may end up with a more favorable appraisal than would otherwise be the case. It is cocky, stubborn, argumentative.

3.   Q2 subordinate behavior is based on the idea that the best defense is a strong defense; what you don't say during an appraisal can't hurt you, so be cautious and don't say much. It is uncommunicative, tense, watchful.

4.   Q3 subordinate behavior is based on the idea that affable behavior generates affable responses, so the best way to have a pleasant appraisal is to focus on pleasantries. It is good-natured, genial, talky.

5.   Q4 subordinate behavior is based on the idea that an appraisal is a good chance to learn and grow, so the best thing to do is to be completely and candidly involved. It is collaborative, businesslike, inquiring, and open.

6.   Virtually all performance appraisal tries to produce a change for the better in the subordinate's behavior. But change is often very hard to effect because we have an emotional investment in our present way of doing things, because some of us are threatened by change, and because change is hard work.

A LOOK AHEAD

Now that we've looked at appraisal behavior on both sides of the desk, we're ready to look at the consequences of the various ways of doing appraisal. Once we see how the consequences of Q4 appraisal compare with the consequences of the other three approaches, we can take a close look at how to do Q4 appraisal. We do both these things in our next chapter.

5

Q4 Appraisal

THE BASIS

We're ready to begin the "how-to" part of our book: how to do Q4 performance appraisal. In this chapter, we give you the "do's" of Q4 appraisal, and we set the stage for the later chapters, which expand each of the "do's" into "how-to's."

We've explained that this book concentrates on Q4 appraisal techniques because these techniques are likely to produce consistently higher results than Q1, Q2, or Q3 techniques. To make this point as emphatic as we can, let's look at the results produced by Q1, Q2, and Q3 appraisal.

THE CONSEQUENCES OF Q1 APPRAISAL

In Q1 appraisal the superior uses a "do as I tell you . . . or else" approach. He tries to produce change through intimidation. "Look," he says, "most people aren't about to improve unless they *have to*. An appraisal gives me a chance to impress my people with the fact that they must change . . . or else they're going to be in trouble. It's amazing how much you can accomplish by shaking people up. The simple fact is that most people have to be made to change . . . and you can do that by making sure they run scared. Worry and fear are great motivators. That's what performance appraisal is for."

Different superiors use scare tactics in different ways. Some are blunt and direct. Others are subtle; their threats are implied, not explicit. But whether the superior uses a sledgehammer or a stiletto, the same results are intended: fear, anxiety, tension, uneasiness.

In Q1 appraisal the superior tries to dominate completely. His mind is made up before the appraisal starts. He tells the subordinate what the latter is doing wrong (he may also mention what he's doing right, but the emphasis is on mistakes), he lectures and warns, and he blames the subordinate, and *only* the subordinate, for whatever problems have arisen. Rarely is there a hint that the superior may be at fault, that he himself may be part of the problem. The subordinate is singled out as the culprit.

Since performance appraisal is supposed to produce change leading to better results, let's ask: Do Q1 tactics do this? The answer is "yes and no."

1. *Some* people *do* change because they're afraid not to. Fear sometimes produces results. The results may not be all that the superior wants, but at least they reflect some improvement in performance.

2. In many cases, however, intimidation doesn't work. For instance, a subordinate who gets bad results because he doesn't *understand* what he is doing cannot be transformed into a wonder-worker by "shape-up-or-ship-out" tactics. And a subordinate who gets bad results because she's bored by her job won't become interested and enthusiastic just because the boss demands it. In many cases, fear does *not* get results.

3. Subordinates who are deeply concerned about their personal security and afraid of taking risks are likely to jump whenever the boss says "jump!". Likewise, subordinates who are eager to maintain good relations with the boss and avoid hassles are likely to succumb to threats. On the other hand, subordinates with strong needs for self-respect, independence, and growth are much less likely to give in to Q1 tactics. Some may respond to intimidation by quitting ("I won't work where I'm not respected"; "I'm sick and tired of being pushed around"). Or they may pretend to go along with the boss while undermining him behind the scenes ("I'll show that so-and-so . . .").

4. So bullying sometimes gets results, but the unintended side effects can be very damaging. Resentment, sabotage, turnover—these are part of the price the "or-else" manager pays.

THE CONSEQUENCES OF Q2 APPRAISAL

As we've just seen, Q1 appraisal tries to produce change by threat, and it frequently backfires. But something must be said for the superior in a Q1 appraisal. While his efforts may be self-defeating, at least he believes that he *can* produce change. He believes he can *do* something to get better results out of people. And, in spite of bad side effects, he sometimes does.

That's not true in Q2 appraisal. In Q2 appraisal the superior is passive about the whole thing. "Don't kid yourself," she says, "people change . . . if at all . . . when they're good and ready to change, and not before. There's little or nothing a boss can do to make people improve. Either they do or they don't. It's up to them. All this talk about motivating people to do things differently is unrealistic. Like it or not, I'm pretty much at the mercy of my people. They decide if and when to improve . . . not me. Sure, some bosses look good because they're surrounded by turned-on people. But they can't take credit for that. They're lucky. If you're fortunate enough to have good people working for you, you're bound to look good yourself. But this is beyond your control. Either you luck out or you don't. If you do, you get the glory. If you don't, you get the blame. But you can't do anything about it, one way or the other."

Then why bother to appraise performance at all? The superior has two answers:

1.   "It's expected of me." Performance appraisal is a "ritual" insisted upon by top management, and the superior is not about to thumb her nose at top management. "If that's what they want," she says, "that's what they get."

2.   "It's a pretty good way to keep people in line." While the superior doesn't believe that appraisal generates change, she does believe it's a useful disciplinary device. "It doesn't hurt," she says, "to remind people occasionally that the organization expects certain things of them. I use these sessions to tell people what management wants them to do. That way, they're less likely to get out of line. Performance appraisal is a good way to funnel messages from the top down."

Little of real consequence happens in a Q2 appraisal, unless by accident. The superior usually deals in symptoms and superficialities. She may say something like: "Your production is down for the last quarter, and the people upstairs aren't too happy about it," but she doesn't go on to find out *why* production is down. She sticks to the surface, for two reasons:

1.   She's convinced that going *below* the surface wouldn't make any difference. ("Why bother? It's not going to do any good for me to know what's bothering one of my department heads, or why production's in a slump. If production is down, he's obviously doing something wrong. But I can't make him do it right. That's up to *him*.")

2.   She's *afraid* to dig beneath the surface. If she does, she may learn something she'd rather not know. Suppose, for example, that she tries to find out why one of her departments is slumping. And suppose the department head replies: "I'm not getting any support from you. You never come down to see what's going on. I need help . . . and I'm not getting it." Or, "Sure, we've got problems. We've got a messy cost problem in our scheduling operation . . . and nobody's doing anything about it. I've sent you five memos on the subject . . . and I'm still waiting for an answer." Or, "What do you expect? Information is always arriving late. We can't prepare reports without information. And every time I call the office about it, I get put off with alibis." In other words, the superior is afraid to dig deep because she may hear something that implicates *her,* that demands action by *her,* that may require *her* to rock the boat. And superiors who do Q2 appraisals don't like to rock the boat.

Subordinates with a strong need to feel secure or to be accepted don't change much as a result of Q2 appraisal. As long as they don't make waves (and people who want to be secure seldom do) the superior sees no reason to get rid of them, and as long as she doesn't insist that they change they see no reason to change. But even if they wanted to change they wouldn't get much guidance. So they usually stay in the same rut, appraisal after appraisal.

Other subordinates, those with strong needs for self-esteem or independence or growth, respond differently. They may get fed up with the lack of challenge, and transfer to another department or quit the company (or, maybe, spot a power vacuum and move in to fill it, displacing the boss and taking over themselves). Either way, the results are rarely what the superior intends.

THE CONSEQUENCES OF Q3 APPRAISAL

Back in World War II, a popular song advised people to "accentuate the positive, eliminate the negative, and don't mess with Mr. In-between." That pretty well describes Q3 performance appraisal. This doesn't mean that the superior talks only about positives and never refers to negatives or in-betweens. It means that he focuses on "good" news, tries to avoid "bad" news (and, when he can't, downplays it, jokes about it, or in some way makes it sound better than it really is), and tries to make even "neutral" news sound "good."

As the superior sees it, this makes sense. "If you want people to do a better job," he says, "you've got to encourage them. Praise, support, applause, all this helps. Whatever you do, don't *dis*courage them. People work best when they feel good. The minute they get disheartened, their work falls off. It's my responsibility to make them feel good, to let them know I'm on their side, that I'm pulling for them. It's up to me to make sure they don't get dejected or up-tight. If they do, their work will suffer."

As a rule, then, three things happen in Q3 appraisal:

1. *Good* news becomes *very good* news. A subordinate who's been doing a good job is told that his work is excellent, great, or even terrific. Positive exaggeration becomes the order of the day. Naturally, the subordinate gets the idea that he doesn't need to improve, that there's no reason to change. Why tamper with perfection, or even near perfection?

2. *Average* performance is inflated into *good* performance. A subordinate who's doing so-so work learns, to her pleasure, that she's doing "just fine," that she's coming along very well, that the boss is "pleased," that she "ought to be proud of herself," and so on. This can be disastrous. After all, the boss is the boss; he's supposed to know what good work is. If *he* says you're doing "fine," why doubt it? Who should know better?

3. Worst of all, *bad* performance is ignored or glossed over. Some superiors never mention it ("Why rub it in? Tell a guy he's doing terrible, and you'll only dishearten him. How can a man improve when his own boss undermines his confidence?"). Other superiors mention bad performance apologetically, suggesting that it's nothing to worry about. For instance, some refer to poor performance with weak jokes ("Well, Wally, you're not exactly a candidate for a prize, but . . ."). Others provide alibis ("Nobody's Superman; nobody succeeds all the time"). This is a way of dodging the hard facts. By using evasive language the superior avoids mentioning what's really wrong. Instead of saying, "Joe, we both know you've fallen far short of your goals this past quarter," he dilutes the truth by saying "Joe, we both know you haven't looked like the world's champion this past quarter." This softens the impact of the comment but it doesn't really help the subordinate.

The problem, then, is that Q2 appraisal is either too emphatic or not emphatic enough. When the superior has something good (or merely adequate) to say, he says it exaggeratedly, so that it misleads. And when he has something bad to say, he says it (if at all) so evasively that it, too, deceives.

What does all this do to the subordinate? That depends on the subordinate. Some (usually those with a strong need to feel secure or well-liked) believe what they hear, and conclude that they don't need to change (which they want to believe anyway). Others get the idea, sooner or later, that the boss doesn't know what's going on, or that he's not very smart, or not sincere. After a while, they grow impatient ("I'm tired of all this Mickey Mouse; I never really learn anything from this guy"), and either become demoralized (which is reflected in their work) or transfer or quit.

WHY Q4?

None of these things is likely to happen as a result of Q4 appraisal. Q4 appraisal, more than any other kind, can be expected to produce change leading to improved performance. That's why the rest of this book is largely concerned with Q4 techniques.

The rest of this chapter describes the typical Q4 appraisal approach— the approach we *recommend*. This chapter provides an overview; later chapters fill in the details.

A Three-Phase Process

Q4 appraisal is a three-phase process:

Phase 1.   Preparation
Phase 2.   The appraisal session
Phase 3.   Review

PHASE 1.   Q4 PREPARATION

Q4 preparation is always done prior to the appraisal session by *both* superior and subordinate, working independently. It should follow a systematic format (we describe such a format in a later chapter), and its results should be recorded in writing. Here are the objectives:

1.   Examine how effectively the subordinate's been performing.
2.   Analyze the reasons.
3.   Evolve action plans.
4.   Figure out the best way to insure collaboration during the appraisal session.

Here's how you and your subordinate, separately and independently, can attain these objectives during preparation:

1.   Sort the subordinate's goals into three groups: (1) those that have been met, (2) those that haven't, and (3) those you're not sure about.

2.   Examine the *met* goals. Determine why they were met. Then develop any further actions or goals that you intend to recommend. Anticipate your subordinate's response and work out ways to handle it.

3.   Examine the *unmet* goals. Determine why they weren't met. Develop any further actions or goals that you intend to recommend. Anticipate your subordinate's response and work out ways to handle it.

4.   Examine the *can't-tell* goals. Determine why you can't tell whether they've been met or not. Develop any further actions or goals you intend to recommend. Anticipate your subordinate's response and work out ways to handle it.

5.   Keep in mind that all your conclusions are tentative and will be discussed during the appraisal session. This discussion should cause some change in your conclusions. At the moment, all you want to do is amass evidence that will be analyzed during the appraisal, and form "perhaps" judgments based on that evidence. Don't try to reach hard-and-fast conclusions during the preparatory period.

PHASE 2.   THE Q4 APPRAISAL SESSION

The Q4 appraisal session—the actual face-to-face meeting between you and your subordinate (which should always follow intensive individual preparation by both of you)—is a five-step process. You're already acquainted with the five steps from Chapter 3: (1) arousing interest and testing readiness to participate; (2) increasing readiness to participate and getting the subordinate's self-evaluation; (3) presenting your own evaluation; (4) venting emotions and resolving disagreements; and (5) working out a final resolution. Now we'll look closer at each step, explaining its *objectives* and the *Q4 way* of achieving them.

Step 1.   *Arouse interest and test readiness to participate*

Objectives.   The purpose of this first step is to make sure your subordinate is really ready to take part in what's coming. If he is, fine. If not, it's up to you to perk up his interest and to find out how willing he is to listen and participate in an open, inquiring, businesslike way. Unless he *is* willing to play an active, collaborative role in the appraisal, there's not much point in proceeding. So the first thing you want to do is arouse interest and test his readiness to participate.

THE Q4 WAY

Here's how to arouse interest and test readiness to participate:

Be Appropriately Sociable.   Your sociability should fit this particular subordinate. Some subordinates need more sociability than others; some become tense if they don't get to chat with the boss for a minute or two, others feel awkward chatting with the boss, some want to get right down to business, others begin to worry if there isn't at least some casual conversation, and so on. Know each subordinate, and be *appropriately* sociable with each.

Explain the Benefit.   Explain how the appraisal can pay off for this particular subordinate. To do this, you have to know what he wants from his job—what *he* considers beneficial—and then you have to tie that to the results of the appraisal. In other words, show him that "if you do thus-and-thus as a result of this appraisal, you can expect to get so-and-so out of it."

Question.   Ask a question (one he can't answer "yes" or "no") to get the subordinate to tell you how he really feels about proceeding. Find out if he's ready to participate constructively, if he's ready to work with you to get at the facts, or if he really wants to do something else (argue, sound off, chit-chat, keep his mouth shut, play verbal "games," etc.).

Size Up His Readiness.   After noting everything the subordinate says and does, size up his behavior and determine if he's ready to go ahead or not. If he's belligerent or sarcastic (Q1 behavior), aloof and sullenly compliant (Q2), overenthusiastic and talky (Q3), *you've got a problem.* These behaviors mean one thing: your subordinate's not really ready to take part in the appraisal in an open, collaborative, fact-finding way. They're signals to you that you must increase his readiness *before* proceeding. On the other hand, if he's showing businesslike, thoughtful, questioning behavior (Q4), then he is ready, and you can get on with the actual evaluation.

Step 2.   *Increase readiness to participate while getting the subordinate's self-evaluation*

Objectives.   You want to do two things in this phase: (1) increase your subordinate's readiness to proceed if it needs increasing (and it usually will) so that you and she can go ahead in a collaborative, Q4 way, and (2) at the same time get her to start evaluating her own performance. Note that the subordinate's self-evaluation should *precede* your evaluation of her performance. In Q4 appraisal both superior and subordinate present their views, but the subordinate presents hers first. That way there's no chance of her being squelched, or of her views being colored by yours.

THE Q4 WAY

Here's how to increase your subordinate's readiness to proceed while starting to get her self-evaluation.

Probe.   Probing is the use of questions, statements, and strategic silences to put another person in a communicative frame of mind and to get that person to share ideas and feelings. Q4 appraisal cannot be separated from skill at probing. There's no way, in fact, that you can get past this part of the appraisal effectively without having a mastery of probing techniques. If you probe in a Q4 way, you can increase your subordinate's readiness to proceed *and* begin getting her to evaluate her performance at the same time.

Promote a Candid, Realistic Self-Evaluation.   Don't settle for just any self-evaluation. You want her to do a thorough self-evaluation that focuses on key issues, explores them in detail, and pulls no punches. To get this, you must know how to probe.

Step 3.   *Present your own evaluation*

Objectives.   Now you want to do three things: (1) assess your subordinate's self-evaluation; (2) if you agree with it, say so; if you don't present your own views; (3) make sure each of you fully understands the other's evaluation.

THE Q4 WAY

Here's how to present your own evaluation.

Weigh Your Subordinate's Self-Evaluation.   Listen carefully and patiently to what he's saying. If you don't understand, ask him to clarify. After he's had a real chance to speak his piece, and when you're confident you understand him, assess his views. Ask yourself questions like: Has he been thorough? Has he ignored or skirted any important matters? Has he backed up his views with evidence? Is it complete and accurate? Has he drawn reasonable conclusions from it? And so on.

Confirm Where You Agree.   If you "buy" any (or all) of his evaluation, say so.

Where You Disagree, Give Your Own Views.   Make sure your views are supported by data. Present your case objectively and unemotionally. Don't blame, scold, or needle. Lay the facts on the line and draw whatever conclusions you think justified. Tell the whole story; don't bury facts, or stack them against the subordinate.

Present Your Views a Few At a Time.   You're not presenting your views just to hear yourself talk. You want them to sink into your subordinate's consciousness. You can make things easier for him (and yourself) if you present your views in small clusters, pausing between each cluster to make sure he understands and to find out how he feels.

Check to Ascertain Your Subordinate's Understanding and Reaction.   If he doesn't understand what you're saying, clarify it. If he doesn't agree, talk about it. You may not be able to get his full agreement, but you must at least get his full understanding.

Summarize Your Agreements and Disagreements.   Once you've presented your evaluation, take stock. List those matters on which the two of you agree or disagree. Don't dodge the disagreements or water them down. Lay it on the line. And don't be startled or upset because there *are* disagreements. If anything, expect them.

Step 4.   *Vent emotions and resolve disagreements*

Objectives.   You want to do two things now: (1) clear the air of interfering emotions, especially those stirred up by differences in the two evaluations—emotions that are slowing down or blocking the progress of the appraisal; (2) resolve any disagreements so that future performance can be based on mutually held perceptions and mutually accepted conclusions.

THE Q4 WAY

Here's how to vent emotions and resolve disagreements.

Encourage Venting.   This is done by probing. The idea is to reduce tensions (and tensions are almost inevitable in an appraisal) because tense people (or angry or elated or worried or suspicious people) aren't able to do a very good job of resolving problems. You want to create a calm, rational, businesslike, trustful climate in which you can achieve the goals of the appraisal. This requires venting.

Discuss.   Once you clear the air of interfering emotions, discuss the differences in a candid, give-and-take way. This may not be easy. It'll take probing and patience on your part. But it must be done. Don't haggle about your disagreements; explore them. Examine (or reexamine) the evidence on which your differing views are based. Once the two of you agree on the evidence, you'll find it easier to agree on an interpretation of the evidence. Try to get complete agreement, but realize that that may be impossible. In any event make sure the two of you understand one another, even if you don't finally agree.

Step 5.   *Work out the final resolution*

Objectives.   Now you want to do three things: (1) develop goals for future performance and plans by which they can be achieved; (2) make sure your subordinate sees the benefit to her of pursuing these goals; (3) check her final understanding and commitment, and set up a review procedure.

THE Q4 WAY

Here's how to work out the final resolution.

Develop Goals and Action Plans.   Before presenting your own thinking, get your subordinate to express hers. Pin this down. Don't settle for vague goals ("Well, I just want to do the best job I can"). Develop specific, detailed goals. Make sure they're neither unrealistically difficult nor unchallengingly easy; set goals that will stretch the subordinate without pulling her apart. If possible, make the goal-setting and action-planning a mutual activity; don't impose your own goals unless you must.

Make the Benefits Explicit.   It's important that your subordinate see how achieving the new goals will pay off for her, for you, and for the organization. Try to get her to tell you what the payoff will be, instead of your telling her. Remember: a benefit isn't really a benefit unless your subordinate genuinely sees "what's in it for me."

Check Understanding and Commitment.   Ask the subordinate to summarize two things: (1) her understanding of what's been decided, and (2) her commitment to it—her willingness to carry out the decisions. If there's still some confusion or resistance, try, one last time, to work it out. Aim at the highest possible understanding and commitment. Then set up a review procedure with a specific date that's agreeable to both of you.

PHASE 3.   Q4 REVIEW

The review session always takes place on a date later than the appraisal session. It's impossible to generalize about when the review should be held—a month later, six weeks, two months, what have you. The date hinges on factors like the significance, complexity, and urgency of the goals, the problems likely to be encountered in working toward them, your availability, the subordinate's availability, and so on. Whenever the review is held, however, it has two objectives: (1) to find out what problems the subordinate may be having with the plan of action devised in the appraisal session, and (2) to work out strategies for overcoming them. The techniques used are essentially the same as those used in the appraisal session, although there's a good chance that the review will take less time.

An Encouraging Word

If our outline seems too brief and too general, don't be discouraged. All we've tried to do in this chapter is present an overview. Everything we've mentioned is explained in detail later. We talk at length about how to present benefits, how to test readiness to proceed, how to probe, and so on. In fact, we start in our next chapter.

SUMMARY

1.   This book concentrates on Q4 appraisal because Q4 appraisal is most likely to produce consistently good results. Q1, Q2, and Q3 appraisal are all likely to produce no change in performance, or the wrong kind of change. Q4 appraisal is likely to produce change leading to better performance.

2.   Q4 appraisal is a three-phase process: Phase 1 is preparation (done prior to the appraisal session); Phase 2 is the appraisal session; Phase 3 is review (done some time after the appraisal session).

3.   Phase 1, preparation, is done separately by superior and subordinate, each of whom systematically examines how effectively the subordinate has been performing and why, anticipates differences in opinion, and gathers data and forms tentative conclusions about both past and future performance, all of which will be used as the basis of discussion in the appraisal session.

4.   Phase 2, the appraisal session, uses a five-step approach:

Step 1.   *Arouse interest and test readiness to participate*
(a)   Be appropriately sociable.
(b)   Explain how the appraisal can be expected to pay off the subordinate.
(c)   Question and probe to learn how the subordinate feels about proceeding.
(d)   Size up the subordinate's readiness to participate by observing his behavior.

Step 2. *Increase readiness to participate and get the subordinate's self-evaluation*
(a) Probe to increase the subordinate's readiness to participate (if necessary).
(b) Promote a candid, realistic self-evaluation.

Step 3. *Present your own evaluation*
(a) Assess the subordinate's self-evaluation.
(b) Confirm where you agree.
(c) Where you disagree, give your own views.
(d) Present your views a few at a time.
(e) After presenting each part of your evaluation, check your subordinate's understanding and reaction.
(f) Summarize the agreements and disagreements between you.

Step 4. *Vent emotions and resolve disagreements*
(a) Encourage venting of interfering emotions.
(b) Conduct a give-and-take discussion to settle any disagreements.

Step 5. *Work out the final resolution*
(a) Develop goals and action plans.
(b) Make the benefits explicit.
(c) Check the subordinate's understanding and commitment; set up a review.

5. Phase 3, review, takes place some time after the appraisal session. Its purpose is to find out what problems, if any, the subordinate is having with the plan of action developed in the appraisal and to work out strategies for overcoming the problems.

A LOOK AHEAD

As our outline shows, one of the first things to do in Q4 appraisal is to explain what's in it for the subordinate. So, in our next chapter we take a hard look at the whole subject of benefits—what they are and how to use them in appraisal.

6

Benefits and Appraisal

Since, in a sense, Q4 appraisal begins and ends with "what's in it for the subordinate," the best way to get into the "how-to" of Q4 appraisal is to zero in on *benefits*.

WHAT IS A BENEFIT?

A benefit is the reward that comes from achieving a goal. When a subordinate asks "What's in it for me?" or "Why should I bother?" he's really asking "What's the benefit?" Whenever you tell a subordinate "If you do this, you'll get that," you're really saying "If you achieve this goal, you'll get that reward." In other words, you're talking about benefits.

This definition makes the whole subject of benefits sound pretty simple. But the minute you start to think about the definition, you realize it raises as many questions as it answers. For example: What is a *reward*? Is it always something tangible? What if the subordinate doesn't want the reward you're offering? What if she wants a reward you're not able to grant? Will a subordinate work hard to achieve a goal even if there is no benefit, or if he doesn't like the benefit? How can you know what a particular subordinate will or will not consider rewarding? And so on. As it turns out, the subject of benefits is complex, and the complexity must be mastered before you can do Q4 appraisal.

THE INGREDIENTS OF BENEFITS

A good way to begin mastering this complex subject is by studying the "ingredients" that make up a benefit. These ingredients are pictured in Figure 6.

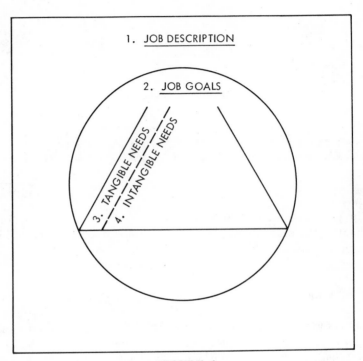

FIGURE 6

Some Definitions

Let's explain the four ingredients: (1) job description, (2) job goals, (3) tangible needs, and (4) intangible needs.

1. Job description. A *job description* (or position description) tells what an employee is supposed to do on the job. It spells out, in general terms, what a job is all about: what activities it comprises and what it's supposed to accomplish. For example, the job description for a *district sales manager* might list as one of the duties of the job: "To optimize sales in his or her assigned district."

2. **Job goal.** A *job goal* is a specific objective. It takes one of the activities listed in the job description and makes it operational. By themselves, the activities listed in the job description are too general to do much with. Only when translated into specific terms can they be carried out effectively. A *job goal* translates one of the general activities in the position description into specific terms. Take the example we just used: "To optimize sales in his or her assigned district." As it stands, this is almost *impossible* to implement; it's too vague, too imprecise. For instance, it doesn't answer any of the following questions:

- What does "optimize" mean? *How many* dollars or units are optimal?
- Are optimal sales strictly a matter of *volume*? Or do other factors (sales expense, profitability, etc.) enter into the definition?
- How about *product mix*? Does "optimal sales" mean a certain *balance* of products sold, or will *any* combination of products do? Are certain products in the line supposed to be emphasized or de-emphasized?
- In *what period of time* must these "optimal" sales be achieved?
- What's meant by "assigned district"? What are its boundaries? Can all prospects within those boundaries be called on, or are some of them "special accounts" handled by the home office? Are calls permitted outside the district? If so, will sales outside the district be included in the "optimal" figure?

The *job goal* answers these questions. It converts a general activity into a specific objective. Here's how "to optimize sales in his or her assigned district" might be translated into a *job goal*:

JOB GOAL

To produce a total of $500,000 in sales of all company products to standard accounts (not special accounts) within the North-Central district, with no more than 20% of this volume being in reversible widgets, between March 1 and February 28.

Job descriptions are usually *im*precise. They establish the overall nature of the job, not its specific demands. *Job goals* are different. They get down to the nitty-gritty.

Are job goals *always* as exact and as easily measurable as in our example? No. Some job goals are less precise. To explain why, let's distinguish between two kinds of job goal:

BUSINESS JOB GOALS

These are the kinds of job goals we've been talking about so far. Here are some more examples:

Decrease rejects at the Lakeside plant by 5% in the next six months.

Pretest our new advertising theme in the Middleborough market and report the results by July 15.

Negotiate a two-year no-strike pact with the union and have the agreement completed at least two months before the present contract expires.

What these, and all *business* job goals, have in common is: (a) they're all relatively *precise*, and (b) they focus on *objective* goals, goals that are not personal in nature.

BEHAVIORAL JOB GOALS

These are (a) usually more *in*exact and harder to measure, and (b) usually involve interpersonal skills. Here are a few examples:

Start standing up to those department heads who make unreasonable demands for computer time.

Resolve your conflict with Joe so that the two of you begin working together effectively again.

Stop belittling those people who disagree with you at weekly staff meetings.

All of these are impossible to measure in the usual sense; they can't be quantified or expressed in numbers. And all of them have a personal quality; they involve changes in the behavior of individuals, not in outside conditions.

To be a *legitimate* behavioral job goal, the behavior that's aimed at—the improved behavior—must be behavior that will make it easier to achieve a *business* job goal. Or, to put it another way, the *present* behavior—the behavior to be changed—must be behavior that has a demonstrably negative effect on the attainment of a business job goal. For example, in order to negotiate a two-year, no-strike pact with the union (business job goal), a company negotiator may first have to learn to control his temper when talking with his counterpart in the union (behavioral job goal). Or, in order to increase production by 3% at the Oceanview plant (business job goal), the plant manager may first have to stop alienating his foreman (behavioral job goal). Behavioral job goals, once achieved, make it easier to achieve business job goals. Changes in behavior that have nothing to do with achieving business job goals are not legitimate behavioral job goals. As we said in an earlier chapter, the question to ask about behavior change is: What difference will it make? If it won't make any difference as far as *business job goals* are concerned, then the change in behavior is not in itself a legitimate goal.

3. Tangible needs. *Tangible needs* are the substantive rewards that the person who's doing the job *wants* from the job. They differ from job goals and from the job description in this way:

- The *job description* tells what the job is all about.
- The *job goal* is what the *company* wants from the job (in business or behavioral terms).
- The *tangible need* is the payoff—the specific, concrete "something"— that the *employee* seeks from the job (for example: a raise in pay, a title, a promotion, a new job assignment, a transfer to another location, an appointment to the executive committee, a chance to work more closely with other people, an opportunity to pursue a line of research, a chance to implement a new idea, and on and on). Some tangible needs are for *material* payoffs ("I want a private office"). Some are for *situational* payoffs ("I want to be given the job of designing the new annual report"). Some tangible needs are for *changes* ("I want to be taken out of marketing and assigned to direct selling"). And some are for a *continuation* of the status quo ("I just want to hold on to what I've got"). What *all* tangible needs have in common is that they represent the "returns"— the "prizes"—that people seek for the effort they expend on the job.

Let's illustrate: Bernie Stewart is a district sales manager. His job goal is to produce the $500,000 in sales in our example. Bernie wants to achieve this goal because, if he does, he'll be the only district manager in the company who's made his assigned quota for 10 straight years, and he'll almost surely get promoted to regional sales manager when the present R.M. retires next year. His *tangible need* is to get promoted. This is something *he* seeks from the job.

Now, here's an important distinction: a *job goal* makes sense no matter who's got the job; a *tangible need* doesn't. Here's what we mean: Suppose Bernie Stewart were to quit his job because he'd been offered the job of marketing director for a larger company. And suppose he were replaced by George Graham, a younger salesman who's been with the company only three years, who has just become a new father and taken a mortgage on a new home, and who worries a lot about how he's going to pay his bills. George, in other words, is deeply concerned about finances, something that hasn't bothered Bernie for many years. Now, as district sales manager, George's job goal would probably stay the same as Bernie's was: to produce $500,000 in sales volume. In other words, the job goal doesn't usually depend on *who's doing* the job. But, while George's job goal is the same as Bernie's was, his reason for wanting to achieve it, his tangible need, is different. Bernie was looking for a title and a promotion, while George is looking for something else: a salary increase so he can meet his bills on time, start a savings account for his new child, buy some much-needed life insurance. That's why his new job is so important to him. If, in his first year as district manager, George produces $500,000 in sales, he'll get a bonus equal to 5% of his annual earnings, and that will give him and his family the money they now lack. George's job goal is the same as Bernie's; their tangible needs are different.

   4. Intangible needs. *Intangible needs* are the reasons why people want the tangibles they seek from their jobs. Intangible needs help us make sense out of tangible needs; they help us understand why Bernie wanted one kind of tangible payoff from achieving his job goal while George wants another kind.

   Tangible needs—the returns we want for doing our jobs—don't "just happen." There's a reason for them, and that reason can be found in our *intangible needs.* Let's expand on this:

- *Tangible needs are always based on intangible needs.* We all share certain basic needs. These basic—or intangible—needs nag at us to be satisfied; if they're not, they continue to "bug" us, and, as a result, we feel tense, discontented, ill-at-ease. (George has security needs that show up as worries about the size of his monthly mortgage payments, about his lack of life insurance, about whether he'll be able to send his child to college, and so on.) That's why our tangible needs are so important; if we satisfy *them,* we begin to fill our basic intangible needs, and *that* makes us feel less dissatisfied, less fretful, less vexed, less troubled.
- *Tangible needs are never random.* We don't pick our tangible needs out of thin air; we pick them because we think they'll satisfy one or more of the intangible needs that's nagging us.

   Take Bernie Stewart. Bernie wants to be the only district manager in the company who's made his quota for 10 straight years, and he wants to become a regional sales manager. Why? Because he has a strong *intangible need* for *esteem*; he wants to be looked up to, admired, regarded as "somebody" in the company. He doesn't like being "just another district manager." He wants to be "special," to stand out. And he *will—if he attains his job goal.* Here's why:

- As the only district manager to make quota for 10 straight years, he'll be guest of honor at a company banquet at which the president of the company will give him a plaque to honor his achievement.
- A whole issue of the company newspaper will be devoted to him. It will contain his photograph and an interview in which he explains the "secret" of his success.
- Almost certainly he'll be made a regional manager within a year. As such, he'll *control* 75 salespeople in six states.

Not bad for somebody who wants to be "special." No wonder Bernie's tangible need is what it is.

What about George Graham? Why is his tangible need different? Because he has a strong *intangible need* for *security*, for making sure he's able to meet his growing family responsibilities. This isn't surprising: he's the father of a four-month-old child, he's just taken on a sizable commitment by buying a new house; and, as he puts it, "We're spending every cent we make; there's nothing left over for savings or emergencies." So, George's *tangible need* is naturally different from Bernie's. If George achieves his job goal, here's what will happen:

- His annual income will increase 20% over last year, when he was a salesman.
- He'll get a 5% bonus—a lump-sum cash payment.
- He'll be able to meet all his current expenses, buy some life insurance, and even start a small savings program.

Not bad for someone with a strong need for security. No wonder George's tangible need is what it is.

A recap

Let's redefine our basic terms.

1. **Job description.** A general explanation of what the job is.
2. **Job goals.** Specific objectives that translate the job description into *operational* terms.

   - *Business job goals:* Fairly specific goals, usually measurable, dealing with objective matters.

• *Behavioral job goals.* Less easily measurable goals, dealing with changes in behavior or interpersonal skills that will help achieve a business job goal.

3. **Tangible needs.** The substantive payoffs the person *doing* the job *wants* from the job.
4. **Intangible needs.**   The reasons *why* people want the rewards they do want from their jobs.

BENEFITS: A BETTER DEFINITION

We're now able to give a better definition of *benefit:*

A benefit is the reward, as the subordinate defines "reward," that the subordinate gets for achieving a job goal, either business or behavioral; the subordinate will define as a "reward" anything that helps him fill one or more of his tangible or intangible needs.

Or, to put it as bluntly as possible, a benefit to the subordinate is whatever the *subordinate* considers a benefit. The fact that you consider it a benefit doesn't make it a real benefit; the subordinate must consider it a benefit. And that won't happen unless it *ties in* with that subordinate's tangible or intangible needs.

BENEFITS AND MOTIVATION

This definition of *benefit* takes us straight to the subject of *motivation.* Motivation is usually defined as the drive to achieve a goal. But why should anyone have such a "drive"? Why should anyone care if a particular goal is achieved or not? Because the person who has the drive *wants the benefit that comes with the goal.* That's why Q4 appraisal starts and ends with a discussion of benefits. If the benefits are *real* benefits, that is, if they're considered benefits by the subordinate, then he'll be motivated to achieve them. Q4 appraisal *motivates.* To make it motivate, four things must happen:

1. You must learn what the subordinate's *tangible* and *intangible needs* are. Find out what the subordinate wants from the job, and why.
2. You must *link* these needs to the subordinate's *job goals.* In other words, you must show how the subordinate can get what he wants by achieving the job goals.

3. This link-up between job goals and needs will give the subordinate a *benefit*, a clear understanding of *"what's in it for me."* (Why should I knock myself out to negotiate the first two-year no-strike agreement in the industry? Because if I do, I'll be made a member of the executive committee with all the recognition that goes with it. Why should I bother to streamline the operation of my profit-centered department? Because if I do, and if profits rise as a result, the company will make a sizable contribution to my profit-sharing account, and I *want* that account to be as big as possible when I retire two years from now.)

4. Understanding the benefit—"what's in it for me"—motivates the subordinate. It produces the *commitment* and drive needed to achieve the job goal. Subordinates work with commitment when they have a personal reason to do so. The job goal becomes something they really *want* to achieve.

The Motivation "Formula"

Motivation cannot really be boiled down to a formula. However, for purposes of clarification, let's look at a useful way of organizing what we've said so far: that performance on the job is a function of benefits. At the risk of oversimplifying, we can summarize the four-part process described above in a simple "formula":

$$J + N \rightarrow B \rightarrow P$$

In this formula

> J is the *job goal*—business or behavioral

> N is the *needs*—tangible and intangible—that the subordinate wants to satisfy on the job

When you link these together ($+$) they lead to ($\rightarrow$)

> B the *benefit*—the subordinate's understanding of "what's in it for me if I achieve the job goal."

This produces commitment—a desire to achieve the job goal—which leads to ($\rightarrow$)

> P—highly motivated *performance*—performance that's enthusiastic, effortful, determined, vigorous, sustained.

To bring this formula—$J + N \rightarrow B \rightarrow P$—to life, we need to say more about *intangible needs*. So far, we've discussed these very generally. But, if you're going to *work* with intangible needs in appraisal, you should understand them in detail.

FIGURE 7.   The pyramid of needs.

Intangible Needs

Figure 7 (adapted from the work of Abraham Maslow, a psychologist who pioneered in this field) depicts on the horizontal layers the six basic intangible needs. (Maslow called these personal needs. From now on, we'll use *intangible needs* and *personal needs* interchangeably.)

We can picture personal needs as the layers of a pyramid. At the bottom are the most basic needs (those most fundamental to life and health). Each higher layer is less crucial to physical well-being but more important to psychological fulfillment. If any of these needs is unfilled, we experience some kind of tension or dissatisfaction. Table 1 defines each basic need and shows what can happen if it isn't filled.

Four Fundamental Points

Before going any further, we'd better emphasize four fundamental points. By doing so, we'll probably answer some questions that may be bothering you.

1. Throughout this book, whenever we talk about intangible or personal needs, we'll be talking about the needs we've depicted on the pyramid.

Table 1. A Closer Look at Intangible Needs

Intangible Need	Definition	What Can Happen When Need Is Not Filled
1. Biological needs	All our bodily requirements for healthy living and functioning	Pain, physical discomfort or impairment, illness
2. Security needs	Needs for assurance that the world is basically stable and predictable, and that our existence is basically safe and unthreatened	Tension, anxiety, worry, fear, panic, danger
3. Social needs	Needs for companionship, love, belonging, affection, acceptance; the need to know that other people find us likable and pleasant to be with	Loneliness, boredom, feelings of being unloved or unlovable, low self-image
4. Esteem needs	Needs for recognition, reputation, status, prestige, approval, self-respect; the need to know that we count for something	Loss of confidence, low self-image, self-doubt
5. Independence needs	Needs for privacy, for not being pushed or manipulated, for a chance to show we're responsible and able to take care of ourselves, for an opportunity to control our own lives	Feelings of frustration, entrapment, exploitation, despair
6. Self-realization needs	Needs to develop in ways that are personally important to us, to feel that we're growing, learning, maturing, increasing our competence and our mastery over circumstances	Feelings of futility, alienation, bitterness, wasted chances, being at a dead-end

(There's one exception to this statement: we won't be talking about biological needs; we focus our attention on the five "higher" needs, from security to self-realization). These needs have two things in common:

- They all manifest themselves in *interaction;* they all affect the way we relate to other people. (They may also, at times, manifest themselves in noninteractional behavior, in things done apart from other people. For instance, a subordinate may spend hours of hard work, at home, polishing and perfecting a report far beyond what's required by management, simply because, as he puts it, "Doing things as effectively as I can is one way I grow; that's how I further my own self-realization." Throughout this book, however, our concern is with the *interactional* manifestations of personal needs.)
- Therefore, the basic personal needs help us make sense out of the behaviors on the Dimensional Model, all four of which are patterns of *interacting* with others.

2.   This doesn't mean that these are the only needs manifested by human beings. Not by a long shot. When we refer to these as *basic* needs, we're not saying that there are no other needs; we're simply saying that these needs are basic to understanding interactional or interpersonal behavior, and *the impact of interpersonal behavior on performance and on performance appraisal* is what this book is about.

3.   As you observe your subordinates (or yourself) on the job, you may well see other needs manifesting themselves: intellectual needs (watch an engineer absorbed in solving a tricky math problem), aesthetic needs (observe an illustrator concentrating on the picture in an ad layout), the need to gratify curiosity (look at a researcher trying an unprecedented experiment "just to see what happens"), and so on. (Psychologists have never agreed on a "complete" list of human needs.) All these "other" needs have two things in common:

- They frequently manifest themselves in *non*interactional performance, in the work people do *alone*. (In fact, some people may deliberately seek isolation so that they can gratify these needs. Think of the researcher who wants very much to spend several days alone in his lab so that he can concentrate on a challenging problem and thereby satisfy an intellectual need—"a need to know.")
- These other needs are not basic to understanding the behaviors on the Dimensional Model, and we do not concern ourselves with them in this book.

4.   We are not, however, denying the importance of these noninteractional needs. Far from it. They *do* affect the things people do on the job, and they can, therefore, be important in a performance appraisal. Any

superior should be aware of them, look for manifestations of them, and consider them when doing appraisal. Nevertheless, we do not concern ourselves with noninteractional needs in this book. Our concern is, as it has been up to now, with *interpersonal behavior and its impact upon performance and performance appraisal.*

A Closer Look at Intangible Needs

1.   We all have the personal needs pictured on the pyramid, but not in the same degree. Some of us, for example, have such a strong need for security that we fret about it much of the time—others of us don't bother much about it; some of us crave esteem and attention—others of us don't; and so on. Generally, the need that "bugs us" the most is the one we try hardest to fill. When it comes to personal needs, the "wheel that squeaks the loudest gets the most grease."

2.   Each of us has his own personal definition of each need. One of us, for example, may define her *social* needs in very expansive terms ("I'm one of these people who needs lots of friends. When somebody new starts working on our department, I go out of my way to be congenial . . . invite her out to lunch . . . spend lots of time getting acquainted with her. I just like to surround myself with friendly people. The more the merrier"). Another of us may define social needs more narrowly ("I've always been satisfied with one or two close friends at the office; I'm not very gregarious"). So what one person means by "social needs" is not necessarily what another means. The same is true of all other intangible needs.

3.   Any *one* intangible need can be translated into *many different* tangible needs. For instance, three superiors working for the same company may have strong esteem needs, yet each may try to fill them in a different way. One superior's tangible need may be to win the Manager of the Year Award ("The only thing I really want is to sit at the awards banquet and get that certificate from the president of the company. When the president honors you, then you know you really count for something"). Another superior's tangible need may be to gain promotion to vice-president ("The only way to be somebody in this company is to have a title on the door. I won't really get any respect around here until I've moved up to a V.P.'s spot"). A third superior's tangible need may be a 10% increase in salary ("Let's face it, you're nobody around here unless you make and spend lots of money. That's all that impresses people: throwing dough around"). To repeat:

- Intangible (personal) needs *underlie* tangible needs.
- Any *one* intangible need can take *many* forms once it's translated into a tangible need.

An analogy may make the connection between intangible and tangible needs clearer. One reinforced-concrete foundation can support *many* different kinds of houses: single-storey ranch houses, two-storey colonial houses, houses of contemporary design, houses that resemble old French chateaus, and on and on. But *without* the foundation there can be no house of any kind. *Intangible* (personal) needs are like reinforced-concrete foundations. One personal need can support *many* different tangible needs. For instance, a subordinate with a strong security need (intangible)—a need to feel safe and protected on the job—many translate it into any of the following tangible needs:

• Work in a department known to have no turnover.
• Work for a particular boss who "protects his people."
• Become fully vested in the company pension plan.
• Get transferred to a job in which you don't have much to do with other people.

And so on. All these tangible needs would help satisfy the need for security; they'd help the subordinate feel safer in his job. But, without the *in*tangible need, none of these tangible needs would make any sense.

4.   Because tangible needs and intangible needs are so close, we've used a broken line to separate them on the pyramid. There's never a sharp, distinct separation between them. Tangible needs are always influenced by personal (intangible) needs.

A Caution

Our "motivation formula" $J + N \rightarrow B \rightarrow P$ talks about *highly motivated performance* (*P*). It does *not* talk about excellent results. There's a reason for this. Without highly motivated performance, it's almost impossible to get excellent results. But highly motivated performance cannot, by *itself*, produce excellent results. Excellent results depend upon other factors as well.

For example, a subordinate whose performance is highly motivated may not produce excellent results if the bottom falls out of the economy, if a competitor comes up with a new product that captures the lion's share of the market, or if other people in the company fall down on the job. And he won't produce excellent results if his job knowledge is weak ("The guy's a real tiger, but he doesn't know what he's doing") or his goals are unrealistic ("He's knocking himself out . . . but nobody in the world could achieve *that* objective"). Motivation *is* important; in fact, it's indispensable. But it's not the whole ball game.

Needs and the Dimensional Model

Q4 appraisal is appraisal that motivates, so we'd better look closer at the subject of motivation. Let's start by asking: "How are *personal* (intangible) *needs* related to the four subordinate behaviors on the Dimensional Model? Figure 8 answers that question.

Figure 8 shows that personal needs underlie—form the foundation for—on-the-job-behavior. What a subordinate does on the job reveals her personal needs. But we never actually "see" personal needs (that's why we call them *intangible;* intangibles are invisible). What we do see is the behavior that's based on personal needs. Needs are demonstrated—made visible—by what people do.

We take a close look at this connection between needs and what people do in our next chapter.

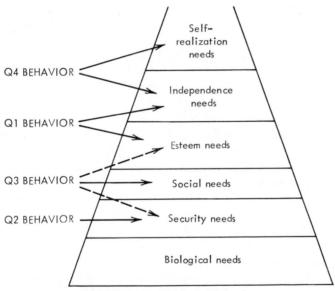

FIGURE 8.   Needs and behavior.

Conclusion

As we've just seen, what people *do* on the job is related to their needs. They behave in certain ways, pursue certain strategies, follow certain paths, because they're impelled by certain intangible needs. On-the-job behavior is, very largely, an attempt to satisfy these intangible needs. Since the satisfaction of personal needs produces *benefits* (when we fill a personal need we feel rewarded), we can say that on-the-job behavior is *benefit-seeking* behavior. Your subordinates may not say this; they may not even think it; but the fact is that what they're doing, much of the time, is striving for benefits as *they* define them. This fact is critically important in Q4 appraisal so we pursue it at length in our next chapter.

SUMMARY

We've covered a lot of ground in this chapter. Let's pause to recap.

1.   Since Q4 appraisal starts and ends with a discussion of benefits, it's important to understand benefits in detail.

2.   A *benefit* can be most simply defined as the reward that comes from achieving a goal.

3.   Four ingredients make up benefits: (a) the job description, (b) job goals, (c) tangible needs, and (d) intangible needs.

4.   A *job* (or position) *description* tells what an employee is supposed to do on the job.

5.   A *job goal* is a specific objective which translates one of the activities in the job description into operational terms. There are two kinds of job goals: (a) business job goals (precise, measurable, and impersonal) and (b) behavioral job goals (inexact, harder to measure, having to do with changes in behavior that would help to achieve business job goals).

6.   *Tangible needs* are the specific, concrete things that the person doing the job wants from the job.

7.   *Intangible* (or personal) *needs* are the reasons why people seek those tangibles in their jobs.

8.   Thus, a *benefit* can be redefined as the reward a subordinate gets for achieving a job goal, either business or behavioral; the "reward" will be considered a reward by the subordinate only if it helps fill one or more of the subordinate's tangible or intangible needs.

9.   *Motivation* is the drive to achieve a goal. People have this drive when they understand, and want, the benefit that comes with the goal.

10.   To motivate a subordinate, four things must happen: (a) you must learn the subordinate's tangible and intangible needs; (b) you must help link these to the subordinate job goals; (c) this link-up must provide a clear understanding by the subordinate of "what's in it for me" (the benefit), so that (d) the subordinate becomes committed to the job goal.

11.   This four-step process can be summarized as: $J + N \rightarrow B \rightarrow P$, where J stands for job goal (business or behavioral); N for needs (tangible and intangible); B for benefit; P for committed performance.

12. There are six basic intangible (personal) needs: biological, security, social, esteem, independence, and self-realization. If any of these needs is unfilled, tension or dissatisfaction results. So, naturally, people try to fill their unfilled needs. They do this by selecting certain tangible needs; when the tangible need is filled, the underlying intangible need is also filled (at least partly), and this provides a benefit. Gaining this benefit (and the good feeling that comes with it) is what motivation is all about.

13. We all have the same intangible needs, but not to the same degree. Each of us defines his intangible needs in his own way. And each of us tries to satisfy his intangible needs by focusing on whatever tangible needs he chooses. Thus, the same intangible need can be filled in different ways by different people.

14. Certain intangible needs underlie certain kinds of on-the-job behavior. Specifically, security needs underlie Q2 behavior, social needs (and, to a lesser extent, security and esteem needs) underlie Q3 behavior, esteem and independence needs underlie Q1 behavior, and independence and self-realization needs underlie Q4 behavior.

15. Thus, what we *do* on the job (our behavior) is related to our *needs*, and the satisfaction of our needs produces *benefits*. To a very large extent, then, on-the-job behavior is *benefit-seeking* behavior. This point is crucial in Q4 appraisal.

A LOOK AHEAD

We've said that on-the-job behavior is largely benefit-seeking behavior, a fact that's crucially important in Q4 appraisal. This means that, to do Q4 appraisal, you must know how to interpret your subordinate's behavior to figure out what his underlying intangible needs are; unless you can do this, there's not much chance you can discuss benefits in a way that will mean something to *him*. And, if you can't do that, there's not much chance you can motivate him to do a better job. So the next chaper explains *how* to interpret behavior, *how* to tie needs to goals, and *how* to develop benefits that produce commitment.

7

How Q4 Appraisal Motivates

As our last chapter showed, on-the-job behavior is like a code. Anyone who cracks a code becomes able to do things he couldn't otherwise do. Anyone who learns to decipher on-the-job behavior acquires abilities he didn't have before. Specifically, once you figure out what a subordinate's behavior means, once you crack the behavioral code and find out what's beneath it, you can:

1. Link each subordinate's job goals to her real needs, instead of her supposed needs.
2. Talk about real benefits for the subordinate, instead of supposed benefits.
3. Produce genuinely committed performance because the subordinate understands "what's in it for me," and because the subordinate considers it worth having.

BENCHMARKS OF NEEDS

Cracking the behavioral code doesn't require the skills of a cryptographer. It requires (a) knowing what to look for and (b) careful observation of what each subordinate says and does. By observing a subordinate's behavior closely and then matching your observations with certain benchmarks, you can pretty well figure out which intangible needs underlie the behavior. Let's look at the benchmarks for deciphering behavior, starting with those for *security* needs, and working our way up the pyramid.

Security (Q2) Needs

There are nine benchmarks, or signs, of security needs: (1) cautiousness, (2) neutrality, (3) procrastination, (4) following the leader, (5) preference for solitude, (6) working "by the book," (7) overly strong respect for tradition, (8) pessimism, and (9) dependence.

1. *Cautiousness.*

The subordinate is guarded and self-protective. He keeps his thoughts to himself, doesn't take strong stands, stays out of controversies, arguments, discussions. He doesn't take chances, prefers the tried-and-true, doesn't want to be the first person to do something different, seldom comes up with a new idea. During appraisal, he "plays it cool."

2. *Neutrality.*

The subordinate doesn't get involved in disputes or take sides. He's closed-mouthed, noncommittal, responds to touchy questions with a shrug or "I'm not sure." He's "hard to read" or "hard to get a handle on." During appraisal, he skirts sensitive or controversial issues.

3. *Procrastination.*

The subordinate puts off certain projects, especially those with high stakes. He delays and postpones. He finds good alibis for holding off, moving slowly, refusing to take chances. He advises "further study" or requests "additional data" before moving ahead. "Let's be sure," he counsels. "We may regret taking hasty action."

4. *Following the leader.*

The subordinate rarely exerts initiative. He looks to you for signals, and follows them unswervingly. He seldom volunteers. He doesn't talk back, question, or express doubt. During appraisal, he's deferential, yielding, submissive.

5. *Preference for solitude.*

The subordinate is a loner. He prefers jobs he can do by himself, away from others. Among people at work, he hangs back, is quiet and restrained, seems shy, awkward, or unsure of himself. He spends much time alone. During appraisal, he's aloof, distant, withdrawn.

6. *Working "by the book".*

The subordinate follows instructions, rules, procedures, policies down to the last word. He does best in structured situations, where he has a detailed plan to follow. He rarely deviates from the routine. If he thinks there's a better way to do it, he keeps it to himself.

7. *Overly strong respect for tradition.*

The subordinate is a strong believer in the status quo—in the way things have always been done. If you ask what he thinks about a new approach, he may answer: "We've done it the old way for years. Why change?" During appraisal, he doesn't suggest innovations, isn't inclined to gamble or take a chance on something new.

8. *Pessimism.*

The subordinate takes a bleak (or at least guarded) view of the future. He's a strong believer in setting something aside for a rainy day. When discussing a course of action, he's excellent at suggesting things that could go wrong. He frequently asks questions that begin "What if . . .?" ("What if the whole market falls apart in the second quarter?" "What if we can't get the production increase we've projected?").

9. *Dependence.*

The subordinate leans on other people. He readily lets others carry the ball, and is never miffed because somebody else gets a challenging or important assignment. He's a willing follower who's most comfortable in supportive or back-up roles. He prefers to follow your lead, to "bring up the rear."

You're not likely to find any subordinate who displays all these behaviors all the time. But if you have a subordinate who displays some or most of them much of the time, you've got a good indicator of strong *security* needs.

Social (Q3) Needs

There are ten benchmarks of social needs: (1) amiability, (2) agreeableness, (3) meandering, (4) striving for acceptance, (5) extreme loyalty, (6) impatience with structure, (7) gregariousness, (8) sensitivity to cues from others (9) tendency to color facts, and (10) indecisiveness.

1. *Amiability.*

The subordinate is very friendly, outgoing, easy to talk to. Her conversation has a highly personal tinge ("How's your family these days?"). She's very accepting of new people in the organization, going out of her way to make them "feel at home." In appraisal, she's affable, good-natured, congenial.

2. *Agreeableness.*

The subordinate usually voices agreement whether she really agrees or not. She rarely takes unpopular stands, seldom argues, belittles, or disagrees. She's quick to compromise, to seek the middle ground. When hearing an argument she often suggests concessions: "If everybody just gives a little, we can resolve this in no time." During appraisal she's likely to give in readily to your views.

3. *Meandering.*

The subordinate has trouble sticking to one task or topic. When doing a job she frequently interrupts herself to chat with her peers. When talk gets heated or unpleasant she shifts to another subject. She's excellent at dodging harsh or disagreeable topics. During appraisal she shows an uncanny ability to switch to topics other than performance.

4. *Striving for acceptance.*

The subordinate works hard at pleasing others, no matter what their level in the organization. She wants to belong, to be accepted, to be "part of the family." To gain acceptance she may pay undeserved compliments to people, invite them out to lunch, spend time in casual chit-chat, send birthday or anniversary cards to everyone in her department, listen patiently as other people unburden themselves, and on and on. During appraisal she shies away from suggestions that she do things that will separate her from the group.

5. *Extreme loyalty.*

The subordinate is a dedicated "team player." She never gripes, or "takes shots" at you, or expresses skepticism about organizational policies. Her attitude is "They know what they're doing . . . it's not my place to question them." She's a booster, frequently praising you ("I've got the greatest boss in the world") or the organization ("This is the best outfit in the whole industry").

6. *Impatience with structure.*

The subordinate is bored by details and unimpressed by procedures. She prefers to "play it by ear." She often says things like: "I don't care how somebody gets a job done as long as she puts her heart in it" or "Why nit-pick? My people do the best they can . . . what more can I ask?" In appraisal she's impatient with "trivial" details, and eager to get on to more "interesting" topics.

7. *Gregariousness.*

The subordinate dislikes being alone. If a group gathers she's likely to be part of it. She enjoys working on committees. She dislikes any task that isolates her.

8. *Sensitivity to cues from others.*

The subordinate is very alert to negative cues from others, and readily adjusts her behavior in response. If she notes displeasure on someone's face she immediately tries to change the look by smoothing over the situation. She seems to have antennas extended in all directions to receive signals from other people.

9. *Tendency to color facts.*

The subordinate exaggerates favorable information so that things sound even better than they are, and she omits or plays down disconcerting information ("It's not as bad as all that"; "I'm sure it'll work out in the long run"). During appraisal she concentrates on positives and eliminates or minimizes negatives.

10. *Indecisiveness.*

Because she wants to please everybody, the subordinate has trouble making firm decisions. She vacillates and delays, trying to keep everyone satisfied. Or she commits herself fervently to one course of action today, only to commit herself, with equal fervor, to a contradictory course tomorrow.

Esteem (Q1) Needs

There are eight benchmarks of esteem needs: (1) boastfulness, (2) domination, (3) positiveness, (4) opinionatedness, (5) high valuation of status, (6) rare credit to others, (7) preference for influential people, and (8) strong need to win.

1. *Boastfulness.*

The subordinate likes to crow. He makes heavy use of "I" and "me." He overstates his achievements, enjoys being the center of attention, and tries to make himself the focal point of any discussion. During appraisal he puffs up his achievements and hogs credit for them.

2. *Domination.*

He monopolizes conversations, squelching others by belittling or putting them down. He listens impatiently and interrupts a lot. Or he listens to the end and then depreciates what he's heard ("Who are you trying to kid? Nobody in his right mind would buy that idea"). If he thinks he can get away with it he may even try to take over the appraisal.

3. *Positiveness.*

The subordinate plays down or ignores anything that might put him in a bad light. In describing his exploits he "rewrites the script" so that he emerges the hero, and other people come off as villains or bunglers. He's skillful at building his own image, usually to the detriment of other people's.

4. *Opinionatedness.*

The subordinate has strong, dogmatic views, and he states them forcefully. He uses few qualifiers ("sometimes," "maybe," "perhaps," "possibly") and many absolutes ("always," "definitely," "never," "absolutely," "unquestionably," "beyond a doubt," "positively"). His air of certainty and finality discourage questions or discussion.

5. *High valuation of status.*

The subordinate is highly impressed by rank and position. He talks a lot about "getting ahead," "moving up," being a "top dog." He disdains people who don't "make it big" ("losers," "second-raters," "chumps").

6.   *Rare credit to others.*

The subordinate is reluctant to credit or praise others. He sometimes appropriates their ideas and passes them off as his own. Or he downgrades them ("It may sound good, but . . . believe me . . . it'll never work"). He may even downgrade other people's success ("Take it from me, the guy's a flash in the pan. He won't last").

7.   *Preference for influential people.*

The subordinate likes to spend time with "big shots" or "comers." He may socialize with his peers, but he rarely socializes voluntarily with his subordinates (even at events like the company Christmas party, he spends most of his time with the "top" people). During appraisal he's likely to resist suggestions that he get "closer" to his own subordinates.

8.   *Strong need to win.*

He likes to win. When he argues he persists until he wears down his opponent. If he's vying for a promotion, he puts heart and soul into the competition. He takes defeat hard and usually explains it as "tough luck" or "a series of bad breaks." He's quick to accuse the winner of "not playing by the rules" or "taking unfair advantage." Almost never does he blame himself for losing. And, in appraisal, he rarely blames himself for failure to reach his goals ("It was an impossible goal to begin with; not even Superman could have made that objective" or "I'd have made that goal easily if the economy hadn't gone to pot").

Independence (Q1 and Q4) Needs

There are many benchmarks of independence. Some are typical of Q1 behavior, others of Q4. We'll consider each group separately.

Q1 INDEPENDENCE NEEDS

Six benchmarks usually reveal the independence needs that underlie Q1 behavior: (1) argumentativeness, (2) rugged individualism, (3) resistance to other people's ideas, (4) taking fixed positions, (5) constant bids for autonomy, and (6) attempts at control.

1.   *Argumentativeness.*

The subordinate is belligerent, argues minor points, and converts differences of opinion into struggles. This is his way of showing that "I do my own thinking . . . nobody imposes his ideas on me." He may not, however, be belligerent during the appraisal. It depends upon whether he thinks he can "get away with it"; in other words, on how tough he thinks you are.

2.   *Rugged individualism.*

The subordinate dislikes supervision, guidance, or control. He's hard to manage, insists that "Nobody has to tell me what to do," and sometimes defies policy or disregards instructions. He has his own ideas on most subjects, and frequently claims that he "knows better" ("I know that's the way it's always been done, but I tell you it doesn't make sense").

3.   *Resistance to other people's ideas.*

The subordinate is quick to knock other people's ideas. He pokes holes in them ("Let me tell you why that will never work"), is sarcastic and mocking ("That's the greatest idea since Napoleon decided to fight at Waterloo"), or belittles the person who conceived the idea ("That guy wouldn't know a good idea if he tripped over it").

4.   *Taking fixed positions.*

Once he makes up his mind, the subordinate refuses to budge. He resists persuasive arguments, and rejects evidence that would undermine his position. He uses phrases like "Don't try to tell me . . ." or "I can prove you're wrong . . ." or "That's ridiculous." But he may mask his behavior during appraisal if he's convinced you "won't stand for it."

5.   *Constant bids for autonomy.*

The subordinate persistently tries to get more freedom of action. If he's assigned to a team, he may tell you: "Look . . . why don't you get these guys off my back and let me do it my way?" Or, accepting an assignment, he may say: "Don't bother with all the instructions . . . just let me handle it."

6.   *Attempts at control.*

Even when working with his peers, the subordinate tries to grab control so that he doesn't feel "crowded" or "constrained." Whenever he can, he strives to be "number one."

Q4 INDEPENDENCE NEEDS

Five benchmarks usually reveal the independence needs that underlie Q4 behavior: (1) self-confidence, (2) collaboration, (3) acceptance of help, (4) full disclosure, and (5) openness to ideas.

1. *Self-confidence.*

The subordinate is self-assured, in a quiet, restrained way. She doesn't brag and bluster, doesn't seem concerned to "prove" anything about herself. Her manner says: "I am what I am, and you'll have to accept me as what I am."

2. *Collaboration.*

The subordinate collaborates willingly with other people. She doesn't feel that teaming up with others "crowds" her; if anything, she's convinced that it may help her achieve more than otherwise. She uses "we" and "us" frequently, as well as "I" and "me." In appraisal she's quick to give credit where credit is due, and to admit that "I didn't do it all myself."

3. *Acceptance of help.*

The subordinate willingly accepts help on projects if she thinks she needs it. She's not worried about looking "weak" or "leaning on other people." "Listen," she says, "I don't pretend I know all the answers. I stand on my own feet when I can, but sometimes I can't." If you suggest, during appraisal, that she needs more training, she isn't insulted or upset.

4. *Full disclosure.*

In presenting her views, the subordinate isn't afraid to give all sides of the story. If she argues for a point, she acknowledges other opinions; she doesn't stack the cards in her own favor. She's candid, direct, and forthright.

5. *Openness to ideas.*

The subordinate is receptive to new ideas, and gives credit to their originators. She isn't threatened by ideas just because they come from somebody else. She's curious, eager to learn, willing to listen, and willing to change her mind if the evidence warrants. During appraisal her respect for evidence, for facts, data, statistics, is paramount; she backs her ideas with evidence, and she accepts other people's ideas *if* they're backed by solid evidence.

Self-Realization (Q4) Needs

There are nine benchmarks of self-realization needs: (1) probing, (2) candor, (3) task-orientation, (4) desire for challenge, (5) risk-taking, (6) preference for the new, (7) willingness to confront differences, (8) sharing ideas, and (9) sensitivity to the needs and ideas of others.

1. *Probing.*

The subordinate is curious and eager to learn. He asks pertinent questions, gets people to open up and talk, and digs for information and ideas. During appraisal, he asks searching questions; he doesn't accept things "on faith" or just because you, the boss, say so.

2. *Candor.*

The subordinate is constructively direct, forthright, willing to level. She doesn't play verbal games (telling the good news while holding back the bad, or exaggerating to make things sound better or worse than they really are). She pays compliments without sounding phony, and levels criticism without being embarrassed, ill at ease, or demeaning the other person. During appraisal, her responses are frank and to-the-point, even if they put her in a bad light.

3. *Task-orientation.*

The subordinate concentrates on the job at hand, and he's interested in the job for its own sake (not just because it will make him look good). He works steadily, without frequently stopping to chat or clown around. He wastes little time on extraneous matters. During appraisal, he doesn't meander or dwell on irrelevancies; he sticks to the subject of performance.

4. *Desire for challenge.*

The subordinate seeks out assignments that are tougher than most, or that give her a chance to try something different. She likes to do things that nobody's done before. Easy or monotonous assignments make her fidgety or frustrated.

5.   *Risk-taking.*

The subordinate isn't afraid to take chances. In fact, he enjoys an element of risk. He's not reckless; he doesn't foolishly gamble the organizations' resources. But he is willing to take calculated chances, and to speak out against stand-pat approaches ("Look, we've been doing it that way for years, and we've never gotten the results we should. Why don't we try a new approach? Let me show you how . . .").

6.   *Preference for the new.*

The subordinate enjoys working with the new and unique. She's easily bored by routine, and scorns "stodgy" or "unimaginative" or "uncreative" ways of doing things. She doesn't accept the new just because it's new; she accepts it only if it works better than the old ("I don't believe in change just for the sake of change"). But she *is* attracted to the new. She's curious about "breakthroughs" and "pace-setting techniques," she enjoys hearing about promising but unproven methods, and she likes investigating novel or original ideas.

7.   *Willingness to confront differences.*

The subordinate doesn't relish conflict, but he faces up to it and tries to resolve it. Instead of turning his back on disagreements, pretending they're not there or that they'll "go away," he acknowledges them, discusses them, and tries to work out settlements that will last. In performance appraisal he faces up to differences between himself and you, and he's not afraid to disagree with you.

8.   *Sharing ideas.*

The subordinate willingly shares ideas with those people who can benefit from them. She doesn't act as if she "owns" a good idea, she doesn't feel powerful or important just because she knows some organizational "secrets," and she doesn't use information as a weapon for putting down other people. When she can (and, many times, she can't), she shares her thinking with people in the organization who can put it to good use.

9.   *Sensitivity.*

The subordinate perceives what other people think and feel, and he responds to it. He doesn't always agree with them, but he is alert to what they're trying to get across and, in turn, he communicates about things that matter to them. To put it another way, he engages in real *dialogue.*

A Caution

In talking about benchmarks of needs, we don't want to convey the idea that every subordinate manifests one and only one set of needs. As we said when we introduced the Dimensional Model of Superior Behavior, all of us display different patterns of behavior at different times and in different situations. So you may observe your subordinates displaying benchmarks that manifest more than one personal need. This is something you'll have to take into account when you do appraisal. Here are a few examples.

Ed Brady is a research chemist for a major chemical manufacturer. When he interacts with his fellow scientists in the company he displays mainly Q2 benchmarks. He shows a strong preference for solitude (he rarely socializes with his peers, and, when he does, he's very quiet and remote); he's exceedingly cautious and noncommittal (when asked for his opinion of a book or movie, he usually shrugs and says "I'm not really sure what my reaction was"); and he willingly follows the leader (when asked to head a committee to plan a retirement party for the boss, he refused and said: "Give the job to somebody else; I'll do whatever I'm told to do to make the party a success, but I don't want to be in charge"). In other words, when it comes to interpersonal relations, Ed is a loner; most of his colleagues call him, behind his back, a "dud."

But, when it comes to research, Ed manifests an entirely different set of benchmarks. In the lab he displays Q4 behavior. He is open to new ideas (he constantly devours professional journals from all over the world in search of what he calls "new directions"); he's a risk-taker (over the years, he's made several groundbreaking discoveries because he's insisted on persevering with research that his peers called "foolish" or "dead-end"); he's strongly task-oriented (he often spends 10 or 12 hours a day in the lab, plus time at home reading abstracts and journals); and he readily seeks out challenge (he often volunteers for assignments that his peers say are "too tough" or "too complicated"). As his boss puts it, "There's no better researcher in the country; the guy's a whiz."

Obviously, Ed Brady is a man who manifests different needs in different settings. When he's interacting with his fellow workers, his *security* needs are paramount; he feels unsure of himself and uncomfortable around people. When he's doing research, his *independence* and *self-realization* needs are paramount; he's self-assured and eager to grow. (Remember: we said in our last chapter than personal needs don't *always* manifest themselves in interaction. They may, sometimes, manifest themselves in the things people do when *by themselves*. In Ed's case, his independence and self-realization needs manifest themselves when he's working *alone* in the lab or at home.)

If you were appraising Ed's performance, you'd probably want to keep both sets of needs in mind. For example, in discussing *behavioral* job goals ("Start communicating some of your ideas to the other people in the lab so that they can benefit from your thinking"), you'd want to be mindful of his *security* needs. In discussing *business* job goals ("We need to finish Project H-12 by March if we're going to beat out competition"), you'd want to keep his *independence* and *self-realization* needs in mind. As we said in our last chapter, motivation *is* complex.

Here's another example:

Sam Elgin is manager of the accounting department. His relationships with the people who work for him are mostly Q1. His subordinates call him (when he's not around) "Terrible-tempered Sam"; as one long-time employee puts it, "When Sam chews you out, you can feel it for weeks afterward." He's strongly opinionated ("Of course I'm right; I'm paid to be right ... and don't you forget it") and boastful ("I learned accounting in night school; that took real strength of character. These people I've got working for me don't know what hard work is ... but, believe me, *I* know"). When he interacts with people, he's loud, cocky, a show-off.

But when it comes to managing *accounting* systems, Sam is quite different. He displays so much Q2 behavior that management complains about his "timidity." He resists change (most of the new systems adopted by his department have been forced on him by his boss); he procrastinates (as one department-head puts it, "Sam never prepares a report today if he can put it off until tomorrow"); and he works by the book (as another department-head complains: "This guy lives and breathes by the book; he's such a stickler for procedure that he drives me crazy"). Thus, as an accounting manager, Sam is cautious, tradition-bound, and afraid of innovation.

Obviously, two sets of needs are at work here. When he interacts with his people, Sam's *esteem* needs come to the fore; when he supervises accounting systems, his *security* needs come to the fore. Once again, we see that motivation is complex.

So here's a word of caution: *be prepared for complex behavior.* Don't be surprised if your subordinates manifest more than one personal need. Most of the examples in this book are deliberately simple; simple examples help to make clear points. But don't expect to see simple, clear-cut behavior all the time in the real world. Observe your subordinates as they *really* are, and deal with them as they really are. Once mastered, the skills described in this book will help you do exactly that.

IS IT WORTH IT?

There's no "quickie" way to find out which personal needs motivate your subordinates. The only dependable way takes considerable time and energy.

You have to observe each subordinate carefully over an extended period, you have to hold probing discussions, you have to listen carefully, you have to sift and analyze and interpret what you hear and see, and you have to match the data you acquire with the benchmarks we've just listed. That's a lot of work. Are the results worth it?

Sure they are. To see why, let's go back to our formula: $J + N \rightarrow B \rightarrow P$.

1. P—committed performance—doesn't just happen. It's the end result of a process that begins when you link job goals (J) with needs (N). (Sure, you may have some subordinates who do committed work without any effort on your part. But you can't expect this to happen very often. In almost all cases committed performance happens because of a process— the *linking* process—and it's up to *you* to see that the process occurs.)

2. P—highly committed performance—happens when the subordinate clearly understands "what's in it for me," and when he *wants* what's in it. Why should anybody work hard to achieve a goal if the payoff isn't one he's interested in? Suppose a subordinate wants greater *independence* on the job, and you tell him that achieving a certain goal will bring him greater *security*. You're likely to turn him off instead of on because "what's in it for him" isn't what he wants. And, because it isn't, he may reject it, and turn in a sluggish performance instead of a committed one.

3. This means that not just any link-up will do. The link-up must be between job goals (J) and the subordinate's *real* tangible and intangible needs (N).

4. Finding out what these real needs are requires plenty of effort on your part. In putting forth this effort, keep two things in mind:

    a. Almost always you have to infer intangible needs from what you've observed about the subordinate. Very rarely will a subordinate say, in so many words, "I have a strong need for security" or "I have very compelling independence needs." Usually, these needs are un-verbalized; you have to figure them out by a process of deduction, in which you add up everything you know about the subordinate and come to a conclusion about his intangible needs. As we said before, you have to break the code; you can't rely on your subordinate to tell you what the code means—you have to determine that for yourself.

    b. Tangible needs are frequently (but not always) verbalized, especially if you ask questions about them. If you ask a subordinate, "What do you want from your job?", he's likely to say something like "A 10% raise" or "A chance to become a section head" or "An opportunity to try out some of my own ideas." All of these are tangible needs, and all of them are easily put into words. But that requires effort on *your* part. Many subordinates won't voluntarily verbalize their tangible needs; they have to be asked.

So, in the great majority of cases, finding out what a subordinate's needs are, either intangible or tangible, takes effort by you. With intangible needs, the effort is usually *inferential;* you have to figure out the needs from evidence you've acquired. With tangible needs, the effort may involve *discussion;* you have to probe the needs. Either way, *you* must take the initiative.

Is it worth it? Yes—as the following example shows.

An Example

To see how important the *right* link-up between J and N is, let's imagine the following: A company has decided to install an electronic-data-processing accounting system (to replace its present manual system). The financial vice president has decided to put the controller of the company, who reports to him, in charge of the project. The exact *job goal* (J) is: oversee the installation of an EDP accounting system and make it operational within six months.

How can the vice president link this job goal (J) to the controller's tangible and intangible needs (N) so that the controller sees the benefit of the project to him (B), is committed, and thus performs in a highly motivated way (P)? The answer depends, of course, on *what the controller's tangible and intangible needs are.* Table 2 (pages 102-103) suggests some possibilities. In reading Table 2, assume that the vice-president (a) has inferred the controller's intangible needs by observing his behavior, and (b) has discovered his tangible needs by discussion with the controller.

Four Vital Points

The table illustrates four vital points:

1. The *same* job goal (J) can be linked to a *wide variety* of tangible and intangible needs (N).
2. The *benefit*—"what's in it for me"—can only be made clear to the subordinate if you link the job goal to the *right* needs—the needs that motivate *him*.
3. The right needs can only be determined if you do the necessary observing, listening, probing, and thinking.

4. If you do all this and do it right, you'll be able to talk the subordinate's language in performance appraisal. And, when it comes to motivating him to do better work, *his* language is the one that counts.

A Managerial Predicament

It would be fairly easy to motivate subordinates if you were always able to gratify their tangible needs. Imagine, for example, conducting the following dialogue with one of your people:

YOU: Helen, what do you want out of your job?
HELEN: I want to be promoted to head of the auditing section.
YOU: Fine. Just complete this assignment successfully and the promotion
       is yours.

If that's all there were to it, motivation would be a snap. But that's not all there is to it. Why not? Because, like every superior, you face the following predicament:

• Tangible needs—the direct rewards that people want from their jobs—
  are important in motivating people.
• But people's tangible needs *exceed* the *supply* of tangible payoffs. You
  can't give a promotion, or a raise, or a bigger office, or a membership
  on the executive committee, to everyone who wants one. When it comes
  to tangible needs, the *demand outruns the supply.*

What *can* you do? Keep these rules in mind:

1. When you can, appeal to tangible needs by offering tangible rewards.
(If a subordinate wants a promotion, say, and if an opening is available,
and if achievement of the job goal justifies the promotion, then offer the
promotion as a reward for attaining the goal.)
2. At the same time, try to satisfy the subordinate's intangible needs.
(Table 3 illustrates how you might fill *both* tangible and intangible needs.)
3. When you *can't* fill tangible needs, try to motivate the subordinate
by at least satisfying his *intangible* needs.

This is *not* a cop-out. It simply recognizes the hard reality: when it comes
to satisfying *tangible* needs on the job, we live in a scarcity economy.
   To show the difference between satisfying tangible needs and intangible needs, we've developed Table 3 on page 104 and Table 4 on page 106.

Table 2. How to Link *J* (Job Goals) and *N* (Tangible and Intangible Needs)

Job Goal	If Controller's Observed Behavior Is:	Controller's Intangible Needs (Inferred from His Observed Behavior) and Tangible Needs (Verbalized) Are Likely to Be:	Benefits Presented to Controller by Vice-President
Oversee installation of an EDP accounting system and make it operational within six months.	Q1—boastful, highly ambitious, domineering. Strongly opinionated. Likes plenty of freedom. Prefers having boss "stay off my back."	*Intangible:* Esteem Independence *Tangible:* "I'd like to accomplish something around here that would gain me some really favorable attention from top management."	1. If you succeed in this assignment, you'll get plenty of attention from important people in the company. 2. This is a chance to stand out from your fellow managers and show how good you really are. 3. This is an opportunity to put some of your ideas to work. You'll have plenty of freedom to do things your way. 4. You'll be in control of a sizable task force. 5. Once installed, this new system will give you tighter control of your department.
	Q2—cautious, follows boss's lead, prefers to work alone, works by the book, has strong respect for status quo.	*Intangible:* Security *Tangible:* "I wish I could exert better control over some of those young mavericks in my department."	1. You'll get plenty of help on this assignment. A sizable task force is being put together to work on the project. 2. Once installed, this new system will make your job easier. You'll come up with better information faster, and cut down on complaints and criticisms from other departments. 3. This EDP system will cut down on "surprises" due to insufficient information, and will give you more time for anticipating and overcoming problems.

4. Successful completion of this project will solidify your position and keep the "Young Turks" in your department off your back.

1. This is a great chance to perform an important service for the company.
2. The assignment will require working with a large group of people in the company, as well as outside suppliers, consultants, etc.
3. Successful completion of this assignment will bring you plenty of approval.
4. Once installed, the new system will give you extra time for dealing with your people by freeing you up from a lot of monotonous, routine, time-consuming chores.

Q3—amiable, agreeable, wants to be widely accepted, loyal, very sensitive to cues from other people, impatient with details and structure.

Intangible: Social
Esteem
Security

Tangible: "I sure would like to get rid of some of the tiresome detail work in my department."

1. This is a demanding assignment. You'll be responsible for working all the bugs out of the system and for meeting a tight deadline.
2. To handle this assignment, you'll have to supervise a sizable task force and get real teamwork out of a bunch of hard-to-handle people.
3. You'll have to make frequent decisions in which large amounts of money will be at risk.
4. Once installed, the new system will provide better and faster data, thereby freeing you up for other tasks and giving you more time for developing new ideas.

Q4—likes challenge and freedom to make decisions. Attracted to new ideas, willing to take risks, enjoys collaborating. Prefers tough unusual assignments.

Intangible: Self-realization
Independence

Tangible: "I'd like a chance to tackle a tougher assignment than any I've tackled before, and succeed at it."

Table 3. Motivating a Plant Manager to Achieve a Business Job Goal by Satisfying Both Tangible and Intangible Needs

Business Job Goal	Observed Behavior	Plant Manager's Needs		What's in it for Plant Manager
		Intangible Needs (inferred)	Tangible Needs (verbalized)	Benefit (what superior might say or evolve from subordinate)
Increase output by 12% over next six months while holding cost increase to $\frac{1}{2}$ of 1%.	Q1	Independence Esteem	"I want to be considered for the production director's job." (Wants a promotion)	*Intangible need:* You'll be spotted as a real comer by management.... *Tangible need:* You'll be a candidate for the production director's job.
	Q2	Security	"I want to be considered for the production director's job." (Attracted by lower-risk aspects of job)	*Intangible need:* You'll further demonstrate your real worth to the company.... *Tangible need:* Same as above
	Q3	Social (also esteem and security)	"I want to be considered for the production director's job." (Wants chance for more contact with people)	*Intangible need:* You'll have to work closely with people you know.... *Tangible need:* Same as above
	Q4	Self-realization Independence	"I want to be considered for the production director's job." (Wants to exercise new skills)	*Intangible need:* This is a chance to test out your new ideas.... *Tangible need:* Same as above

In the examples in Table 3, the superior's task is made easy by the fact that the production director's job is *open*. But, in Table 4, things are much tougher, for two reasons:

1. The tangible need (production director's job) *cannot* be filled, so the superior can't offer a tangible reward.
2. We've added a *behavioral* job goal to the business job goal. This complicates things, because now, if the subordinate is to reach his *business* job goal, he'll have to make a change in his *behavior* as well.

Therefore the superior must link *both* job goals, the business and the behavioral, to the subordinate's *in*tangible needs (remember: he has no tangible rewards to offer) and demonstrate a benefit to the subordinate. Table 4 shows how this might be done.

The point is this: *most of the time* you're in a bind because you don't have enough tangible rewards to go around. Table 4 illustrates what your "fallback" position should be.

Three Costly Mistakes

$J + N \rightarrow B \rightarrow P$ means: When you link job goals to tangible needs and intangible needs, the benefit of pursuing the goals should become clear to the subordinate, who will then perform in a committed way. There are three reasons why this formula might *not* work:

1. You may not know what the subordinate's needs are because you haven't studied his behavior. We've discussed this at length.
2. You may not bother to make the link-up at all. You may establish the job goals but fail to connect them to the subordinate's needs. This is what's wrong with many Management by Objectives programs; the superior sets clear objectives to be used as a compass for guiding individual effort, but he *doesn't* take the next step and *link* these objectives to each subordinate's needs. As a result, subordinates don't always see why they should make the effort to attain the objectives, and they don't really try. In many cases superiors fail to link objectives to needs because they *assume* that "everybody can figure out the benefits for himself." They take it for granted that the benefits are implied by the goal; all they have to do is state the goal and—presto!—the subordinate understands the benefit. This is just plain wrong. If you don't make the benefit explicit by linking job goals to needs (either directly or by getting the subordinate to make the link-up for himself) the benefit may never become clear to him.

Table 4. Motivating a Plant Manager to Achieve *Both* Business and Behavioral Job Goals by Satisfying Intangible Needs *Only*

| Business Job Goal | Behavioral Job Goal | Observed Behavior | Plant Manager's Needs | | What's in it for Plant Manager |
			Intangible Needs (inferred)	Tangible Needs (verbalized)	Benefit (what superior might say or evolve from the subordinate)
Increase output by 12% over next six months while holding	Reduce the open antagonism between you and Johnson, the head of Industrial Engineering.	Q1	Independence Esteem	"Production director's job" (not possible)	You'll have a better chance to get that 12% increase in output, hold down costs, and be recognized by management as a real comer if you lessen the antagonism between you and Johnson.
cost increase to ½ of 1%	Increase your contacts with Johnson so that you start making better utilization of the I.E. section.	Q2	Security	Same as above	You'll have a better chance to get that 12% increase, hold down costs, and further prove your real worth to the company if you beef up your contacts with Johnson.

Reduce the irritation that Johnson in I.E. feels with you because of all the talking and chit-chatting you do.	Q3	Social (also esteem and security)	Same as above	You'll have a better chance to get that 12% increase, hold down costs, and work closely with the people in I.E. if you talk to the point and thereby reduce Johnson's irritation.
Learn the details of Johnson's valuable I.E. techniques so you can use some of them in your own operation.	Q4	Self-realization Independence	Same as above	You'll have a better chance to get that 12% increase, hold down costs, and test out your new ideas if you learn some of Johnson's I.E. techniques.

3.   Here's another common mistake: you may link the job goals to what you *assume* are the subordinate's needs, and you may assume they're the *same* as *your* needs. For instance, a superior whose behavior is Q1 and who is seeking more independence, esteem, and power assumes that everybody wants independence, esteem, and power; a boss whose behavior is Q2 and who seeks mainly stability and security takes it for granted that everyone craves stability and security, and so on. In those few instances where the superior's needs *do* coincide with the subordinate's, this approach produces pretty good results. But in most cases, where the subordinate's needs *differ* from the superior's, this approach does more harm than good.

SUMMARY

1.   Once you can figure out what a subordinate's on-the-job behavior means, you can (a) link her job goals to her real needs, (b) talk about real benefits, and (c) produce committed performance.

2.   Deciphering on-the-job behavior requires matching (a) your observations of that behavior with (b) certain benchmarks. The resulting match will give you a good idea of the intangible needs that underlie the behavior.

3.   The benchmarks of Q2 security needs are: cautiousness, neutrality, procrastination, following the leader, preference for solitude, working "by the book," pessimism, dependence, and overly strong respect for tradition.

4.   The benchmarks of Q3 social needs are: amiability, agreeableness, meandering, striving for acceptance, extreme loyalty, impatience with structure, gregariousness, sensitivity to cues from others, a tendency to color facts, and indecisiveness.

5.   The benchmarks of Q1 esteem needs are: boastfulness, domination, positiveness, opinionatedness, high valuation of status, rare credit to others, preference for influential people, and a strong need to win.

6.   The benchmarks of Q1 independence needs are: argumentativeness, rugged individualism, resistance to other people's ideas, taking fixed positions, constant bids for autonomy, and attempts at control.

7.   The benchmarks of Q4 independence needs are: self-confidence, collaboration, acceptance of help, full disclosure, and openness to ideas.

8.   The benchmarks of Q4 self-realization needs are: probing, candor, task-orientation, desire for challenge, risk-taking, preference for the new, willingness to confront differences, sharing ideas, and sensitivity to the needs and ideas of others.

9.   Committed performance doesn't happen automatically. It happens when the subordinate says: "I know what's in it for me if I pursue the goal, and I want what's in it." This understanding of the benefit usually

occurs only if you link the subordinate's job goals to the subordinate's real needs *or* help him work out this link for himself.

10.   In determining what these real needs are, remember that intangible needs almost always have to be inferred by you from what you've observed about the subordinate; tangible needs are frequently verbalized, especially if you ask about them.

11.   Any one job goal can be linked to a wide variety of tangible and intangible needs. It's up to you to make sure that each goal is linked to the *right* needs.

12.   There are always more tangible needs to be satisfied than there are payoffs with which to satisfy them. So a good rule-of-thumb is: (a) when a suitable payoff is available, appeal to the subordinate's tangible need by offering the payoff; (b) at the same time, try to satisfy the subordinate's intangible needs; (c) if no suitable tangible payoff is available, and the tangible need cannot be satisfied, concentrate on satisfying the intangible needs.

13.   There are three reasons why $J + N \rightarrow B \rightarrow P$ might not work: (a) you may not know what the subordinate's needs are because you haven't studied them; (b) you may not link the job goal to the needs because you think the subordinate will do that for herself; (c) you may link the job goal to the wrong needs because you mistakenly assume that the subordinate's needs are the same as yours.

A LOOK AHEAD

In discussing benefits we've naturally talked a lot about *job goals*. In our next chapter, we take a closer look at job goals; we examine the role they play in appraisal, and how they should be set. And we make the point that, if you want to motivate your subordinates to perform in a committed way, you not only have to zero in on their real needs—but also you have to present them with *Q4* job goals. Motivation is a matter of linking genuine needs to Q4 goals. Chapter 8 tells what it is that makes goals Q4.

8

Q4 Goal-Setting

Our last chapter may have left the impression that you can motivate a subordinate by linking his needs to *any* job goals. If so, the impression is wrong. Just any job goals aren't good enough. The link-up must be to *Q4 job goals*. This chapter focuses on Q4 job goals—what they are and how they're set. (Since this is not a book on goal-setting—a long and complex subject—we'll cover only these aspects of the topic that are necessary for doing Q4 appraisal.) Let's start by defining our basic term.

WHAT MAKES JOB GOALS Q4?

A job goal is Q4 when it produces *optimal results* for the organization, for the subordinate, and for you. Or, to put it differently, when a Q4 job goal is achieved, *everybody involved wins*—and everybody wins by an *optimal* score. Let's examine the phrase *optimal results* since it's the key phrase in our definition. An optimal result is the *best* possible result for a *particular* person in a *particular* set of circumstances. Let's look at an illustration:

Suppose you're the Vice-President—Production of XYZ Company, and you're setting production-cost goals for your plant manager for the coming year. In setting these goals, you know the following:

1. This year's labor contract has two more years to run, and no additional hiring is contemplated for next year, so next year's labor costs aren't expected to exceed this year's.

2. New equipment, now being installed, should reduce considerably the amount of down-time that has plagued the plant this year, when frequent equipment breakdowns sent repair costs soaring. The cost of the new equipment will be written off as a general expense; it will not be charged against the plant.
3. The engineering department has developed a production technique that will completely bypass one step in the present production operation. This should shorten production time per unit by 12%. It should also make it possible to reduce the work force by 4%.
4. A brief wildcat strike early this year proved extremely costly. The underlying issue has since been resolved, and no further labor turmoil is expected next year.

Let's suppose, now, that with this information in hand, you decide to set next year's production-cost goal at exactly the same level as this year's. Would the new goal be *optimal*? Probably not. Knowing what you know, you'd have good reason to shoot for *lower* production costs next year; a *reduction* in these costs would seem reasonable. So, unless you had *other* information to offset the facts just given, the new goal would not be optimal because it wouldn't produce the best results *under the circumstances*.

Let's take one more example:

Suppose you're the district sales manager for ABC Corporation, and you're presently setting sales objectives for next year. To help you set the objective for the Southwestern territory, the market-analysis department has come up with the following data:

1. Several new plants, all prospective users of your product, have moved into the territory in recent months. This should increase the potential for sales by 16%.
2. A competitive manufacturer, with excellent sales in the Southwestern territory, will next month discontinue manufacture of the product that competes with yours. This means that your company will have a chance to pick up as much as 22% new business from sales that are now going to your competitor.
3. Nationally, an increase of 4% in the demand for your product is forecast.

In addition to this information, you know two other things: (1) several innovations in your product should give your company a sizable edge over all competitors, especially since the innovations have not been accompanied by a price increase; (2) the salesperson in the Southwestern territory will continue to be one of your most experienced and successful people. In view, of all this, the market-analysis department has projected a "windfall increase in sales in the Southwestern territory next year, possibly as high as 12%, even if competitive activity increases substantially."

Knowing this, you say to yourself: "It's unreasonable to ask anybody to come up with a 12% increase in sales. Too many things could go wrong . . . too many unforeseen factors could intervene. If I set the increase at 12%, I'll end up looking stupid if we don't get it. It's better to play it safe." So you set a sales goal that calls for a 5% increase over this year's sales. Is this an optimal goal? No. Not *under the circumstances*. This is a *Q2* goal (cautious and pessimistic), not a Q4 job goal (the one that's calculated to produce the best results under these particular conditions).

FOUR CRITERIA OF Q4 JOB GOALS

A Q4 job goal meets these four criteria:

1. It's realistic, requiring optimal effort by the subordinate.
2. It's specific—or as specific as circumstances permit.
3. It's comprehensive.
4. It's understandable.

Let's look at each criterion in turn.

1. Realism and Optimal Effort

To make sure the job goal is realistic and requires optimal effort, keep three guidelines in mind:

1. *Don't make it too easy.*

If you do, one of two things will probably happen. (1) Some subordinates will put forth just enough effort to attain the goal, but not a bit more. They'll do their jobs "by the numbers," without much initiative ("If that's what they want, why should I knock myself out?"). (2) Some subordinates will put forth *some* extra effort, but, discouraged by the lack of challenge, they may begin to feel restless and dissatisfied. This group will probably contain those subordinates who have the *most* to contribute. Some of your people, of course, will probably be happy to learn that you've given them a "cinch" goal, but your *best* people—the most dynamic and innovative ones—are likely to be turned off. The plain fact is that many people *want* tough, challenging job goals. They enjoy stretching, striving, exerting—and effortless goals deprive them (some would say "cheat" them) of the chance. This may contradict the conventional wisdom, but it's been demonstrated again and again in studies by behavioral scientists.

2.   *Don't make the job goal too hard.*

Many people want—in fact, *seek*—rigorous, demanding goals. But there's a point at which any job goal can become so arduous, so burdensome, that it becomes self-defeating. At this point two things are likely to happen: (1) some subordinates won't even make a serious effort ("Why bother? There's *no way* I can make that goal"); (2) some will become edgy, anxious, perhaps slightly panicky—they'll strain to achieve the goal, and, as they do, tensions will rise, mistakes and snafus will increase, and the situation in general will deteriorate.

3.   *Find the "golden mean."*

The ancient Greeks used to recommend the "golden mean"—the point between two extremes at which everything comes into proper balance— as the best course of action. It's a good idea to keep in mind when setting goals. At one extreme the need to put forth excessive effort can be disruptive, even incapacitating; it reduces the chance of achieving the job goal. On the other hand, the need for practically *no* effort can be demoralizing and debilitating; the goal may be reached, but it only produces stagnation. What's needed is a goal that calls for an *optimal* amount of effort (which is rarely the same as the *maximal* amount). The trick is to set goals that require the right amount—not too much and not too little—of stress, urgency, exertion. Make the goal tough enough to stimulate extra effort, but not so tough that it makes people feel hopeless. Make your subordinates stretch, but don't ask them to break in half.

Stated differently, job goals should be neither easy to achieve nor near impossible; they should be *realistically difficult.*

These three points can be illustrated graphically. The graph in Figure 9 would have to be modified to fit any particular situation, but, in general, it shows what happens when goals are too easy, too tough, and optimally challenging.

We are *not* saying that optimal effort always falls halfway between "no effort" and "extreme effort"; we are *not* saying that the "golden mean" is always "in the middle." This graph would have to be varied for each real-life situation. All we're saying is that, as a rule, the *optimal* effort lies *somewhere* between "no effort" and "extreme effort." This raises a question: In any given situation, *how much* effort is optimal?

HOW MUCH IS OPTIMAL?

In any given situation, *how much* challenge is motivating? The answer, unsatisfactory as it sounds, is: *it all depends*. It all depends on the nature

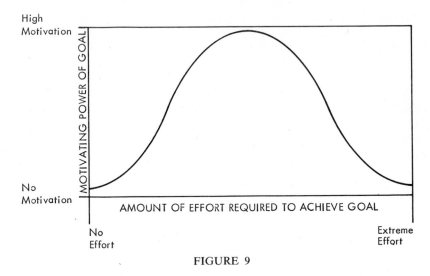

FIGURE 9

of the job to be done and the people who will have to do it. For example, a job goal that seems "tough but achievable" to one of your subordinates may seem "impossible" to another; a goal that stimulates one may frustrate another; and on and on. You can't set optimal goals (except by sheer luck) unless you *know* each of your people: her capacities, skills, ambitions, and hang-ups. To repeat a point we've made before: you cannot do Q4 appraisal (which includes setting Q4 goals) without first studying each of your subordinates.

Finally, it's important to emphasize that the goal must be considered realistic by the *subordinate*. If, after thorough discussion, his reaction to the goal is "You've got to be kidding" or "Aw . . . c'mon now" or "I can't believe you're serious" or "Who do you think I am . . . Superman?", then you'd better reexamine your own thinking. It isn't good enough for *you* to consider the goal realistic; *he* must see it that way, too.

2. Specificity

The second criterion of Q4 goals is that they be specific. Vague goals cannot produce optimal results—because they don't explain what's "optimal." If you tell a production manager to "increase production as much as possible," nobody in the world can tell whether or when the goal has been achieved. But if you tell a production manager to "increase #7 widget production between January 1 and December 31 by 10% over the amount produced the preceding year," you've got a goal that means something.

As we'll see in a minute, this is still not a true Q4 job goal, but at least it has one essential Q4 characteristic: it's specific.

3. Comprehensiveness

One reason the goal we just mentioned isn't really a Q4 goal is that it isn't comprehensive enough. It doesn't tell the whole story. Suppose, for example, that the production manager were to achieve the goal and increase production costs by 15% while doing so. Would that be "optimal"? Who knows? The goal never mentioned costs, so there's no way of answering the question. Or what if he achieves the goal while rejects soar higher than ever. Would that be optimal? Once again, who knows?

To be Q4, then, a job goal should be not only specific, but comprehensive. It should cover all the conditions that would make achievement optimal: times, dates, deadlines, quantity, costs, and so on. Here's an example:

Increase #7 widget production between January 1 and December 31 by 10% over the amount produced last year, while holding quality to the specifications most recently established by the engineering department, and permitting an increase in rejects no greater than 2% over last year and an increase in costs no greater than $\frac{1}{2}$ of 1%.

WINDFALLS

Q4 goals should require optimal effort by the person to whom they're assigned. But occasionally a goal that *sounds* Q4 gets achieved with no effort at all—at least not by the person to whom it's been assigned. The subordinate, in other words, is the beneficiary of a windfall. This could happen with the goal we just looked at. Suppose, for example, that on June 30 (six months into the period covered by the goal) the production manager has realized *no* increase in production; production is lagging at last year's rate, and there appears to be no chance of this year's goal being met. Then suppose that on July 1 new equipment is installed in the plant. The production manager deserves no credit for this equipment; in fact, he strongly opposed its installation, but was overridden by the Industrial Engineering department. Thanks to the new equipment, production suddenly zooms upward, and, by year's end, has increased by *15%* over last year. Here's the dialogue that might ensue when the production manager gets his performance appraisal.

SUPERIOR.   Frank, you've done a lousy job this past year.
SUBORDINATE.   Whaddya mean, "lousy"? I've done a great job and you know it. A 15% increase in #7 widgets, when I was only expected to come up with a 10% increase. How can you call that lousy?

SUPERIOR.   You don't deserve credit for that. You fell into it.
SUBORDINATE.   Fell into it? You've got to be kidding.

An so on. The point, of course, is that the superior is on very weak ground. The fact is that the goal—*as written*—was achieved. And since the goal never said that the achievement had to be attributable to the production manager's own efforts, his boss doesn't have much of an argument.

Can situations like this be prevented? Sure they can. All that's necessary is a stipulation, in the goal itself, that the goal must be achieved by the efforts of the person to whom it's assigned. In the goal we've been talking about, for example, the addition of the following sentence would have helped:

This goal is to be achieved solely through your own managerial efforts; any production increase realized as the result of actions not attributable to you will not count as part of this goal.

4.   Understandability

The final criterion of a Q4 goal is that it be understandable. An optimal goal is one that's readily and completely comprehensible to the subordinate. It's worded in plain English or in a specialized jargon that's thoroughly familiar to the subordinate. It speaks *his* language, not just yours.

Sometimes written goals look forbiddingly legalistic, with numerous qualifying clauses and modifiers. There's nothing wrong with this *as long as the subordinate clearly understands what the goal says.* In fact, the use of qualifying clauses may be a good way to make the goal specific and to eliminate ambiguities. By itself, there's nothing wrong with legalistic language or with a specialized vocabulary or with technical terminology *as long as* the subordinate "gets it." The important question is not: How is the goal phrased? The important question is: Does the subordinate thoroughly understand it?

BEHAVIORAL VS. BUSINESS JOB GOALS

Everything we've said so far makes sense as long as we're talking about business job goals. But how about behavioral job goals? Can these measure up to our four criteria? Let's see:

Realism and Effort

When it comes to behavioral job goals, windfalls are less likely than with business job goals. Take the following example of a behavioral job goal:

In the next six months cut down the number of departmental errors attributable to "misunderstood instructions" from five a week to no more than one a week.

It's always possible that there will be no departmental errors during the next six months not because of any *effort* by the department head (whose goal it is), but simply because of luck. But it's unlikely. Generally, behavioral job goals are achieved because the person who is assigned the goal changes his behavior. That takes effort, and no windfall is likely to help very much.

Specificity

Behavioral goals obviously cannot be as specific as business goals. Nevertheless, they should be as specific as you can make them. The fact that you can't reduce a goal to numbers doesn't mean that you can't make it fairly precise. A few examples will show what we mean by "precise" behavioral goals:

VAGUE.   Resolve your differences with Webster.
PRECISE. Get Webster to understand that you're not trying to take over his department, so that sometime during the next three months he expresses a willingness to have you back as a member of his task force.
VAGUE.   Toughen up.
PRECISE. Start displaying leadership and discipline in your department so that, starting 30 days from now, there are no instances of unauthorized absences.
VAGUE.   Improve your communication skills.
PRECISE. In the next six months, cut down the number of departmental errors attributable to "misunderstood instructions" from five a week to no more than one a week.

These examples help us to make three points:

1. One good way to make behavioral goals specific is to say, in the actual wording of the goal, what should *happen* if the goal is met. In each of our three examples there is a statement of the *event* that will establish whether or not the goal has been achieved.

. . . so that sometime during the next three months he expresses a willingness to have you back as a member of his task force.

. . . so that, starting 30 days from now, there are no instances of unauthorized absences.

. . . cut down the number of departmental errors from five a week to no more than one a week.

Another way to put this is this: a *behavioral* goal will be more effective it it is tied to a *business* goal, or at least to a business activity of some kind (being a member of a task force, cutting down on unauthorized absences, cutting down on departmental errors, etc.). Unless this is done, the behavioral job goal is likely to be hopelessly vague.

2.   One specific element that can always be included in a behavioral job goal is *time*. Never made a behavioral goal open-ended. Always state *when* it should be achieved.

3.   While it's true that behavioral job goals can't always be quantified, that doesn't mean they can *never* be quantified. As our third example shows, numbers can sometimes be used to make behavioral goals more specific.

Comprehensiveness

As with business job goals, behavioral job goals should include all necessary details: what is to be achieved, when, for what purpose, under what limiting or influencing conditions. Here is an example of how all these factors can be covered in one behavioral goal:

WHAT IS TO BE ACHIEVED.   Take steps to tighten your control of your department and see to it that there are no policy infractions. . . .
WHEN.   During the next six months. . . .
FOR WHAT PURPOSE: So that we have no further run-ins with the Vice-President of Administration.
LIMITING CONDITION.   Do it without increasing turnover in the department.

Understandability

It's frequently much tougher to make a behavioral job goal understandable than it is a business job goal. Behavioral goals often seem quite clear—when actually they're loaded with ambiguities. The result is that they can mean almost anything to anybody. Who knows, for example, what the following so-called "behavioral goals" *really* mean?

Take it easy.
Learn to relax.
Don't be so uptight.
Assert yourself.

These, and many other "behavioral job goals," are subject to multiple interpretations. The superior thinks they mean one thing; the subordinate thinks they mean something else. The only way out of this semantic trap is to (1) make the goal as specific as possible and (2) tie it to a business job goal. We've already seen how behavior goals can be tied to business goals; let's see how vagueness can be turned into specificity.

Vague	Specific
Take it easy.	Don't start shouting the minute Kelly makes what appears to be a mistake. Get his side of the story. Find out why he does things the way he does them and then discuss better ways, so that he begins to improve instead of making one mistake after another.
Assert yourself.	In discussions with Morgan, don't passively accept everything he says. If you don't agree with him, ask him to justify his views; if you still don't agree, present your own, so that he doesn't always impose his ideas on your operation.

When it comes to behavioral goals, understandability and specificity are two sides of a single coin.

THE GOAL-SETTING PROCESS

The *content* of goals—what they say and how they say it—is, as we've just seen, fundamentally important. Equally important, however, is the *process* by which they're set. That process depends, in large part, on the climate or environment in which they're set. Let's look now at some of the factors affecting this environment and, in turn, affecting the way goals are set.

You're in the Middle

So far, we've talked as if you have complete freedom when it comes to setting job goals. Actually, of course, you haven't. The truth is that, in setting job goals—especially *business* job goals—you're very much in the middle of pulling, pushing, tugging forces. Let's look at these, because understanding them and being able, to some degree, to control them is crucial to Q4 appraisal. These forces fall into three categories: forces from above, forces from below, and forces from the sides.

Forces from Above

Before you can do effective job-goal setting, you have to reckon with at least three sets of forces from above: (1) the general *nature* of your organization's goals; (2) the general *system* by which goals are set; and (3) the *behavioral* characteristics of your own superior.

1.   *The general nature of the organization's goals*

Ideally, all of an organization's goals should be like a set of Chinese boxes, with those at each level fitting smoothly into the ones above. (This is the basic principle of MBO.) No superior, obviously, should set job goals at variance with those at the next higher level. If the overall goals of the organization can be compared to a cube, then all the lower-level goals must be cube-shaped too; no single department can set goals shaped like octahedrons, for the simple reason that octahedrons don't fit smoothly into cubes. (If an organization has a formal MBO program, then it has a system for insuring that all of its goals "fit." But the principle, of course, applies to any organization, with or without MBO.)

2.   *The general system by which goals are set*

Organizations vary widely in the amount of autonomy they give to superiors in setting business job goals. These "grants of independence" range on a continuum between "no autonomy" to "complete autonomy." In a no-autonomy situation you're really a pipeline, transmitting goals set by somebody else to your own people; in a complete-autonomy situation you're told by your superior: "You're on your own; set your objectives as you see fit, and let me know what you decide." Most job-goal setting probably takes place in the large area between these two poles.

3.   *The behavioral characteristics of your own superior*

The troublesome fact is that the basic content of any one message can have *several different meanings*—depending upon who transmits it. Different superiors can deliver pretty much the *same content*, but each delivery may carry a *different meaning* because of the superior's different behavioral characteristics. This can play havoc with goal-setting.

For example, suppose you're a district sales manager for XYZ Widget Company, which sets annual sales quotas in this way: the General Sales Manager, working with his market-planning staff, analyzes each district's past sales and future potential and then sets a 12-month dollar-volume objective. Suppose the GSM is now ready to transmit next year's district-wide quota to you. Table 5 lists *four* ways in which this *single* job goal might be transmitted, depending upon the GSM's *behavioral strategy*; it also lists the different *meanings* underlying each transmission. Note that in all four cases the basic *content* is pretty much the same, but the underlying—and significant—*message* is different. (See Table 5, next page.)

The consequence of all this is that you must make sure you're getting the right message from your boss before you set goals with your own people. You must translate *content* into *meaning*. By itself, the explicit content of any instruction may not tell you everything you need to know. The explicit content must be deciphered—interpreted—so that you get to what really counts: the *implicit meaning*. Then, once you know the implicit meaning, you must answer several crucial questions before you begin your own job-goal setting. For example:

• Suppose the boundaries within which I'm supposed to operate have been set by my boss in a dogmatic Q1 way. Suppose they seem arbitrary and unreasonable. Can I do *nothing* to change them? Am I stuck with un-realistic and unachievable goals?
• Suppose the boundaries have been set in a cautious Q2 way. Can I pin the boss down and make him say exactly what the boundaries are? Or, is he really implying that I'm free to modify the goals in any way I want; is the boss abdicating responsibility?
• Suppose the boundaries have been set in a keep-'em-happy Q3 way. Can I get the boss to stiffen the goals? Can I stiffen them myself? Does "keeping 'em happy" *really* take precedence over performance?
• Suppose the boundaries have been set in a pragmatic Q4 way. Do I have the data I need for determining if the goals are really sensible? If they seem unfair or unachievable, can I *prove* it? Can I hold my own in a give-and-take discussion with the boss?

These questions boil down to this: Can you *manage* your own superior? If not, you're going to have trouble when it comes to goal-setting.

Forces from Below

The forces from below are your own subordinates. As we've already stressed, you must know their tangible and intangible needs and their abilities and potential before you can do Q4 goal-setting.

1. If you don't know their abilities and potential, you can't set job goals that will call forth optimal effort. Optimal effort is an individual matter, and varies with the skills and capacities of the subordinate.
2. If you don't know their tangible and intangible needs you can't develop benefits that will fully motivate. Benefits are an individual matter; they vary with the needs and ambitions of the subordinate.

Table 5.   One Content—Four Meanings

Q1 TRANSMISSION.   Your quota is $1,200,000. That's 20% over this past year . . . and I don't want to hear any ifs, ands, or buts. As far as I'm concerned, $1,200,000 is an absolute *minimum*. I expect you to *exceed* it. If you don't there's something wrong with your district . . . and I intend to find out what.

THE Q1 MEANING.   The new quota is beyond discussion. It's an edict. If it's not achieved, you may suffer dire consequences. In fact, if you *merely* achieve it, you're still likely to pay a penalty, since your boss expects to *surpass* it. This message really means: a decree has been handed down; follow through or else.

Q2 TRANSMISSION.   According to the market-planning people, it looks like your new quota is $1,200,000. I sure hope you can make it.

THE Q2 MEANING.   The new quota is tentative, uncertain. In fact your boss isn't even willing to put his own weight behind it; instead of saying *he* set the quota, he says "according to the market-planning people." And, instead of saying that the quota is *settled*, he says, "It looks like your new quota is $1,200,000." What does *that* mean? Is it or isn't it? To top it all off, he implies that achievement of the quota is optional: "I sure hope you can make it." This message has no fixed meaning at all; it's so ambiguous that you can interpret it several ways.

Q3 TRANSMISSION. We've worked out a figure of $1,200,000 this year. Now . . . before you get all worked up . . . let me tell you that I realize that's a pretty stiff increase. I admit it. And I sure hope it doesn't get your guys all hot and bothered. Whatever you do, when you present the figure to them, don't make it sound like a command. We don't want a rebellion on our hands.

THE Q3 MEANING. The new quota isn't really a quota, but a hope. It can and will be scaled down if it gets "the guys all hot and bothered." In fact, you're explicitly instructed *not* to make it "sound like a command," which means you're not supposed to make the figure sound too serious. This message really means: it would be nice to make the new quota, but not at the risk of making the sales force unhappy.

Q4 TRANSMISSION. With help from the market-planning people, I've come up with a quota of $1,200,000. Based on all the figures, we believe it's fair and achievable. It is 20% more than this year, but we think that the potential's there. Let me explain our computations to you . . . then you tell me if you see any flaws in our thinking. If you do, now's the time to adjust the figures . . . either up or down. If you don't, I'll expect you to hit the $1,200,000 mark.

THE Q4 MEANING. The new quota is "fair and achievable," and it *will* be the quota—unless *evidence* is produced that it should be changed. If it is changed, it may be either down or up; it all depends on the facts. The purpose of the discussion between the boss and you is to make sure, through mutual discussion of hard data, that the final quota is "fair and achievable." That's the sole criterion. This message really means: let's both make sure we tap the real potential of this district next year.

3.   Therefore, if you understand a subordinate's needs but don't know what her abilities and potential are, you are likely to link strong benefits to weak goals. If you know her abilities and potential but don't understand her needs, you are likely to link strong goals to weak benefits. Either way, you're not likely to get what you want: optimal performance and optimal results.

Forces from the Sides

The forces from above (mainly your own superior and the way goals are set in the organization) and the forces from below (mainly your subordinates) are *internal* constraints—limitations *within* the organization. The forces from the sides, however, are both inside and outside the organization. Let's look at both kinds.

INTERNAL FORCES

These include all your relationships with other departments and other superiors in the organization, the policies and procedures you're expected to follow, and so forth. These forces limit you in two ways: some of them dictate things you *cannot* do, and some of them indicate things you can but *should not* do.

Things You Cannot Do.   We don't have to belabor this topic since you can easily think of plenty of things you cannot do when you set job goals. If you're a sales manager, for example, you cannot set sales objectives based on increased advertising when the advertising department is planning ad cutbacks; you cannot set goals that involve getting sales reports daily if the accounting department only produces such reports weekly; and on and on. (This is not to say that you can't lobby for change in these areas, but, until a change is effected, you must live with the situation as it is.) In job-goal setting you must accept certain *givens*, certain hard, unyielding facts. Like it or not, these inhibit your freedom.

Things You Should Not Do.   Many job goals can only be achieved in cooperation with, or, at the very least, without the opposition of, other departments in the organization. When setting goals, you can, if you wish, make action-plans that are sure to inconvenience other departments; you can fail to consult a fellow superior with whom you must work closely; you can ignore the people on whom you must lean for support, and so on. You *can* do these things, but, if you want your goals achieved with a minimum of stress and trouble, you obviously *shouldn't*. One way or another, by direct conflict or by indirect sabotage, your peers will get back at you, or at least try to. So any superior who's not bent on undermining himself will give careful thought to his peer-relationships before he begins setting goals. Peers (and peer departments) are a force from the sides that can play havoc with job goals.

EXTERNAL FORCES

A complete list of these would fill at least a thick book. Government regulations, legal restrictions, standard business practices, economic conditions, relationships with the public, union contracts, insurance requirements, pressures from outside groups, and numerous other factors circumscribe what you can do in setting goals.

SUMMARY

1. In Q4 appraisal the subordinate's needs aren't linked to just any job goals; they're linked to Q4 job goals.
2. A job goal is Q4 when it produces optimal results for the organization, for the subordinate, and for you.
3. An optimal result is the best result in a particular situation. What's optimal under one set of conditions won't necessarily be optimal under another.
4. A Q4 job goal must meet four criteria: (a) it must be realistic and require optimal effort, (b) it must be specific, (c) it must be comprehensive, (d) it must be understandable.
5. Behavioral job goals can't always meet these criteria as well as business job goals, but they should come as close as possible. The key to developing optimal behavioral job goals is to make them as specific as you can.
6. You can be reasonably sure you're building optimal effort into a job goal if you do three things: (a) make sure it isn't too easy, (b) make sure it isn't too tough, and (c) find the "golden mean" for the subordinate who's supposed to achieve the goal.
7. You rarely have complete freedom in setting job goals. Usually, you have to contend with three sets of forces that limit what you can do in setting goals, or at least make your job more difficult. These are: (a) forces from above, (b) forces from below, and (c) forces from the sides.
8. The forces from above include: (a) the general nature of your organization's goals, (b) the system by which goals are set, and (c) the behavioral characteristics of your boss. The last can be especially trouble-

some, because, in passing along goal-setting instructions to you, the boss also passes along certain implied messages that may modify his actual words. Unless you interpret these "hints" correctly, you may find yourself in difficulty when you try to carry out his directives. Knowing what the boss is "really" saying requires a knowledge of his general behavior.

9. The forces from below are your own subordinates. To do Q4 goal setting, you must know, and take into account, their needs (tangible and intangible) and their abilities (actual and potential).

10. The forces from the sides include your relationships with your peers, the regulations governing what you cannot do, the conditions governing what you should not do, and external forces impinging upon the organization.

11. All these forces must be considered in setting job goals. If they are, and if you know the criteria of optimal goals, you should be able to set Q4 goals. Unless you do, you won't be able to do Q4 appraisal.

A LOOK AHEAD

In Chapter 5, when we laid out the approach used in Q4 appraisal, we talked about *readiness to participate* and about *probing*. Like benefits, goals, and goal-setting, these are "must" topics. Without mastering them, there's very little chance you can develop benefits that motivate or set goals that produce optimal results. And if you can't do these things, you can't do Q4 appraisal. So we look closely at both topics—*readiness to participate* and *probing*—in our next two chapters.

9

Receptivity

In our next two chapters we cover two of the most fundamental Q4 skills—
skills without which you cannot do Q4 appraisal: (1) increasing the subordinate's readiness to participate, and (2) probing. Since both of these
are *communication* skills, we'd better dispose, right now, of two very common
misconceptions about communication. Unless we do they'll come back to
haunt—and confuse—us later in the chapter.

Many people wrongly believe that:

1. Communication is a matter of *words*, so that anyone who uses
   words well communicates well.
2. Anyone who uses words the right way can communicate almost
   anything *to* anyone.

Put another way, many people wrongly believe that communication is
verbal, and that it's something someone does *to* someone else.

The facts are different. Actually:

1. Communication is a matter of *behavior* (and words are only part of
   behavior).
2. Communication occurs *between* people; we only communicate *with*,
   never *to*.

Put another way, communication is *behavioral* and *interactional*. That last
sentence is pretty abstract. Let's bring it down to earth.

1. *Communication is behavioral*

This means what it says. People communicate with *all* their behavior, not just with their words. A subordinate can *tell* you, during an appraisal, that he's interested in what you're saying, but you'll get a different message if he continually fidgets, yawns, and stares absentmindedly into space. A subordinate can *insist* that she's deliriously happy with the outcome of her appraisal, but you'll get a contrary message if she's scowling. *Everything* we do communicates, and our *full* behavior frequently delivers messages that contradict our words.

2. *Communication is interactional*

Real communication (communication in which each person really gets through to the other) requires the active participation of *two* (or more) people. It requires dialogue. And dialogue requires listening as well as talking; it requires give-and-take, back-and-forth responses. You can no more communicate by yourself than you can play tennis by yourself. Communication is always *two-way;* the listener is just as active, just as involved, as the speaker. (That's why so many TV commercials don't get through: the listener isn't *really listening*. The speaker does his part, but the process is all one-way. As a result, the message may be eloquent, but there is *no* communication.)

So, when it comes to communicating in performance appraisal, *verbal* skills alone won't do the job. Sure, they'll help, but you also need listening skills, questioning skills, analytic skills, and observational skills. And you can't take anything for granted. A good communicator never *assumes* she is getting through; she never flatters herself that her subordinate *really* understands just because he *says* he understands. The glib nod, the quick "I get it," the instant "Okay," often cover up doubt and bewilderment.

Management theorist Peter Drucker has said that, contrary to common belief, speakers do not and *cannot* communicate. They can only make sounds. These sounds *become* communication, that is, they get a *message across*, only if the listener lets them get through. Thus, says Drucker, it's really the *listener* who communicates—not the speaker. This may seem strange but it's a simple statement of fact. Words are only noises unless the listener lets them through; this is just another way of saying that communication is not verbalization—it's *interaction*.

Usually, a superior who says "We've got a communication problem" really means "We've got a *no*-communication problem." That's because so-called communication is so often only noise making—sounds falling on closed, and therefore deaf ears. Ironically, some superiors who consider themselves excellent communicators (because they're constantly being praised for their silver-tongued use of words) do consistently poor jobs of *getting through*, while others, who are far less eloquent, really *do* communicate. Skill with words is only part of a very complex *two-way* process.

Small wonder, then, that so many superiors are frustrated during performance appraisal. Small wonder that they come up against misunderstanding and confusion. And small wonder that performance appraisal leaves them wrung out. Communicating is hard work.

GETTING OVER THE OBSTACLES

One reason communication is such hard work is that you *can't* communicate, can't create two-way understanding, unless you can overcome the obstacles described in this chapter. And this takes effort. Communication—especially in a touchy situation like appraisal—is almost never easy. It's not like walking along a well-paved road; it's more like scaling a mountain, with crags, boulders, slippery places, and perilous drop-offs at every point. This may sound far-fetched, but it's not. As we show, communicating in appraisal is demanding and fatiguing; the minute your attention flags, the minute your skills let you down, you're in danger of plunging into trouble.

RECEPTIVITY

The commonest obstacle to communication is a situation known as *low receptivity*. *Receptivity* is what we called, in Chapter 5, "readiness to participate." From now on, we'll use the shorter term.

Receptivity is the willingness to listen to the other person and consider what he's saying. It's the willingness to take in (receive) what the other person knows, believes, thinks, and feels. It's the willingness to pay attention, to concentrate, to weigh, to evaluate, to mull over. In other words, the receptive person is willing to give the other person a chance to get through; he's willing to cooperate in the communication process. This doesn't necessarily mean he'll agree with what he hears; it only means he'll consider it. In an effective performance appraisal, *both* people—superior and subordinate—are receptive to each other. Each is ready to give the other a chance to state his case and to have it judged on its merits.

The word *receptivity* stems from *receive*. And, *receive* has two meanings that are important for our purposes. One is *to take in or acquire*, as in

"I received a thousand dollar bonus." The other meaning is *to meet with*, as in "I received friendly treatment from the people in the department." Now, the point is this: the *receptive* communicator does both things. He *acquires* and he *meets with*.

1. He *acquires*—takes in—whatever the other person is trying to communicate.
2. He does this by making his mind *meet with* the mind of the other person.

The receptive communicator isn't a passive lump; he doesn't just let the other person's words fall on him like rain. His mind actively meets the other person's. When two minds meet, so that what's in one can be understood by the other, you've got *high receptivity*.

A good definition of *high receptivity*, then, is this: *high receptivity is the readiness to collaborate in the communication process*. It's the readiness to participate, to join in, to get involved in the communication process. Or, in even plainer English, *high receptivity is the willingness to work with the other person in getting through to one another*. We emphasize the words *collaborate* and *work* because we want to drive home the idea that the highly receptive person takes an active part in the communication process. This active role always includes the readiness to:

1. Listen carefully and with an open mind.
2. Give thoughtful and objective consideration to what's been said.
3. Answer questions raised by the other person.
4. Ask questions in an effort to clarify what the other person means.
5. Provide the other person with needed information.

Once again, let's state a key point: high receptivity is not necessarily the same as agreement. High receptivity is *open-mindedness*—willingness to listen and consider and collaborate in the communication process. After he's listened and considered and collaborated, the receptive person may agree or disagree. But, whatever he finally decides, whether he agrees or disagrees, he does so *as the result of attentive listening and thoughtful consideration*. Whether he accepts or rejects, he does so only after participating in the communication process.

What Difference Does It Make?

Why all this fuss about receptivity? What difference does it make if it's high or low? *Plenty*. The painful fact is that you're not likely to communicate—only make noise—at low receptivity. No matter how eloquent, logical, coherent, fluent, or articulate you may be, you stand little chance of getting through to a subordinate if his receptivity is low. All the eloquence and logic and good sense in the world will have a hard time penetrating a closed-mind; the mind should be opened first. Low receptivity must be increased to high receptivity before the most effective communication can take place. Articulateness, fluency, coherence, foolproof logic, strong arguments, impressive data are all likely to be wasted at low receptivity. Until receptivity is high, chances are that you're going to spin your wheels.

THE RECEPTIVITY CONTINUUM

We've been talking as if there are only two kinds of receptivity: high and low. Actually, in an appraisal (or any other situation) your subordinate may display many different degrees of receptivity, ranging from low to high. These degrees can be ranged on a continuum which can (theoretically) be numerically graduated (Figure 10). In actuality, of course, we can't achieve such precision.

The continuum can also be pictured as shown in Figure 11.

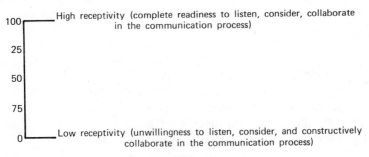

FIGURE 10

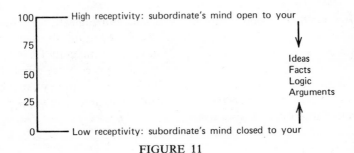

FIGURE 11

The continuum shows that it's not realistic to think of the subordinate as having either an entirely open or entirely closed mind. Many times, you'll find your subordinate's receptivity somewhere between low and high. The ideal, of course, is continuous high receptivity. Achieving this takes lots of know-how and lots of hard work on your part.

A Matter of Timing

We've just said that you don't have much chance of getting through at low receptivity. This means that communication—getting through—depends upon *timing*. In any appraisal, there's a *right* time and a *wrong* time to "unload" your ideas, your logic, and your information on the subordinate.

- The *right* time is when the subordinate's receptivity is *high*.
- The *wrong* time is when it's *low*.

If your timing is off, you're sure to communicate less effectively than you should.

- If you bring in your arguments at *low* receptivity, you'll probably communicate very little. Much of what you say will fall on deaf ears or else be rejected outright. No matter how eloquent or how sensible you are, you'll actually be making *noise*.
- If you bring in your arguments at *moderate* receptivity, you'll probably communicate more, but not an optimal amount. You'll utter a *mixture* of communication and noise.
- *Only* when you bring in your arguments at *high* receptivity will you communicate at the optimal level.
- Your task, then, is to introduce your ideas at those times when your subordinate's receptivity is as *high as possible*.

A WARNING REPEATED

We repeat: the words and sentences coming out of your mouth may be forceful, intelligent, commanding, polished, and logical; they still won't communicate *optimally*—they'll have trouble getting through—if your subordinate's receptivity is low. You'll have great difficulty forcing ideas— *no matter how good they may be*—on a closed, nonreceptive mind. This is a hard fact to accept, but it is a fact. If you refuse to accept it, to acknowledge the importance of proper *timing* in communication, you're likely to do ineffective performance appraisals.

Fluctuations in Receptivity

In an appraisal (or any other communication situation) receptivity can, and probably will, *fluctuate*. The possibilities are endless. Receptivity can go from low to high and then slide back to low again. It can be driven down from high to low and then be raised back up. It can slide back and forth along the continuum. These fluctuations may be due to matters beyond your control (maybe the subordinate's wife is sick, and, no matter how hard you try to rivet his attention, he tunes you out from time to time and thinks about her instead; maybe he had an argument with one of his peers earlier in the day, and, instead of paying close attention to what you're saying, keeps thinking about what "I should have told that guy"; and on and on). On the other hand, the fluctuations may be due to things that have happened between you and your subordinate. Whatever the reasons, the important point is that receptivity can, and often does, fluctuate.

Not only can receptivity change—it can change very rapidly. It can go from high to low to high in a matter of seconds. What can you do about these fluctuations? Before you can do anything else, you must learn to differentiate high and low receptivity.

How to Recognize Low Receptivity

How do you know when a subordinate's receptivity is high or low? By *observing his behavior*. Subordinates signal their level of receptivity by the way they behave. Here are some typical signals.

LOW RECEPTIVITY (Q1 BEHAVIOR)

- *Arguments.* If the subordinate dares (this depends on how tough she thinks you are), she may argue with you, challenge you, try to bait or entrap you.
- *Negative flat assertions.* A flat assertion is a statement that's absolute and unqualified ("I can't imagine anything dumber than that"). *Negative* flat assertions ("You're dead wrong"; "That's the craziest thing I ever heard"; "He's never told the truth in his life"; "You're always on my back"; "You never give me a chance"; etc.) are a clear sign of low receptivity. Flat assertions can be recognized by their use of superlatives ("stupidest," "silliest," "most unfair," "most unreasonable," etc.) and unconditional words ("always," "never," "ever," "absolutely," "positively," etc.).

- *Impatience.* The subordinate is visibly, perhaps insolently, impatient and inattentive. There's an impudent, defiant air to her impatience: she may yawn conspicuously, stare into space, fidget. Once again, she seems more intent on baiting you than on paying attention.
- *Interruptions.* Interruptions indicate two things: that the subordinate is more concerned about what's on her mind than what's on yours, or that she's being intentionally rude.
- *Negative acts and emotions.* There's an endless list of these: curses, shouting, sarcastic remarks, slamming a fist on the desk, blaming, threatening, and on and on.

All of these—arguments, negative flat assertions, impatience, interruptions, negative emotions—are signs of *low* receptivity. They indicate that the subordinate is *not* ready to listen to and consider what you have to say. She's *resisting.* Either she's not bothering to listen at all, or, if she does listen, she's not willing to consider what she hears. She's either not paying attention, or she's paying attention and instantly rejecting. Or, just as bad, she's *mishearing*—getting only part of the story or getting it wrong. All of these signals point to one fact: you aren't getting through; you aren't communicating.

LOW RECEPTIVITY (Q2 BEHAVIOR)

- *Silence.* The subordinate says virtually nothing. He may shrug, grimace, nod, or grunt, but he doesn't *talk.* He's unresponsive. He gives virtually no clues to what he's thinking or feeling; his face is impassive, expressionless.
- *Apathy.* The subordinate doesn't seem to care. Good news doesn't cheer him, and bad news doesn't appear to bother him. He seems detached, unconcerned, unemotional.
- *Inattention.* The subordinate fidgets, tries to stifle yawns, stares absent-mindedly into space.
- *Nervousness.* The subordinate is visibly uneasy, even jittery. He crosses and uncrosses his legs, drums his fingers on the arm of the chair, fiddles with his necktie, and so forth. If he says anything, he stammers or falters, or speaks in a barely audible voice.

Silence, apathy, inattention, nervousness—these are signs that a subordinate either isn't listening, or that he is listening and feels so threatened that, instead of considering what he hears, he nervously *withdraws.* He, too, may mishear; he may pull away from threats that don't exist. One thing is sure: he's not letting you *get through.*

LOW RECEPTIVITY (Q3 BEHAVIOR)

- *Unquestioning compliance.* The subordinate goes along with whatever you say. Her failure to ask questions doesn't necessarily mean she's listening and considering; it probably means that she just doesn't want to "embarrass" you or "cause problems." She seems to be paying attention, while actually daydreaming or thinking her own thoughts.
- *Meandering.* Whenever the subordinate starts hopping from topic to topic, it's a sure sign that she's not receptive. If she were, why would she try so hard to change the subject?
- *Overagreeableness.* The subordinate expresses eager, but phony, agreement. Underneath her ready assents ("Wonderful," "That's great," "And how!") there's doubt or reservation. When she says "I agree completely," she may really mean: "I don't get it" or "I'll go along but I'm really skeptical."
- *Selective questioning.* The subordinate either doesn't ask questions at all or, what's more likely, she asks "harmless" questions that can't possibly make you feel uneasy. She never asks questions that throw you off balance or that force you to defend your position.

Unquestioning compliance, meandering, overagreeableness, selective questioning—these are signals that the subordinate isn't listening or that she feels threatened, and that she doesn't want you to know it. So she disguises her boredom or her concern and *pretends* that she's receptive. If you're taken in by this, you have only yourself to blame.

DIRECT AND INDIRECT REJECTION

One big difference between a subordinate with strong Q1 esteem and independence needs and a subordinate with strong Q2 security or Q3 social needs is that the first sets up barriers that are much easier to spot. There's no mistaking an argument, or a negative flat assertion, or an interruption, or an outburst of anger or indignation. These are all *direct* rejections, in which the subordinate openly repudiates you or your ideas. But subordinates with strong security or social needs use *indirect* rejection. Indirect rejection is much harder to interpret. Take silence, for example. When a subordinate sits back and keeps his mouth shut that may be a sign of low receptivity, a signal that he's not listening or that he's not willing to voice his objections. But it may also be a sign that he is listening and that he's giving due consideration to what he hears. As a rule, it's much harder to spot indirect rejection than direct rejection. The only way to make sure that you're dealing with indirect rejection is to probe. We'll talk about probing in our next chapter.

How to Recognize High Receptivity (Q4 Behavior)

Here are some common signals of high receptivity:

- *Qualification.* A qualified response is usually a sign of listening and *considering.* Compare these two responses: "You're absolutely wrong" (flat assertion) and "I'm not sure I buy that" (qualified response). The first really says: "There's no need to continue talking . . . my mind's already made up . . . as far as I'm concerned, the matter is settled." The second really says: "I'm inclined to disagree with you . . . but I'm not really certain . . . so continue to talk while I continue to consider what you're saying." The first response (the flat assertion) means: "You don't stand a chance in the world of convincing me." The second response (the qualified response) means: "You still have a chance."
- *Approval.* There are two important differences between Q4 approval and Q3 overagreeableness: (1) Q4 approval comes *after* a period of careful listening and, probably, of questioning, whereas Q3 overagreeableness begins *very early* in the discussion; (2) Q4 approval is usually less *exuberant* than Q3 overagreeableness. In Q4 communication the tone is more deliberate, more thoughtful; when the subordinate says "Fine" or "Okay," it's obvious that he's given the matter some sober consideration. But, in Q3 communication, the tone is *automatically* lavish and overstated; the subordinate is so quick to agree that it's obvious he hasn't given any real thought to what he's saying. Here's an example:

SUPERIOR.   Joe, I'd like to talk to you about a new assignment.
SUBORDINATE.   Fine!
SUPERIOR.   I've been thinking of transferring you to the auditing section while Harry's on vacation.
SUBORDINATE.   That's great!
SUPERIOR.   If your work is okay there, I may make the assignment permanent.
SUBORDINATE.   Hey, I'd really like that.

And on and on. In cold print, this looks unrealistic. But that's often the way subordinates with strong social needs *do* talk; they voice enthusiasm without first thinking. This is a far cry from Q4 approval, which is always premeditated.

- *Involvement and debate.* Willingness to give and take, to ask questions, to provide thoughtful, complete answers, to discuss, to broach alternatives, all of these are signs of listening and considering. They're signs of participation and collaboration. So is *debate.* But there's a big difference between *Q4 debate* and *Q1 argument.* In Q1 argument the subordinate argues for one reason: to win. She wants to assert her independence and put you down at the same time. She's stubborn and closed-minded. She ignores or twists evidence. She's smug and sarcastic. In *Q4 argument* the subordinate argues for a different reason: to settle a matter on which she and you genuinely disagree. Her primary interest is in gaining understanding rather than winning. She's open-minded and thoughtful. She considers evidence carefully. Her manner is tentative and provisional. A *Q1 argument* is frequently a squabble—haggling in an effort to prove that "I know my own mind." A *Q4 debate* is a discussion—a constructive clash of ideas, a consideration of pros and cons in an effort to learn what's what.

- *Questions.* Questions, as long as they're businesslike, pertinent, and to-the-point, are one of the surest signs of high receptivity. Every question really says: "I'm considering what you've said . . . and I want to hear more."
- *Openly expressed doubts.* When someone voices a doubt (provided that it's not a flat assertion), he's really saying: "Let's consider that." Willingness to *consider* is a sign of high receptivity. Phrases like "I'm not so sure I agree with you . . . ," "That doesn't sound right to me . . . ," "Are you really sure about that . . . ?" "It didn't impress me that way . . . ," all have one thing in common: they all leave the door open for further discussion.

All of these—qualification, approval, involvement, questioning, open expression of doubt—are signals of *high receptivity.* They're signs of a willingness to listen, to appraise, to evaluate, to consider, to examine, to assess, to judge. They're signs, above all, of a readiness to work together with you in the communication process, to make it a collaborative, two-way affair. Without this, there can be no communication, no getting through. There can only be *noise-making.*

A Caution

We've been talking as if low receptivity (signalled by Q1, Q2, or Q3 behavior) can always be raised to high receptivity (signalled by Q4 behavior). That, of course, is what you'd *like* to do, but it's not always possible. There may be many times when the best you're able to do is decrease the *intensity* of the Q1, Q2, or Q3 behavior so that it becomes less Q1, Q2, or Q3. This will lead to higher receptivity, but it won't lead to full Q4 receptivity.

A couple of diagrams may help to clarify this. Suppose you're appraising a subordinate who's behavior is heavily Q2—unresponsive, tense, watchful,

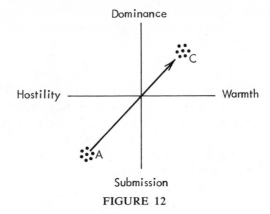

FIGURE 12

secretive. Let's chart this behavior at area A on the model in Figure 12. Now, what you'd like to do is to change that behavior so that it becomes Q4—open, candid, cooperative. In other words, you'd like to move the behavior from area A to area C.

It is very unlikely that you're going to achieve this ideal. What *is* likely is that, after considerable effort, you'll get your subordinate to the point where he's somewhat more responsive, somewhat less tense, somewhat less watchful, and somewhat less secretive. The behavior will still be Q2, but *less intensely* Q2. You won't move your subordinate all the way to area C, but you will move him to area B, as shown in Figure 13.

Is this smaller and less dramatic move worth the effort? Yes. In appraisal, *some* receptivity is much better than *no* receptivity. *Some* listening, some

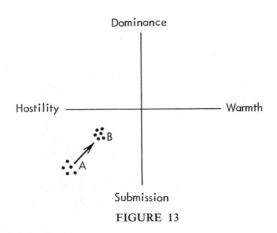

FIGURE 13

consideration, some collaboration are better than none. Aim at complete receptivity, but be realistic enough to know that it's the exception, not the rule.

A RESTATEMENT OF FUNDAMENTALS

The points we've made in this chapter are so fundamental to Q4 appraisal that we're going to restate them:

1. You can't communicate effectively in an appraisal unless you're alert to your subordinate's *receptivity*.
2. If receptivity is *high* at the outset, you can *immediately* get down to the nitty-gritty, the basic issues. High receptivity assures that you can hold a fruitful discussion and that your views will be heard and considered by the subordinate. Whether or not the subordinate *accepts* those views depends upon two things: (1) how sound they are and (2) how persuasively they're presented. But, at the very least, you can be sure that, *as long as the subordinate's receptivity remains high*, your thinking will be listened to and will be considered.
3. If receptivity is *low* at the outset, you'll waste time and effort by immediately presenting facts, ideas, and logic. Low receptivity means that the subordinate will not wholeheartedly collaborate with you, and that your views will *not* be listened to and considered. They either won't be heard at all or they'll be heard and promptly rejected. One thing is sure: your views will not be mulled over, they will not be weighed and measured and evaluated, so there's *no* possibility that they'll be thoroughly understood, or that they'll generate commitment. And understanding and commitment are the final aim of the appraisal.
4. Complete receptivity is the ideal to aim at, but it's frequently unattainable. You may not be able to get maximum receptivity, but you should be able to get optimal receptivity—the highest possible receptivity under the circumstances.
5. What should you do to attain optimal receptivity? *Probe.* Probing is the best way to raise low receptivity to the highest degree possible under the circumstances. Only then do you stand a realistic chance of motivating committed performance.

There Is Another Way, But . . .

We've just said that probing is the best way to raise low receptivity to high (or at least optimal). We didn't say it's the *only* way. There is another way, but it's one that you rarely have an opportunity to use. This is to offer a benefit so impressive that you immediately capture and hold your subordinate's attention ("Play ball with me, and I'll see to it that you're promoted to General Manager at a 50% increase in salary"). A "carrot" of this size, dangled in front of an uncollaborative, inattentive subordinate, is almost sure to grab and hold his attention. And it will do it much more quickly than probing, which is slower and less dramatic. But how often do you have a carrot this big?

As we said earlier, big carrots are in very short supply. If you want to be able to raise receptivity more often than the supply of available carrots permits, you must know how to probe.

SUMMARY

1.   Contrary to popular belief, communication is not simply a matter of words, and it's not something that somebody does to someone else. It's a matter of behavior, and it happens between people.

2.   Communication—getting through to the other person so that he understands what you're trying to say—is hard work. One reason is that the other person frequently sets up obstacles to communication. The commonest obstacle is low receptivity.

3.   High receptivity is the readiness to collaborate in the communication process. It involves the willingness to (a) listen carefully and with an open mind, (b) give thoughtful and objective consideration to what's been said, (c) answer questions, (d) ask questions in an effort to clarify what the other person means, and (e) provide the other person with needed information.

4.   When a subordinate's receptivity is low, you will have trouble getting through. Many of your facts, logic, and arguments will be wasted until you increase the receptivity to its optimal point—the point that's the highest possible for the particular subordinate in the particular appraisal.

5.   Actually, a subordinate's receptivity may be low, high, or somewhere in-between. During an appraisal, it may fluctuate considerably, depending upon many factors, including what happens between you and him.

6.   Low receptivity can be recognized by the following Q1 signals: arguments, negative flat assertions, impatience, interruptions, and negative acts and emotions; by the following Q2 signals: silence, apathy, inattention, and nervousness, by the following Q3 signals: unquestioning compliance, meandering, overagreeableness, and selective questioning.

7.   High receptivity can be recognized by the following Q4 signals: qualification, approval, involvement, questions, and openly expressed doubts.

8. The best way to raise low receptivity is by probing. A faster way is to capture and hold attention by promising a dramatically appealing benefit. But this way is seldom available to you, so a knowledge of probing is a must.

A LOOK AHEAD

Since a knowledge of probing *is* a must, we devote all of our next chapter to it. The question we ask and answer is: How can you create in a subordinate a willingness to collaborate with you in doing Q4 appraisal? How can you make a subordinate receptive to a thorough, searching, candid analysis of his performance?

10

Probing

We closed our last chapter by asking a question that we have already answered. The question was: How can you create in a subordinate a willingness to collaborate with you in a thorough, searching, candid appraisal of his performance? The answer was: by probing. But that raises a number of other questions that must be answered before you can do Q4 appraisal: What exactly is probing? How does it work? How do you do it?

It's no exaggeration to say that *if you cannot probe effectively, you cannot do an effective performance appraisal.* That's a strong statement, but it's valid. So let's take a very close look at the whole subject of probes and probing.

PROBING: A DEFINITION

A *probe* is a communication technique that's used to investigate or explore a topic, so *probing* is the act of investigating a topic by using such techniques. *Probe* comes from a Latin word meaning *examine*, and probing is exactly that: the act of examining what's in the other person's mind. But probing not only helps to examine, to discover, what's in the other person's mind; it also helps *raise the other person's receptivity.* We're going to look at both these functions: raising receptivity and finding out what the other person thinks and feels. Both of them, of course, are vital to Q4 appraisal.

Raising Receptivity

As we've seen, getting through to a subordinate in an appraisal is a matter of timing. The best time to get across your facts, ideas, and viewpoints is when the subordinate's receptivity is high. When it's low, you should avoid presenting your ideas, and concentrate on raising the receptivity. Getting through comes *after* raising receptivity. As we said in the last chapter, a basic tool for raising receptivity is probing. So skill at presenting ideas doesn't mean much without skill at probing. Probing is not an "optional" communication skill; it's a fundamental skill that you cannot do without.

Uncovering What a Subordinate Thinks and Feels

Probing serves a second major function in appraisal: in addition to raising receptivity, it helps you find out what's in the subordinate's mind and heart—what he *really thinks* and *really feels*.

Subordinates have plenty of reason to withhold or disguise their real thoughts and feelings during an appraisal. Because the appraisal is a confrontation, because it generates fear or concern or tension, it often leads subordinates to "play games" with the boss. As a result, many appraisals degenerate into "hide-and-seek," with the subordinate evading and dodging the superior. *Unless you can break through his evasion, the appraisal is doomed to fail.* And the surest way to break through, to reach the subordinate's true thoughts and feelings, is by probing.

So we're faced with two questions: How does probing raise receptivity? How does it uncover what the subordinate thinks and feels?

HOW PROBING RAISES RECEPTIVITY

Probing raises the subordinate's receptivity by helping to fill his *unsatisfied personal* (intangible) *needs*. As we've said, unsatisfied needs create tension, uneasiness, stress. They demand attention; they distract us from other concerns. A subordinate who comes into an appraisal with, say, a strong security need comes in strained and worried. His attention is focused on *himself;* he's inclined to engage neither in productive self-evaluation nor to consider what you say. His receptivity is low because his self-concern is high. His unfilled personal needs block communication.

Probing changes this. When you probe, you help satisfy unfilled personal needs. As you do this, the needs diminish; they become less intense. The subordinate's attention is thus "freed up" for a constructive dialogue.

To see how this happens, let's look at an example. Let's say that Elaine Browning is personnel director for a large manufacturing company, and that she has four subordinates whose performance she must appraise: Ken Polk, who has strong security (Q2) needs; Angela Bowman, who has strong social (Q3) needs; Harley Flynn, who has strong esteem and independence (Q1) needs; and Dorothy Knight, who has strong self-realization (Q4) needs.

When Elaine appraises Ken Polk (who has strong *security* needs) she knows his receptivity is low because he's unresponsive and nervous. As she probes to raise his receptivity, he gets this message:

Elaine's not trying to ramrod her ideas down my throat. She's giving *me* a chance to express my ideas . . . she's showing patience and a willingness to hear me out. I was expecting a pressure-cooker situation, but I was wrong. She's not hurrying me . . . she's not trying to make me accept her thinking. In fact, she seems honestly interested in what I think. This isn't the ordeal I anticipated.

As this message sinks in, Ken's insecurity lessens. As it lessens, he's able to loosen up, to devote less attention to his own fears and more attention to the appraisal task at hand. That's what's meant by "spinning up receptivity."

When Elaine appraises Angela Bowman (who has strong *social* needs), she knows Angela's receptivity is low because she chit-chats incessantly and shows no concern for getting down to business. As Elaine probes to raise Angela's receptivity, Angela gets this message:

Elaine's concerned about me. She keeps asking me questions . . . and she keeps bringing me back into line . . . but everything she's asked shows that she's really interested in *me*. Not only that, but she's willing to listen . . . and I can tell from her responses that she really *is* listening. It's reassuring to have a boss like her . . . a boss who accepts you as a person . . . a boss who's not distant and unconcerned.

As it becomes plain that Elaine is *not* distant and unconcerned, that she *is* friendly and interested (in a businesslike way), Angela's social needs become less pressing. As they do, she's able to shift her focus from her own concerns to the job of evaluating her performance and considering her superior's ideas. Her receptivity rises.

When Elaine appraises Harley Flynn (who has strong *esteem* and *independence* needs), she knows his receptivity is low because he has a chip on his shoulder and makes sarcastic remarks. As she probes to raise his receptivity, he gets this message:

Elaine's interested in *my* ideas . . . and she respects them. She really wants to know what *I* think. She's not crowding me . . . she's giving me a chance to say what *I* want to say. She obviously believes that I'm *worth* listening to.

As this message comes across, Harley's *esteem* and *independence needs begin filling up.* He no longer feels it's necessary to resist Elaine's ideas in order to prove what a "hot shot" he is. He's able to divert his attention from his *own* concerns to the task of thinking through his own notions and listening to Elaine's ideas.

The situation is somewhat different with Dorothy Knight, who has strong self-realization needs. Dorothy comes into the appraisal with high receptivity. She considers it a growth-producing opportunity; she wants to engage in self-discovery as well as consider what Elaine has to say that will help her grow on the job. What Elaine must do in this case is *keep* Dorothy's receptivity high. She does this by probing. Dorothy responds to the probes by thinking:

This is a fine experience. I'm discovering something about myself . . . I'm getting a chance to present some new ideas I've been thinking about . . . and I'm even getting an opportunity to debate some points with the boss. This is a challenging, stimulating session.

Feeling this way, she naturally remains receptive.

In every instance, probing raises receptivity by helping to gratify needs that would otherwise nag at the subordinate and preoccupy his attention.

HOW PROBING UNCOVERS THOUGHTS AND FEELINGS

Probing not only raises receptivity; it also helps you find out what your subordinate thinks and feels. It does this in five ways:

1. *Probing gets the subordinate to participate*

A major purpose of probing is to get the subordinate to respond. Probes are phrased so as to get a reaction or a reply. Once you voice a probe (and this usually takes only a few seconds), the thing to do is shut up and give the subordinate a chance to talk. This creates interaction; it gets *both* of you into the discussion. And interaction—exchange of ideas coupled with involvement—is the very heart of communication (as opposed to noisemaking).

2. *Probing elicits information*

Probes draw out information, ideas, and feelings that haven't been volunteered. Subordinates may withhold information because they're afraid you'll use it against them. They may also withhold it because they don't know what information you want. And they may give you useless information because they don't know what information you need. *Probes tell them.* They help you guide the discussion.

3. *Probing makes the appraisal meaningful to the subordinate*

If people are interested in anything, it's their own words. By probing you can make the appraisal meaningful to the subordinate by letting her speak her own ideas, sentiments, and concerns. This lets her inject her own needs into the appraisal. It makes the appraisal more personal and more relevant.

4. *Probing vents interfering emotions*

Strong emotions, positive or negative, usually hinder the clear, objective thinking that's so vital during an appraisal. By probing, you can help your subordinate vent these emotions—get rid of them (or at least neutralize them) by expressing them. Once they've been vented, you'll be able to get down to the real business of the appraisal.

5. *Probing forces you to listen attentively*

When you probe, you *must* listen attentively because probes are usually *serial,* one following another until you have the information you want. In order to phrase each new probe intelligently, you must understand what the subordinate has just finished saying. Each probe produces an answer; the answer is followed by another probe that builds on the *previous* answer and leads to the next answer; and so on. So the value of any probe depends upon how well you've heard and understood the last answer. This takes high receptivity on *your* part.

A Caution

We're not saying that communication depends only on probes. Getting through to subordinates depends upon many skills besides probing. You can probe effectively and still have trouble during an appraisal if you haven't planned ahead, if your thoughts are disorganized, if your logic is weak, if your choice of words is poor, if you bunch your ideas instead of spacing them out, if you neglect the emotional impact of language, and so forth. Getting through depends upon many skills; we'll talk about the others later. All we're saying now is that no communication skill is *more* important, or more neglected, than probing.

PROBES AND PERFORMANCE APPRAISAL

There are three things you *must* do in a Q4 appraisal, and all of them require probing.

1. You must get the subordinate to *open up* and tell you what he thinks and feels.
2. You must get the subordinate to *keep on talking*, so that you get a complete picture of what he thinks and feels. If you get only a partial picture, you're likely to draw some wrong conclusions.
3. You must *make sure you understand* what's on the subordinate's mind. If you don't, much of the appraisal will probably be a waste of time—or worse.

There are eight basic kinds of probes. One easy way to remember what they are and what they do is to group them under one of the three functions we've just listed.

A LOOK AT EACH PROBE IN DETAIL

1. Probes That Get the Subordinate to Open Up

OPEN-END QUESTIONS

Examples.   Open-end questions help you get a wide-ranging response about a broad topic. Here are some examples:

How do you see foreign competition affecting our domestic marketing plans next year?

Tell me what impact you think this unionization drive will have on us.

What do you feel we can expect in the way of government regulation over the next couple of years?

What Open-end Questions Do

They *draw out* the subordinate—get him involved—by giving him a chance to say what's on his mind about a given subject. They give him freedom to speak out, to voice what he knows, what he thinks, what he feels.

They tell the subordinate that he's an *important* part of the appraisal, that his thinking *counts*. As long as a subordinate is restricted to "yes" or "no" answers, he can't feel that he's a significant part of things. But open-end questions cannot be answered "yes" or "no." They demand more than that; in doing so, they let the subordinate know that his ideas matter.

They help you come to grips with *negative emotions*. If a subordinate seems tense or uneasy about something you've said, but hasn't openly said so, open-end questions can get him to voice his feelings and explain them ("How do you feel about that?" "What's your reaction?"). Similarly, if a subordinate *has* voiced negative feelings, open-end questions can get him to explain them and *examine* them ("Why do you feel that way?" "Tell me why you're so upset"). But the questions must be asked in a concerned and nonpunitive way. If the subordinate thinks he's going to get clobbered, he'll dodge the question.

They help you handle flat assertions. Flat assertions are usually exaggerated ("That's the dumbest idea I ever heard"). But there's often a kernel of truth to them (the idea may not be the "dumbest," but it may be somewhat unworkable). Open-end questions do two things: (1) they let the subordinate think through, and then modify, his flat assertions, and (2) they give him a chance to isolate the kernel of truth (if any) at the heart of the assertion. In the following example, open-end questions (combined with other probes) get a subordinate both to voice opinions and examine them.

SUBORDINATE.   That's the screwiest suggestion I ever heard. Smith must be out of his mind to recommend a thing like that to you.

SUPERIOR.   What makes you say that? (Open-end question)

SUBORDINATE.   Well . . . the idea will never work . . . never in a million years. We tried something like that a few years ago and it fell on its face . . . remember?

SUPERIOR.   Tell me more about it. (Neutral question)

SUBORDINATE.   The H-12 project . . . remember? It was almost identical to what Smith's recommending now. And nobody understood it . . . so the whole thing bogged down.

SUPERIOR.   Why do you think that happened? (Open-end question)

SUBORDINATE.   I just told you . . . nobody understood it. The plan was okay . . . but you can't make something work if you don't understand it . . . and nobody in the department understood it. We needed training . . . and we never got it.

SUPERIOR.   So it wasn't the idea that was nutty. It was lousy training. (Summary statement)

SUBORDINATE.   Yeah, that's right. The idea's okay . . . but it'll never work unless we train people first.

Open-end Questions and Subordinate Behavior

Q1.   Anger, belligerence, and other negative emotions are typical of Q1 behavior. Open-end questions (combined with reflective statements) are helpful in venting these feelings.

Example.   I can tell you're sore. What's bugging you? (Reflective statement followed by open-end question)

Q2.   Silence or terseness are typical of Q2 behavior. Open-end probes (combined with pauses) are useful in loosening up taciturn or tight-lipped subordinates.

Example.   Tell me why you feel Shelton can't be trusted with the job.

Q3.   Chatty, verbose meandering from topic to topic is typical of Q3 behavior. *Don't* use open-end probes in this situation. You'll only encourage more talkiness when you should be encouraging less. Here's an example of what should *not* happen:

SUPERIOR.   Joe, how do you think things are going in Davis's territory?
SUBORDINATE.   I'm glad you asked that, Al . . . really glad. I was talking to Davis just the other day. In fact, I spent time with him in the territory. You'd never recognize the guy. He's lost 45 pounds . . . jogs a mile every day . . . and has stopped smoking. He's become a real health fiend. Seems his doctor insisted on it . . . etc., etc.

Q4.   A willingness to disclose significant information, fully and candidly, is typical of Q4 behavior. Open-end questions are excellent for starting this disclosure:

Example.   How do you think you've been doing on the Eastgate project?

Some Cautions

• As we just said, use open-end questions sparingly with very talkative subordinates. If you ask too many open-end questions of a long-winded subordinate, the appraisal will probably last much longer than it should.

- Use open-end questions sparingly with subordinates who meander a lot. Subordinates who have a hard time sticking to the subject may use an open-end question as an opportunity to "take off" on a whole series of irrelevant topics.
- Don't contaminate or influence the response by voicing *your own* opinion along with the open-end question. Here's an example: "I think the Common Market approach is sure to prove beneficial to us. What do you think?"

2.   Probes That Get the Subordinate to Keep On Talking

PAUSES

Examples. It's obviously impossible to give an example—in print—of a pause. A pause is a deliberate *silence*, a brief period of *no* talking, a short, temporary break in the dialogue.

What Pauses Do

- They give the subordinate a chance to mull over what she's heard, so that she can absorb it and evaluate it.
- They give her time to formulate a response, to think through what she's going to say next.
- They relax the pace of the appraisal so that the subordinate doesn't feel pressured. A dialogue is a back-and-forth conversation, but it shouldn't be a game of verbal ping-pong. In ping-pong the idea is to beat your opponent; in an appraisal, the idea is to *mutually* work out better ways of doing things. That requires an unpressured, deliberate pace, and pauses help to establish such a pace.
- Pauses give *you* a chance to think and plan, too. (Don't of course, get so wrapped up in your own thoughts that you fail to pay attention to the subordinate's response to the pause.)
- Pauses are especially useful for drawing out the silent, unresponsive subordinate. I' you ask a question and then *wait* for an answer without saying anything more, the subordinate will frequently break the silence in a matter of seconds. Unhappily, many superiors feel awkward if a silence falls between themselves and the subordinate. So here's what typically happens: the superior asks a question, gets no *immediate* response, and then, embarrassed by the silence, goes on to do some more talking *herself. This only gets the subordinate off the hook*, and guarantees

that the appraisal will be a monologue instead of a dialogue. Here's an example:

SUPERIOR.   What do you think, Carol? Can we meet these new figures?
SUBORDINATE.   (No immediate response)
SUPERIOR.   (Hurriedly) Well . . . I can understand your not wanting to commit yourself. I know that's a tough question. So let me ask you this. Do you think maybe we ought to scale down the figures?
SUBORDINATE.   (A thoughtful look on her face, but no immediate response)
SUPERIOR.   (Without waiting) Well . . . let's come back to that later. I know these are sticky issues we're talking about.

And on and on. Many superiors in the real world—like the one in our example—need to master the art of keeping their mouths shut at times.

Pauses and Subordinate Behavior

Q1.   Wisecracks, sarcasm, baiting remarks are all typical of Q1 behavior. Don't give in to the urge to strike back immediately with your own provocative remark. Your subordinate will probably interpret your action as proof that the "needle" has scratched a sore spot. Instead, *pause*. Give yourself time to frame a thoughtful, deliberate response, to think through the possible consequences of whatever you're going to say next.

Q2.   As we've said, pauses are especially useful with quiet, withdrawn Q2 behavior.

Q3.   Use pauses sparingly with talkative subordinates. Windy people like nothing better than a chance to rush in and fill a verbal vacuum with their own words.

Q4.   Use spaced pauses to give candid, open subordinates time to organize their thoughts and thereby make a more coherent presentation of their ideas than they would if they felt rushed and pressured.

Caution.   Not *every* silence should be considered a pause. There's a difference between a real pause—sometimes called a pregnant pause—and embarrassed silence. A pregnant pause is a deliberate silence in which you give the subordinate time to formulate a response. The pregnant pause is designed to *bring forth* a reaction. An embarrassed silence, on the other hand, is simply a sign that you don't know what to say. It's an awkward lapse, not a deliberate silence.

REFLECTIVE STATEMENTS

Examples.   Reflective statements indicate that you *understand,* are *aware of* (but not necessarily that you *agree* with), the subordinate's feelings and sentiments. These feelings can be either negative or positive. Here are some examples of reflective statements dealing with *negative* emotions:

I can see you're worked up about this.
It's pretty clear that you're angry.
I can tell you feel hurt.

And here are some reflective statements dealing with *positive* emotions:

I can tell you're happy about the situation.
It's pretty obvious that you feel proud.
You're certainly enthusiastic about it.

What Reflective Statements Do.   Reflective statements vent emotions, positive or negative, that interfere with rational discussion. They relax the situation and pave the way for a businesslike exchange by letting the subordinate get rid of his highly charged feelings. Here's an example:

SUPERIOR.   Joe, how do you feel about the progress you've made in the last six months? (Open-end question)
SUBORDINATE.   (Heatedly) That's a laugh. Progress! Hell ... I'm going backwards around here ... not forward. (His voice rising) In fact, if you want to know the truth, I think I'm getting lousy treatment around here. I can name at least six people in this department who are trying to cut my throat because they know there's no other way they can compete with me ... and the worst of it is, I think you're in cahoots with them. I mean it!
SUPERIOR.   It's pretty plain that you're angry, Joe. (Reflective statement)
SUBORDINATE.   (More intensely) Sure I'm angry. You'd be, too, if you were as isolated as I am. I don't have one ally in this department ... not one person who's willing to work with me. Only a bunch of jerks who are trying to give me a hard time.
SUPERIOR.   I see ... you're really fed up. (Reflective statement)
SUBORDINATE.   (Calmer) Yeah ... I really am, Fred. And I'd really like to talk with you about it. There are some things going on around here that I don't think you're aware of.
SUPERIOR.   Go ahead, Joe, I'm listening.

This is a very brief example. Venting may take longer in real life; it may well require a series of reflective statements, not just one or two. But the point is this: *reflective statements help to do the venting.*

Reflective Statements and Subordinate Behavior

Q1.   Anger, indignation, scorn, haughtiness, the feeling of being "misunderstood" or "unappreciated," all of these and numerous other negative emotions are common elements of Q1 behavior. Reflective statements are very useful for venting these feelings.

Example.   You're really worked up about this . . .

Q2.   Tension, nervousness, apprehension, deep uneasiness, all of these are typical of Q2 behavior. Reflective statements can help to dissipate these expressions of anxiety.

Example.   It's apparent that you're uncomfortable about this.

Q3.   Exuberant, high-spirited, effusive chatter is a common manifestation of Q3 behavior. Reflective statements can help clear the air of these distractions.

Example.   You really seem wound-up about it.

Q4.   At any time during an appraisal, a subordinate whose behavior is mainly Q4 can slip into one of the behaviors described above, perhaps due to something *you've* said or done. If she does, you'll probably have a need for one or more reflective statements.

Example.   My last remark seems to bother you.

Cautions

- Be sure to use enough reflective statements to vent the feelings *fully.* As a rule, the more *intense* the emotion, the more reflective statements you'll have to use. That's because, at first, venting usually leads to *stronger* expressions of feeling; thus, an angry statement, once reflected, often leads to an even angrier outburst. In other words, the emotion initially *builds up.* This is known as "peaking." Only after the emotion has peaked will it begin to subside. This usually requires *several* reflective statements.

- On the other hand, don't *overuse* reflective statements. You don't have to reflect every sentiment and emotion expressed by a subordinate. Reflect the troublesome ones, those that show the subordinate is genuinely upset or bothered, or that he's too "high" to settle down to business. In other words, reflect those emotions that must be dispelled before the appraisal can be conducted in a businesslike way.
- Don't use reflective statements in a "light" or "kidding" way. Remember: whatever the subordinate is angry (or elated) about isn't funny to him. Make sure your reflective statement shows you take him seriously, and that you respect his position.
- Don't fall into the trap of "taking sides" by agreeing with the subordinate's sentiments—unless you're sure you want to. Here are some examples of very risky statements that not only reflect angry sentiments but go beyond that and state or imply agreement.

I can sure see why you feel so indignant.
You're obviously upset, and *I would be too, if I were in your shoes.*
I don't blame you a bit for feeling sore.

Statements like these can return to haunt you, so don't make them unless you're sure you *mean* them and are ready to state them aloud.
- Don't forget to use reflective statements to vent overly positive feelings (many people use them only for negative feelings). A subordinate who's feeling intense positive emotions is just as unreceptive as one who's feeling intense negative emotions. (For example, a subordinate who's "brimming over" with excitement because 10 minutes ago his daughter gave birth to his first grandchild, may be just as unresponsive to your ideas as a subordinate who's angry because 10 minutes ago some "jerk" ran into his brand-new automobile.)

NEUTRAL QUESTIONS AND PHRASES

Examples.   Neutral questions and phrases get the subordinate to elaborate on some aspect of a subject already under discussion. Sometimes, they *sound* very much like open-end questions. They ask for amplification of some *facet* of a topic that's already been broached. They zero in on *part* of a subject and ask for more information about it. Here are some examples:

Fill me in *further* on why you prefer to do it at the Fenway plant.

Tell me *more* about why you're so pessimistic about this quarter's profit picture.

Give me some *additional* reasons why you keep insisting that Webster ought to be transferred.

What Neutral Questions and Phrases Do

- They help amplify the flow of information. (Open-end questions *start* the flow, while neutral questions keep it going.)
- They get the subordinate to *go deeper* into pertinent topics. (Open-end questions permit more general responses which often stay on the *surface* of things.)
- They let the subordinate know that your interest is continuing, that you want to know more. Few things will do more to raise a subordinate's receptivity than the knowledge that you, the boss, want to understand in *depth* something that she's talking about.

Neutral Questions and Subordinate Behavior.   Neutral questions and phrases are useful no matter what your subordinate's behavior. Whenever you want more information about a subject, whenever you need elaboration or amplification of something the subordinate's said, whenever you need a topic expanded or clarified, you'll find neutral questions and phrases helpful.

Caution.   Keep your neutral questions neutral. Don't phrase them so that they stifle candor. For example, "Why in the hell *don't* you think Morgan can do the job?" is a *belligerent* question—not a neutral one. It tells the subordinate that you already disagree and that you may be ready to start an argument. There's a good chance that a question like this will *squelch* the flow of information.

BRIEF ASSERTIONS OF INTEREST

Examples

I see.
Keep going.
Hm-m-m-m.
Yes.
(Nod of head)

What Brief Assertions of Interest Do

- They encourage the subordinate to *continue* sharing her thoughts.
- They draw out *further* information. When the subordinate continues talking about a topic, she almost always adds to or expands upon what she's already said.
- They increase *receptivity*. Subordinates are more likely to listen willingly to you when you show that you're listening willingly to *them*.

Brief Assertions and Subordinate Behavior.   Brief assertions are useful with any kind of subordinate behavior, but two situations deserve special comment.

Q2.   A tense, unsure subordinate usually gives very short responses to questions. Brief assertions are especially helpful in getting the insecure subordinate to amplify his very brief (and often not very informative) answers.

Q3.   Use brief assertions *minimally* with highly talkative subordinates. These subordinates will usually amplify their ideas without encouragement from you. The problem is that many of their ideas ought *not* to be amplified because they're not relevant to the appraisal. Be careful; if you use brief assertions without first thinking about what you're doing, you may add fuel to the fire. The talky subordinate may get the idea that you're eager to hear more of whatever he's talking about, and start to unload all sorts of trivia on you. Don't encourage communication unless the communication is worth encouraging.

Cautions

- Use brief assertions only when they're *true*. Saying "I see" when you don't see can only increase the confusion.
- Don't use too many brief assertions in too brief a time. A whole string of "Uh-huhs" and "I understands" and "Keep goings" may sound mechanical and phony. Ironically, if you use too many brief assertions, the subordinate may get the idea that you really *aren't* interested—that you're only *pretending* to be.
- Of all probes, brief assertions are the easiest to use mechanically. It takes some thought to frame a good open-end question, say, or a reflective statement, but it's easy to say "Uh-huh" without giving it any thought at all. Don't do this. Use brief assertions only *after* you've considered their possible implications and consequences.

3.   Probes That Help You Make Sure You Understand

CLOSED-END QUESTIONS

Examples.   Closed-end questions are worded so as to get very narrow and exact answers to very precise questions. There are three kinds.

1. *Fact-finding* questions that start with *who, when, where, how much.*
2. *Commitment* questions that can be answered *yes* or *no* (without leading).

3. *Option questions* that can be answered by selecting one of two or more alternatives.

Here are some examples of all three types:

1. Fact-finding questions

Whom do you recommend for the job?
How many units can you produce by Tuesday?
When do you plan on starting the new operation?
Where did the shipment originate?

2. Commitment question

Do you think this objective is realistic?
Are you willing to accept Ralph as a co-worker on this assignment?
Does this approach strike you as sensible?

3. Option questions

Shall we get together to check it out on Wednesday morning or Wednesday afternoon?
Would you prefer to work with Doris ... or Ken ... or both of them together?

What Closed-End Questions Do

- They help you get precise, explicit facts or opinions.
- They help you test final commitment ("Yes," "You bet," "Sure").
- They tell you whether your reaching for commitment is premature. Here's an example:

SUPERIOR.   How about it, Frank ... are you ready to give it a try?
SUBORDINATE.   Hold on, Lou ... not so fast. I'm not even sure I fully understand what you're asking me to do.

This example illustrates two points: (1) the answer to a closed-end question may tell you that you've got to go back and retrace some of your steps; (2) closed-end questions don't *always* produce short, precise answers. In fact, any closed-end question can be answered in a long-winded manner. But *usually* closed-end questions elicit brief responses, specific bits of information, or "yes" or "no" answers.

Closed-end questions help raise *receptivity* by controlling *meandering*. The only way to keep some subordinates from flitting from topic to topic is by restraining their freedom of movement; they must be made to stick to the subject. By permitting limited answers, closed-end questions restrict mobility; it's pretty difficult to go off on a tangent when responding to a question like: "Do you think you can make the 10% increase?" (Of course, the subordinate could respond with something like: "Well . . . that's a pretty tough question to answer. . . . In fact, it reminds me of the time. . . ." If he does, the only thing to do is *repeat* the question, even if that means interrupting the subordinate. "Joe, pardon me . . . but it's important to settle this one point. Do you think you can make the 10% increase? *Yes* or *no*?")

Closed-End Questions and Subordinate Behavior

Q1.   Subordinates whose behavior is mainly Q1 sometimes make grandiose and unrealistic commitments. Closed-end questions are useful for bringing these commitments down to earth.

Examples

Are you quite sure you don't want to scale down this objective a bit?
Is there any chance that you're aiming too high?

Q2.   Subordinates whose behavior is mainly Q2 prefer to straddle the fence. Option questions (prefaced by a brief statement of the reason for asking the question) are especially useful for getting them to take a stand.

Examples

Grace, it would help us both if we could settle on a specific figure. Which goal do you feel makes the most sense: 10% in three months or 15% in four?
Ken, I'm still not clear on which way you think we should go. Do you think we'll do better at the Fernwood plant or the Pine Ridge plant?

Q3.   Subordinates whose behavior is mainly Q3 often have to be restrained from meandering. As we've said, closed-end questions are excellent for this purpose. It's usually a good idea to preface the question with a reminder of the need to get back on track.

Example

Wayne, it's important that we settle the matter we were talking about originally. Do you think Marlowe can handle the assignment?

Q4. Subordinates whose behavior is mainly Q4 can usually be relied upon to provide details without much prodding by you. But they still need to know precisely which details you need. Closed-end questions tell them. They say, in effect, "Zero in on *this*." Without this kind of direction, the subordinate may provide the wrong details.

Cautions

• Don't ask too many closed-end questions early in the appraisal. A series of early, rapid-fire closed-end questions will make the appraisal sound like an interrogation—a "third degree." And that will make information gathering harder to do. Instead, use open-end questions early to start the flow of information, follow with neutral questions and phrases to get more data on pertinent topics, and begin to use closed-end questions sparingly as you approach the end of the discussion of a topic. And, to avoid the "interrogation effect" at any point in the appraisal, explain why you're about to ask a closed-end question before you ask it.
• Remember: with tight-lipped, unresponsive subordinates, too many closed-end questions can be counter-productive. If you ask enough of them, the subordinate can coast through the appraisal with mostly nods, grunts, and shrugs. You'll learn very little about his real thoughts and feelings this way. So use them, but use them sparingly, with those subordinates whose behavior is mainly Q2.

LEADING QUESTIONS

Examples. Leading questions contain their own *yes* or *no* answers. The answer is built into, implied by, the question. Here are some examples:

You want to do the kind of job that'll help you get more money, don't you? (Answer: Sure!)

It's not worth the extra time, in view of the cost problem, is it? (Answer: No.)

You wouldn't want to get a reputation as a troublemaker, would you? (Answer: Of course I wouldn't.)

What Leading Questions Do. They help you find out if the assumption that you've built into the question is correct. It's okay to use leading questions to get the subordinate to *agree* with you, but *only after full discussion*. Don't use them too early in the discussion of a topic; if you do, they'll be interpreted as *overcontrol*, and that may stifle discussion *or* generate resistance. Here's an example in which leading questions are *mis*used—and thereby generate resistance.

SUPERIOR.   Al ... so help me ... if you don't stop undermining this policy, I'm going to blow the whistle on you. You wouldn't want to find yourself in hot water with the General Manager of the division, would you?

SUBORDINATE.   Frankly, John, I couldn't care less. The policy is stupid ... and, if necessary, I'll say so to the General Manager.

SUPERIOR.   C'mon, Al ... be reasonable. If you antagonize him, it could be curtains for your career with this company. You don't want that to happen, do you?

SUBORDINATE.   I'm not so sure, John. The way I feel now, maybe that would be the best thing that could happen to me."

Leading Questions and Subordinate Behavior

Q1.   Be careful; this subordinate may resent what he considers an effort to "lead him by the nose." If he does, he may stiffen his resistance to your ideas. But there may be times when a leading question, combined with a reflective statement, is useful for crystallizing the consequences of unthinking actions.

SUBORDINATE.   (Very self-righteously) I don't care what you say, Hank. I'm going to barge into Dryden's office when I leave here and tell him exactly what I think about the stupid way this operation's being run. I'm sick and tired of being the fall-guy around here, and I'm gonna let him know it.

SUPERIOR.   I can see you're really hot about this. (Reflective statement) But Earl ... you don't really want to make an enemy of the man who's going to be the next president of this company, do you? (Leading question)

SUBORDINATE.   (Subsiding somewhat) No ... I guess not. But I can tell you this: I'd sure *like* to tell him off someday.

Q2.   Leading questions, used late in the appraisal, can help to get a commitment from an indecisive subordinate who prefers not to commit herself.

SUPERIOR.   Martha ... do you think we ought to go with Omnidigit or with Trans-binary? (Closed-end question)

SUBORDINATE.   (Slowly) I'm just not sure.

SUPERIOR.   But you do feel, don't you, that we ought to go with the supplier with the best track record? (Leading question)

SUBORDINATE.   Yes . . . of course.

SUPERIOR.   And you wouldn't want to be stuck with a system that might give us problems, would you? (Leading question)

SUBORDINATE.   Oh, no.

SUPERIOR.   Well, then, based on the tests you ran, which supplier has the best track record and is least likely to give us problems? (Closed-end question)

SUBORDINATE.   (Slowly) Well . . . I guess Omnidigit comes closest to filling those two requirements.

SUPERIOR.   Okay. Then let me ask you this: Can you see any good reason *not* to go with Omnidigit?

SUBORDINATE.   (Still very slow to respond) No . . . no I can't.

SUPERIOR.   Then, since Omnidigit has the best track record, is least likely to give us problems, and you can see no good reason not to give them the contract, would you say we ought to go with Omnidigit? (Leading question)

SUBORDINATE.   Yes . . . yes I would.

Q3.   Subordinates whose behavior is largely Q3 are frequently unwilling to make firm decisions, since decisions usually require saying *no* to somebody. Here again, used late in the appraisal, leading questions may help you guide such subordinates towards a specific commitment.

Q4.   You may well go through an entire appraisal with a subordinate whose behavior is mainly Q4 and not need a single leading question. At most, use them very sparingly.

Cautions

- Don't use leading questions too early.
- Use leading questions *very sparingly* because they may cut off information.
- Remember: *too many* leading questions will make the appraisal seem manipulative, as if you're playing games with the subordinate by repeatedly backing him into a corner.
- Leading questions can be nothing more than *threats*. As such, they're going to be resented. Here are a couple of examples:

You don't want to join the ranks of the unemployed, do you?
You wouldn't like to find yourself out on the street, would you?

SUMMARY STATEMENTS

Examples. These sum up briefly, in your own words, information you've received from the subordinate. They show her that you've absorbed what she's said, and that you're now checking to make sure you understand it. They do *not* imply agreement. Here are some examples:

As I understand it, Marie, you think we'd get better results by committing the whole budget to TV and eliminating print ads entirely.

If I hear you right, Stan, you're concerned that Franklin is too green for this assignment and that Stevens is too likely to antagonize people . . . so we'd better find somebody else.

Your thinking . . . as I get it . . . is that these figures are completely outside your control and that nobody in the company could have done any better under the circumstances.

What Summary Statements Do:

- They help you ascertain that you really have been hearing what you think you've been hearing.
- They bring crucial points into focus, so that both you and the subordinate can examine them.
- They tell the subordinate whether or not she's been getting through. Sometimes, on hearing you summarize your understanding of what she's said, your subordinate will realize that she hasn't made herself clear. She can then correct the situation. Here's an example:

SUPERIOR.   As I understand it, Sue, you're suggesting that we scrap the art department in the coming year and rely entirely on freelancers for our illustrations . . . and that we'll end up saving money if we do.

SUBORDINATE.   No, Joyce . . . that's not exactly what I meant. I think we should *experiment* with the idea next year . . . maybe by cutting our art department by a third and letting freelancers do that part of the job. If this saves money . . . and I think it will . . . then we can decide what to do about the rest of the department. Scrapping the entire department now would be premature. All I'm suggesting is that we *experiment* with the idea . . . *not* that we put the whole thing into effect at once.

Summary Statements and Subordinate Behavior

Q1.   You're likely to encounter a whole series of disagreements from a subordinate whose behavior is mainly Q1. One way to handle this is to summarize them first, then deal with each on a one-by-one basis. This not only helps you to organize his disagreements into some kind of coherent whole, but it also gratifies him by proving that you've been listening.

As I get it, Stu, you're saying that I'm not giving you enough credit for landing the Lakeland account . . . that it's unreasonable to expect you to land four target accounts in a three-month period . . . and that you'd be able to land at least three if Production wasn't hampering your efforts. Let's discuss each point in turn.

Q2. You probably won't have as much chance to use summary statements with Q2 behavior as with Q1, because there will be less to summarize.

Q3. Meandering subordinates are sometimes hard to follow. One good way to eliminate some of the confusion, focus on the pertinent facts, and separate the relevant from the irrelevant, is by summarizing *only* those matters that deserve to be summarized. It's usually a good idea to preface your summary statement with an explanation of what you're trying to do.

Maureen . . . let me see if I can boil down what you've been saying to essentials. As I understand you. . . .

Q4. Summary statements are always useful for making sure you understand what the subordinate's been trying to tell you. Even when a subordinate is candid and open, you can't be certain you understand him until you summarize it and then have your summary confirmed.

Cautions

- Don't use a summary statement to make a speech or take over the dialogue. Make your summaries brief and to-the-point; focus on what the *subordinate's* been saying—not on what you would like to say. Either you check for understanding, or you voice your own thinking. You *can't* do both at once.
- Don't put words in the subordinate's mouth. Say what you actually *heard*, not what you *wish* you'd heard. If you voice your ideas, but pretend they're your subordinate's, you're likely to generate resentment.

SUMMING IT UP

We've covered so much ground in this chapter that it would probably be a good idea to tie it all together in one package. So we've included Table 6 to summarize what we've said about probing.

Table 6. Probes: What They Are and What They Do

Function	Probe	Definition	Characteristics	Useful in Dealing with Following	Cautions
1. Getting the subordinate to open up	Open-end questions	Questions worded so that they get a wide-ranging response on a broad subject	Usually begin with *what, why, how do, tell me*. Get subordinate involved in appraisal by giving him a chance to tell you what he knows or thinks.	*Q2 silence*: in combination with a pause, opens up closed-mouth subordinates. *Q1 negative emotions*: in combination with reflective probe, helps vent anger and hostility.	Avoid using with a subordinate who's meandering in a Q3 way; you'll only give him a chance to meander some more.
2. Getting the subordinate to keep on talking	Pauses	Silences that permit subordinate to make sense of what he's heard and respond to it	Relax pace of the appraisal so subordinate doesn't feel pressured. Give you a chance to collect your thoughts and plan what you're going to say next. Excellent for dealing with uncommunicative subordinate.	*Q2 silence*: encourage withdrawn or reticent subordinate to consider and respond.	Don't end the pause too quickly; don't start talking again before your subordinate has had a chance to say something. Be patient.
	Reflective statements	Statements that show you understand how the subordinate feels (without implying that you agree)	Help clear air so subordinate can think more clearly. Help vent and drain overly negative or positive emotions.	*Q1 anger*: vents negative feelings. *Q2 silence*: helps subordinate acknowledge his tension and become more responsive. *Q3 exuberance*: vents overly positive emotions.	Voice your understanding of how the subordinate feels, but be careful not to voice agreement unless you're sure you want to.
	Neutral questions and phrases	Questions that get the subordinate to elaborate on some aspect of a topic	Somewhat more focused than open-end questions Help subordinate un-	Useful across the board .: with *Q1, Q2, Q3* behavior. Helps gain more information and	Be sure you zero in on significant aspects of the topic. Don't encourage subordi-

	Technique	Description	Uses / Benefits	Special applications	Cautions
		...already being discussed	...derstand what *further* information you need.	show subordinate you're listening.	...nate to talk about trivia
	Brief assertions of interest	Short statements that encourage subordinate to keep on talking	Help establish and maintain good rapport. Usually produce additional information.	*Q2 terseness:* helps subordinate expand and amplify his brief responses.	Too many of these start to sound mechanical or absent-minded.
3. Making sure you understand	Closed-end questions	Questions worded so that they get a very precise answer to a very specific question	Excellent for getting subordinate to voice his final commitment. Excellent for gathering specific facts.	*Q3 meandering:* focuses on specifics and thereby controls wandering from topic to topic. *All others:* helps you learn details and fill in gaps in knowledge.	Be careful how you word these; otherwise, you may get a clear-cut answer to the wrong question.
	Leading questions	Questions that suggest their own answers	Excellent for getting subordinate to commit self. Help you check your understanding by telling you whether the assumption you've built into the question is correct.	*Q2 and Q3 indecision:* used late in appraisal to guide and move subordinates to action.	Use this sparingly, or the subordinate will think you're trying to trap him.
	Summary statements	Statements that summarize facts obtained from the subordinate	Focus on facts, not on emotions. Help subordinate clarify own thinking by hearing it summed up by somebody else.	*Q1 multiple disagreements:* help you summarize multiple disagreements by subordinate so they can be dealt with one by one. Gratifies his esteem need by showing him you've been listening. *Q3 confusion:* focuses on relevant facts. Helps separate wheat from chaff.	Don't put words in the subordinate's mouth; summarize what you *heard* him say, not what you *wanted* him to say.

RESTATING THE THEME

The theme of the last two chapters is so important that it's worth restating:

1. Communication is both behavioral and interactional, which means that any appraisal is likely to be loaded with obstacles, barriers, traps, pitfalls—you name it.

2. One of the worst of these obstacles is *low receptivity*. A subordinate whose receptivity is low is unwilling to engage in constructive self-evaluation or to *consider* what you say. *His mind is closed.*

3. This means that, during the appraisal, there's a right time and a wrong time to present your ideas and information to the subordinate. The *right* time is when the subordinate's receptivity is *high*—when he's willing to listen and consider. The *wrong* time is when his receptivity is *low*—when his mind is closed.

4. If you try to communicate information and ideas at low receptivity, you'll waste some of your best and most valuable points. This will happen no matter how sensibly or eloquently you present your ideas.

5. Therefore, if your subordinate's receptivity is *low*, the only thing to do is raise it, and *then*—when it's as high as you can get it—present your information and ideas. High receptivity must always be present to some degree if you're going to communicate instead of make noise.

6. You can detect a subordinate's level of receptivity by *observing* his behavior during the appraisal. A subordinate will *signal* whether his receptivity is high or low by the things he says and does.

7. A useful way to raise low receptivity is by *probing*. Probing raises receptivity while, at the same time, it tells you what the subordinate thinks and feels. Therefore, *effective performance appraisal is impossible without effective probing.*

SUMMARY

1. A probe is any communication technique that's used to investigate or explore a topic. Probing does two things: it helps you raise a subordinate's receptivity, and it helps you find out what the subordinate thinks and feels.

2. Probing raises receptivity by helping to fill the subordinate's unfilled personal needs. Unfilled personal needs monopolize attention. Probing can be used to gratify unfilled needs for security, sociability, esteem, independence, and self-realization. As this happens, the subordinate becomes

less self-concerned and can turn his attention to self-evaluation and to your opinions.

3. Probing uncovers the subordinate's thoughts and feelings by (a) getting her to participate, (b) eliciting information, (c) making the appraisal meaningful to the subordinate, (d) venting interfering emotions, and (e) forcing you to listen attentively.

4. There are eight basic kinds of probes. Table 6 defines them and summarizes their characteristics.

5. Effective performance appraisal is impossible without effective probing.

A LOOK AHEAD

Probing is a vital communication skill, but not the only one. Other communication techniques must be mastered if you're going to do Q4 appraisal. We look at these other techniques in our next chapter.

11

Q4 Communication

Once you've spun up your subordinate's respectivity, you can't assume that the appraisal will be clear sailing. You still face some problems:

1. How can you keep receptivity high?

Now that your subordinate is ready to do serious self-evaluation, to collaborate, to listen, to consider your point of view, how can you make sure he stays that way? How can you make sure you don't drive down his receptivity by upsetting, or boring, or distracting him?

2. How can you get your ideas across clearly and persuasively?

When his receptivity is high, how can you make sure you don't waste your chance by conveying your message in a muddled or unconvincing way?

We answer these questions in this chapter and offer some guidelines.

STAY ALERT TO SIGNALS OF HIGH AND LOW RECEPTIVITY

The fact that your subordinate's receptivity is high doesn't mean it's going to stay high. So stay alert to the behavioral signals that tell you if receptivity is dipping downward (Q1, Q2, or Q3 behavior) or remaining high (Q4 behavior). At the first sign of diminishing receptivity, spin it up again. Never take it for granted that receptivity will stay high automatically.

KEEP YOUR SUBORDINATE INVOLVED

The best single way to keep receptivity high is by keeping the subordinate involved in a collaborative, Q4 effort. To do this, you must probe *throughout* the appraisal. Don't make the mistake of assuming that once you've raised receptivity, you can "take over" the appraisal and transform it from a "duet" into a "solo." You *can* do that, of course, but only if you want to drive receptivity back down. If you drive it back down, the only person who will pay attenton to your solo is you.

If you want to see exactly what we mean by saying that you must probe throughout the appraisal, turn back to Chapter 5, where we outlined the format for a Q4 appraisal session. If you'll reread the outline, you'll notice that, *at every point*, the appraisal is a two-way affair. At *no* time is it a solo operation. When the subordinate presents his own evaluation of his performance, the superior must ask questions and request information whenever he feels he needs it. Even when the superior presents *his* evaluation, he must pause frequently to make sure the subordinate understands; he must check that understanding with frequent probes. At *no* time does Q4 appraisal degenerate into a monologue.

So, to repeat: if you want to keep receptivity high, keep your subordinate involved. Let him collaborate with you. To do this, use probes throughout the appraisal.

CHOOSE YOUR WORDS CAREFULLY

If you want to maintain high receptivity and get your ideas across, watch your language, especially the words you use. Words are like booby traps; if you don't pick your way among them carefully, they're liable to blow up in your face. *This is especially true in a situation as sensitive as performance appraisal.* Once a subordinate's receptivity is high, she's going to be listening carefully to everything you say, and she's going to take it *seriously*. To her, the appraisal is serious business, so any words that come out of your mouth carry weight. There are three reasons why.

1. Your words are a good clue to what's going to *happen* to the subordinate. Throughout the appraisal, she keeps wondering: "Am I in trouble? Will this affect whether I get a raise? Will he discipline me . . . put me on

probation . . . give me a hard time . . . bawl me out . . . promote me . . . demote me . . . freeze me in my present job?" and so on. Everything you say is interpreted by the subordinate in the light of concerns like these. If you say something as simple as "You're doing fine," the subordinate may interpret that to mean, "I'm off the hook" or "I don't have anything to worry about." So you'd better say only what you really mean.

2.   There's a second reason why your words are so important: in the eyes of most subordinates, you're an *authority*. Your words carry extra weight just because you're the boss. Even if a subordinate doesn't accept what you say, you can still back up your words with action. Suppose you tell a subordinate, "You're doing a rotten job." He may hear this and think: "You're crazy . . . you don't know what you're talking about." But— crazy or not—you have clout; you can act upon your statement by firing the subordinate, or by other punitive action. So what you say *is* significant.

3.   Finally, your words are important because, if you are not careful, they can drive high receptivity back down to low. Remember: receptivity starts to rise as unfilled personal needs begin filling; as long as our needs are unfilled, we focus our attention on ourselves; when our needs become gratified, our attention is "freed up" and we can focus it on other matters. *The process works the other way, too.* As our filled needs "empty out," so that they no longer feel gratified, we begin to refocus our attention on ourselves; we withdraw our attention from other matters and start concentrating on ourselves and our unfilled (or rapidly emptying) needs. As this happens, high receptivity decreases until it becomes low receptivity.

What this means in an appraisal is this: The minute you say something that threatens to "empty out" or degratify a filled personal need, you may drive receptivity down. This is especially true if you say something that drains away gratification from a particularly *strong* need.

For example, suppose a subordinate has strong *security* needs which, thanks to your efforts, are presently gratified. Her receptivity is therefore high. Now suppose that, without intending any harm, you tell her: "Doris, you don't seem very enthusiastic about all this. If you don't believe in this project, just say so, and I'll look for somebody else to do it." This statement is almost sure to drive her receptivity down. Why? Because Doris will withdraw some of her attention from the appraisal and focus it on *herself.* She'll begin to worry: "What does the boss mean by that? Is she really saying that I'll be fired? Or demoted? If she gets somebody else to do the job, what will that do to my future? Should I pretend to be more enthusiastic than I am? Or should I tell her why I'm not enthusiastic? If I do, will she be upset with me? Do I run a greater risk if I keep my mouth shut or if I tell her what I really feel? Is it too late to save the situation?" And on and on.

Suppose a subordinate has strong *esteem* needs which, because of your probing skills, are presently fulfilled. His receptivity is high. Now suppose that, without carefully considering what you're saying, you tell him: "Doggone it, Lou . . . that strikes me as a pretty stupid thing to say. Especially for a guy like you, with 12 years of experience. Don't you know better than that by now?" You can pretty safely bet that these words will drive down his receptivity. He's almost sure to divert some of his attention from the *appraisal* and focus it on his own immediate concerns: "That's a lousy thing to say to a guy who's been around for 12 years. A lot he knows! I'm trying to get the truth through that thick skull of his . . . and he calls me stupid. Somebody's stupid alright . . . but it's not me. He's gonna pay for that. I'm gonna needle him for the rest of this appraisal. I'll show him he can't talk to me that way." And so on. Unless you do something to bring receptivity back up, the appraisal is likely to deteriorate.

Thus, your words are important for three reasons: (a) they're used by the subordinate as clues to his future; (b) they're given extra weight because you're the boss; and (c) they may, if they're the wrong words, drive down receptivity. So it's critically important to choose your words carefully. Here are some guidelines.

Pick Words That Say What You Want to Say

This isn't as easy as it sounds. An example will show why:

Edward is a copywriter in the advertising department. His work is excellent but he frequently misses his deadlines. One reason is that he writes very slowly, sometimes taking several hours to find the "right word." He's a painstaking writer who refuses to put anything down on paper unless he's sure it's "exactly right." As a result, he turns in first-rate copy, but it's usually late. In appraising Edward, there are several different things you might say. For example: "Ed . . . it's no wonder you turn in so much late copy. You're a *nit-picker*. You're too *uptight* about your copy. You exaggerate the importance of every little word. You're *over-scrupulous*."

Two things are wrong with this approach. (1) You are using a large number of emotionally loaded, negative words; this is sure to drive down Edward's receptivity. (2) You are leaving the impression that it's bad for a copywriter to be conscientious about words, and that, of course, is wrong; copywriters are supposed to be conscientious about words, but they're also supposed to get their copy completed on time. Your statement almost implies that it would be better for Edward to be sloppy about words. Obviously, that's not the message you want to convey, but, because of the words you've chosen, it is the message that comes across.

Here's another way you might broach the subject:

Ed ... you're a very *conscientious* craftsman ... a diligent writer with a *good feel* for language. You *appreciate* the importance of every word. But ... unfortunately ... your concern for the right word seems to be slowing you down to the point where a lot of your copy is turned in late. What we need is *both* your concern for language *and* the ability to meet deadlines. What are your ideas on how you can do both?

In this example (assuming that you mean what you're saying, and that you're not "soft-soaping" Edward) your words say exactly what they should say: that conscientious use of language is a virtue in a copywriter, but that it must be *coupled* with the ability to meet deadlines. By saying what you *intend* to say, by avoiding negative emotional language, and by probing to get Edward involved, you're almost sure to spin up his receptivity and get him to work with you toward a solution of the problem. If you *keep* him involved, you've got a good chance to keep his receptivity high.

Avoid Emotionally Loaded Negative Words

They usually *lower* receptivity by making the subordinate resentful, defensive, and resistant. One of your major responsibilities in an appraisal is to lower the emotional temperature of the meeting; negative language *raises* it. For example:

1. A subordinate may stubbornly refuse to accept other people's ideas, and this may have a bad effect on her performance, but she's not likely to discuss the matter in an open, constructive way if you tell her she's *pigheaded, thick-skulled, obtuse, closed-minded, narrow, self-righteous, arrogant,* and so on.

2. A subordinate may be too easygoing and quick to compromise, and this may have a bad effect upon his performance, but he's not likely to be receptive to your ideas on the subject if you tell him he's a *creampuff,* a *chump,* a *pushover,* a *patsy,* and so forth.

We're not saying that you shouldn't make value judgments. It's impossible not to, since value judgments are basic parts of the appraisal. But, whenever possible, phrase your value judgments in cool, unemotional language.

DON'T USE ANALOGIES THAT OBSCURE THE REAL ISSUES

An analogy compares something to something else. Comparison often helps to clarify a point, or to make it more colorful, or more emphatic. That's why we used an analogy earlier, when we said: "Words are like booby traps; If you don't pick your way among them carefully, they're liable to blow up in your face." But, all too often, superiors use analogies to avoid saying something in plain English. When this happens, analogies obscure the real issues; they become a way of evading touchy situations. Here is an example:

John . . . you remind me of a guy who used to pitch for our college baseball team. He knew how to throw a baseball, but he lost a lot of games because base-runners were always stealing bases on him. Once a batter got on base, this pitcher would just lose track of him. You're a lot like that.

Nobody could blame a subordinate for being confused by this. Here's what the superior *should* have said, in plain English:

John . . . the problem is that you don't do two things well at one time. The minute you start concentrating on a task, you let other things get away from you. Most of the difficulty stems from the fact that you lose control of the rest of your projects as soon as you start a new one.

Here's another example of evasion by analogy:

Ken . . . I've always said that nobody should be made a quarterback unless he can do the whole job . . . throwing, running, blocking, calling plays . . . inspiring the team. A quarterback who can't do all these things is going to miss a lot of scoring opportunities.

This is baloney. Here's a translation of what the superior really means but is unwilling to say:

Ken . . . you're not ready to be promoted because you still lack the skills the job requires. I won't promote anybody into that position who can't do it all . . . organize the district, get those salespeople moving, do some selling on his own, provide me with good competitive data, and cut selling costs. So far, you haven't shown me that you've got the organizational skill . . . or that you're sufficiently concerned about selling costs.

To repeat: there's nothing wrong with using analogies to clarify or emphasize. But they shouldn't be used as an excuse for not being candid.

USE CONCRETE WORDS; AVOID ABSTRACTIONS

People "catch on" more quickly when they can "see" things with the mind's eye. The trouble with abstractions is that they don't give subordinates anything to "picture." Compare the following examples:

ABSTRACT.   Joe . . . you're doing a fairly good job . . . but, of course, I expect you to do better next quarter.

CONCRETE.   Joe . . . you're at 92% of quota for this quarter. I expect to see you at 105% next quarter . . . which will help us pick up some of the slippage we've suffered the past three months.

ABSTRACT.   Janet . . . it would help a lot if you got those reports in earlier.

CONCRETE.   Janet . . . it would take a lot of pressure off the programmers if you got those reports in by nine o'clock every Thursday morning.

These examples illustrate two points:

1.   Vague, abstract language provides an easy "out" for subordinates. If you tell a subordinate you want him to do better, you can't blame him if he doesn't do *enough* better, since, after all, he doesn't know exactly what "better" means anyway. But the minute you define "better" as "105% next quarter," you've made it impossible for him to say, in his next appraisal, "I don't know what you're complaining about . . . you told me to do better, and I hit 101% of quota. That's better, isn't it?"

2.   One excellent way to make your language concrete is to use *numbers*. You can't do this all the time, of course, but when you can, you should. Quantification helps people understand *exactly* what's expected of them, and it enables you to measure performance.

There is one other reason to avoid abstractions: abstract language doesn't give people anything to "picture," it doesn't rivet their attention. In fact, it's likely to bore them, and when people are bored their attention wanders. So, if you use a lot of vague words, words that can't be envisioned, words that don't have sharp, clear meanings, you're likely to drive down receptivity. Once a subordinate starts responding to your ideas with a "ho-hum," the appraisal is in trouble.

SPACE OUT YOUR IDEAS; DON'T BUNCH THEM

If you ever were to eat a bunch of bananas at one sitting, you would probably have a terrible time digesting them. The eating of bananas should be spaced out; an interval between each helps the digestion.

Ideas are like bananas in this respect. Anybody who tries to digest a bunch of ideas in very rapid succession will probably have trouble doing so. Ideas should be spaced out; an interval between ideas helps the understanding. It also helps to keep receptivity high.

When you hurl bunches of ideas at a subordinate, she may feel threatened ("Why is he clobbering me like this? Why is he trying to overwhelm me with all these ideas?"), even though you don't mean to threaten her. This feeling of "being bludgeoned" may stir up security or esteem needs, and once these needs are aroused, receptivity will go down.

The best rule is: Don't throw a whole bunch of ideas at a subordinate at one time. Space them out, singly or in small groups depending upon how complex they are. Leave an interval between each idea or small group of ideas, so that she has time to mull it over. If you dump a whole bunch of ideas on a subordinate without spacing them out, you'll probably create confusion, and drive down receptivity.

Another way to put this is: Present your ideas *continually*—not continuously. Something that's done continuously is done without any interruption whatever; it goes on and on and on. But something that's done continually is done at intervals; there are gaps in the activity.

What should you do during these gaps? *Probe.* Probe to make sure that you're getting across, that you're understood. Give the subordinate a chance to respond, to ask questions, to express uncertainty.

It's especially important to space your ideas (1) if they're new, unusual, or unfamiliar to the subordinate; (2) if they're complicated; and (3) if there are a lot of them. But, whatever their nature, the safest general rule is: present them continually—not continuously.

WHAT YOU SAY AND WHAT THE SUBORDINATE HEARS MAY BE TWO DIFFERENT THINGS

Much of what you say in an appraisal is *heard* by the subordinate in a way different than you intended. Here are some possibilities to keep in mind.

The Subordinate May Not Hear You *At All*

He may tune you out. If you're boring him, if you're saying something he doesn't understand, if his mind is on something else, he may literally not hear you. Minutes after the appraisal, he may not recall your having said something that *you* consider important. That's why you must pause from time to time to probe whether he's been listening. The only way to make sure is to ask. Open-end questions are ideal for this ("How does that strike you?" "What's your reaction?" "Tell me how you feel about it"). All of these are ways of finding out if the subordinate has been following what you've been saying.

Keep two cautions in mind:

1. If you want to make sure a subordinate has been listening, *don't* use closed-end probes, because they won't tell you what you want to know. If you ask, "Do you agree?" he can easily answer "Sure" even though he hasn't heard a word. Use questions that require more than "Yes" or "No." If you get a vague, evasive or embarrassed answer, it could mean that he hasn't been listening. *Probe* until you know for sure; there's no point in continuing if he hasn't heard what you've said up to this point.

2. It may be your fault that the subordinate tunes you out—which is another way of saying that her receptivity drops. You may drone on too long, your manner may be drab, you may talk about something she's not interested in, and on and on. These are all things you can do something about. But sometimes a subordinate will tune you out for reasons that are beyond your control. If so, it's probably best to postpone the appraisal until a better time. For example, it might be a waste of time to do an appraisal with a subordinate at the same time his child is undergoing surgery, or on the same day that he's scheduled to appear in court for a divorce hearing, or on a morning when he's been in a serious traffic accident on the way to work. Whether or not a scheduled appraisal should be delayed is something only you can decide in the light of the facts. But there may be times when postponement is the only practical course.

The Subordinate May Exaggerate What You Say

This is especially likely if he has a strong need for approval or reassurance. For example, you may say: "That's not a bad idea." He may hear: "That's an excellent idea." Or you may say: "I'll have to think about that." He may hear: "No." Once again, the only way to make sure your ideas aren't being distorted is to probe. If you don't, you may find yourself going through the following dialogue several weeks *after* the appraisal.

YOU. How come you never checked with me on that idea we talked about?
SUBORDINATE. *Checked* with you? Why should I? You told me no.
YOU. No I didn't. I told you I'd have to think about it.
SURORDINATE. Gee . . . I thought you'd turned me down.

The Subordinate May "Level Down" What You Say

When this happens, she makes your ideas *less important* than you intended. Here's an example:

SUPERIOR.   Helen . . . as far as I'm concerned, this is your number one goal . . . and it takes precedence over everything. I can't see anything else that's as urgent as this.
SUBORDINATE.   (To herself) Sounds fairly important. I guess I'd better do something about it pretty soon . . . after I clear my other projects out of the way.

What accounts for leveling down? Lots of things. The fact that the subordinate has her own priorities, that fact that she doesn't really believe you ("The boss calls *everything* number one"), the fact that you aren't emphatic enough ("If it's really so important, why does she sound so blah about it?"), the fact that the subordinate wasn't paying close attention, and so on. The important thing to remember is that leveling down is *common*; it happens frequently. Once again, only probing can detect it.

The Subordinate May Erase What You Say

If it's threatening enough, he may literally blot it out. In other words, he may hear it and almost immediately forget it. This explains why subordinates sometimes insist, weeks and months *after* an appraisal, that they never heard something the superior clearly remembers having said. Very often, what the subordinate really means is that he *did* hear the message, but— because it made him very uneasy—he erased it. And, since he really doesn't remember having heard it, he can honestly say, "I never heard you say that."

You obviously cannot prevent this. If a subordinate chooses to forget something, you can't stop him. What you *can* do is ask him to summarize *his* understanding of what you've said, to make sure he's heard it. It's harder for a subordinate to forget something that he himself has repeated out loud.

WHAT YOU SAY TO THE SUBORDINATE MAY NOT BE WHAT HE SHOULD HEAR

So far, we've been talking about selective listening, in which, to a degree, the subordinate chooses what she hears and how she hears it. But it's also true that you do *selective talking* during the appraisal. You choose what you want to say and how you want to say it. And just as your subordinate may not hear what she should hear, you may not *say* what you should say. Here are some points to help you say what *ought* to be said:

- Don't focus only on *negatives* (unless, of course, there are no positives). This is Q1 communication; it deprives the subordinate of a balanced view of her performance.
- Don't focus on *inconsequential* matters. This is Q2 communication, talking about issues that can't possibly rock the boat because nobody really cares much about them one way or the other.
- Don't focus only on *positives* (unless, of course, there are no negatives). This is Q3 communication; like Q1, it can only produce a badly distorted picture.

The best rule is: Tell the subordinate *everything* she ought to hear— good and bad. Try to present a full, complete, candid picture of her performance as you see it.

SUMMARY

1.   Once you've spun up a subordinate's receptivity, you still face two communication problems: (1) keeping receptivity up, and (2) getting your ideas across clearly and persuasively. There are several ways to overcome both problems.

2.   Stay alert to signals of high and low receptivity. Remember that high receptivity can drop.

3.   Keep the subordinate involved. Don't change a duet into a solo.

4.   Choose your words carefully. Remember that they carry special weight because you're the boss. Anything you say may (a) be used by the subordinate as a clue to his future, (b) be given extra weight by the subordinate because of your authority, (c) drive down receptivity. So pick words that say what you want to say, and that aren't emotionally loaded.

5.   Don't use analogies that obscure the real issue. Say things in plain English.

6.   Use concrete words; avoid abstractions. Words that give the subordinate something to picture communicate best.

7.   Space your ideas; don't bunch them. Between each idea or small group of ideas, probe.

8. Remember that the subordinate may hear something different from what you say. She may not hear it at all, she may exaggerate it, she may level it down, she may erase it.

9. What you say may not be what the subordinate should hear. You may select mainly positive, negative, or trivial matters on which to focus, thereby presenting a distorted picture of the subordinate's performance. Try to present a complete and balanced picture.

A LOOK AHEAD

All the Q4 skills we've talked about so far—presenting benefits that motivate, setting optimal goals, raising receptivity, communicating clearly and persuasively—thrive best in a *trustful* climate. Unless you can establish such a climate—what we call a win-win climate—you may still be unable to do Q4 appraisal. Q4 appraisal depends not only on Q4 skills, but on a Q4 environment in which to use them. In the next chapter, we show how to develop a Q4, win-win environment.

12

Developing a
Win-Win Climate

Q4 performance appraisal can *only* be done in a win-win climate. In a win-win climate, *everyone*—the subordinate, the organization, you—*gains.* Everyone should be *better* off as a result of the appraisal; everyone should win.

To understand what win-win is all about, let's compare the Q4 appraisal climate with Q1, Q2, and Q3 appraisal climates.

FOUR APPRAISAL CLIMATES

Q1 Climate

The superior wins (or *thinks* he does). He gets to show "who's boss." He gains self-esteem. But, as a rule, the *subordinate* loses. He may lose face or self-respect, fail to get a balanced view of his performance, fail to grow. He may come out of the appraisal resentful, frustrated, angry. The organization loses, too, because instead of getting *optimal* performance out of the subordinate, it's likely to get sullen, unwilling performance.

Q2 Climate

Nobody wins much of anything. The *superior* keeps the boat from rocking (she may consider this "winning"), but that's about all. The *subordinate* learns little or nothing, and is given no impetus to improve her performance. The organization gets a continuation of the status quo, nothing more.

Q3 Climate

The superior wins acceptance, he feels assured that the subordinate thinks he's "okay." But the *subordinate* loses because he gets a lopsided view of his performance, a view that's heavily (and falsely) weighted with positives. Because he gets little stimulus to change, the organization loses, too.

Only a Q4 Appraisal Is Win-Win

Only a Q4 appraisal fulfills the criteria that define what a performance appraisal should be:

Performance appraisal is a formal discussion between a superior and a subordinate for the purpose of discovering and evaluating how and why the subordinate is presently performing on the job, and how the subordinate can perform more effectively in the future, so that *the subordinate, the superior, and the organization all benefit.*

We've emphasized the last phrase because it makes our point. The ultimate purpose of an appraisal is to develop and maintain win-win working environments in which *everybody* benefits.

But win-win working environments cannot be established where *trust* is lacking. In fact, it's impossible to create win-win situations unless the subordinate has confidence in—*trust* in—his superior's integrity and intentions. Without this, none of the skills we've described in this book is worth very much.

TRUST: A DEFINITION

Trust is the conviction held by the subordinate that you genuinely want to *help* him. It's the belief that you will not knowingly take advantage of, manipulate, or deceive him. It's the assurance that you won't "use" him. It's the confidence that you'll make every effort to say and do what's in his best interest.

Obviously, you can't have trust without *honesty*. This point is so basic that we won't dwell on it. Everything in this book assumes that the superior is a person of integrity—that he is, in fact, *trustworthy*. Otherwise, it's pointless even to talk about trust, and it's impossible to do Q4 performance appraisal.

An Ironic Situation

Ironically, many superiors who *are* trustworthy nevertheless evoke distrust. They have the subordinate's best interest at heart, but the subordinate doesn't see it that way. Their motives are basically good, but the subordinate suspects those motives. Here are three examples.

Many superiors who practice Q1 management justify their behavior this way: "Sure, I lean on my people pretty hard. But they need a strong hand to guide them. If it weren't for me, they'd be in big trouble most of the time. When I lay down the law, *it's for their own good*." But that's not necessarily how the subordinates see it. From their viewpoint, the superior "doesn't care about us."

Many superiors who practice Q2 management justify their behavior this way: "Sure, I do a routine job of appraising performance. What's to be gained by going into a lot of details and agitating everybody? There's enough turmoil around here without my creating more. Nobody wants a boss who's constantly making waves. When I refuse to rock the boat, *it's for my subordinates' own good*." But that's not necessarily how they see it. From their viewpoint, the superior "isn't interested in us."

Many superiors who practice Q3 management justify their behavior this way: "Sure, I take it easy with my subordinates. They do their best work when they're not under pressure . . . when they're relaxed . . . when their morale is high. I admit it: I pull my punches . . . but *it's for their own good*." But that's not necessarily how the subordinates see it. From their viewpoint, the superior is so easygoing that "we never learn anything in an appraisal."

In each case, the problem is not one of honesty. The problem is that the superior (1) makes wrong assumptions, and (2) bases ineffective behavior on those assumptions.

TRUST-BUILDING SKILLS

Integrity *is* essential to building trust. But, it may not be *enough*. What's needed are *skills* with which you can demonstrate that you have the subordinate's best interest at heart. You need some way to show your concern for his well-being. Unless you do, your interest may be misinterpreted as *lack* of interest or as insensitivity. Let's take an overall look at the skills needed to build trust and establish a win-win, Q4 appraisal climate.

Build a Foundation of Trust Everyday

As we said in Chapter 2, you can't turn trust off and on like a faucet. Either it's there most of the time, or you're in trouble. The time to begin building trust is not at the start of the appraisal; the time to begin building trust is in your day-in, day-out interactions with your subordinates. If they know, from daily experience, that you deserve their credence, they'll have no reason to change their minds when the appraisal begins. The trust will be there when you need it.

Ask the Subordinate to Prepare a Systematic Evaluation of His Own Performance Before the Appraisal

This shows him that you respect his opinion, and that you expect him to be an active—*not* passive—participant in the appraisal. Even more important, it shows him that you want him to be prepared—that you have no wish to take advantage of him during the appraisal by surprising him or catching him off guard. This will intensify his feelings of trust.

Take Time to Do the Job Right

It takes time and patience to discover all the facts about how a subordinate is doing on the job, but that is the only way to stimulate real change. "Quickie" performance appraisal doesn't work. Raising receptivity, probing, listening, discussing, evaluating—these take time, but they're vital.

Q4 appraisal takes more than time. It takes concentration. Make the appraisal your *sole* concern. Cut off telephones, bar interruptions, put aside other projects, no matter how pressing. Focus exclusively on the subordinate. Q4 appraisal is never casual; it's demanding—and usually tiring.

Make It Plain That Your Ideas Are Not Fixed and Unchangeable

You're bound to have some definite ideas about any subordinate, but don't chisel them in granite. Stay open—*really* open— to new information, new viewpoints. Be willing to *learn* from your subordinate; make it plain at the outset that you want to know how he sees things, and what evidence he has for his views. Make the appraisal a session in which both of you learn.

This is basic: If you go into an appraisal with your mind made up, you *cannot* do Q4 appraisal. If you are convinced you have all the answers, that you *know*—beyond a doubt—what is "wrong" with the subordinate, then the result will be Q1—autocratic, arbitrary, dogmatic. To do Q4 appraisal you must be willing to change or moderate your views in the light of new evidence. Where is this new evidence likely to come from? From the exchange of information between you and your subordinate during the appraisal. That's one of the "bonuses" you get from synergistic appraisal: new information that neither of you had before.

Get the Subordinate to Analyze Her Own Performance

As we've said all along, Q4 appraisal is a *joint* activity—a *partnership*—in which you and the subordinate collaborate in evaluating her progress and in planning her future. Don't squelch this analysis. Don't present your own ideas too early and thereby stifle her views. Don't deliver a monologue. Make the appraisal a dialogue—a real give-and-take—in which the subordinate feels free to present her own ideas. Q4 appraisal is a prime example of *two-way* communication.

Here are some ways to help the subordinate analyze her own performance.

PROBE IN DEPTH

This is the best way to get a subordinate to give as well as take. Do the probing *in-depth*. Don't depend on one probe to get involvement. Use a *series*, all on the same topic, so that the subordinate realizes that you really *are* interested. Dig *deep*; let her know that you're serious about wanting her opinion.

EXPLAIN THE PURPOSE OF YOUR PROBES BEFORE YOU USE THEM

This is especially important early in the appraisal, when you are trying to establish rapport. If you ask a series of questions (especially closed-end probes) without explaining why, you are likely to come across like a lawyer in cross-examination, and the subordinate may wonder: "What's he so nosy for? Why is he prying like this? What's it to him?" Most subordinates will tell you more if they understand the *purpose* of your questions.

START WITH PROBES THAT ARE EASY FOR THE SUBORDINATE TO HANDLE

Remember: You're trying to *gain involvement*. You are *not* trying to paint him into a corner. Never begin with probes like these.

Kay, I'm really curious: how come there's so much trouble in your department these days?

Dave, I won't beat around the bush. I keep hearing nothing but complaints about your department messing up shipments. What's wrong?

Instead, start out with probes that pull the subordinate into the dialogue *without* threatening or accusing:

Kay, how do you feel things are going in your department these days?

Dave, how's your department doing in getting out shipments?

LISTEN TO IRRELEVANCIES AND EXPLORE THEM

Don't "put down" or ignore a subordinate just because she says something that doesn't seem to "fit in." What seems pointless to you may be significant to her. Showing an interest in her "irrelevant" remarks doesn't mean you agree with them; it means you're interested in finding out why they're important to her. If they weren't, she wouldn't voice them. So probe these remarks in depth, even if you can't see any point to them; if you probe, the point will sooner or later become clear, and you'll learn something about the subordinate in the process.

We are *not* advising that you probe every bit of trivia and every trifle that comes out of the subordinate's mouth. Probe those comments that seem related to *performance* but that don't seem to "tie in" with the general drift of the dialogue. Probing frivolous chit-chat only wastes time; probing remarks that have to do with performance but that seem tangential —that digress from the main topic—may reveal things you should know.

Listen at a Thinking Level

Make sure you know what the subordinate means. Ask yourself: "Do I really understand what he's trying to tell me? Do I know *why* he's telling me this . . . why he considers it important? Do I understand how this ties in with everything else he's told me? Do I follow his logic? Am I getting the main point?" *Never assume that the answer to these questions is "yes."*

Test your understanding by probing. Two probes are especially good for this purpose:

- *Summary statements.* Briefly restate what you think he's said, and find out whether he agrees or disagrees. If he agrees, fine; let him continue. If he disagrees, probe to find out *why.*
- *Reflective statements.* If he's been expressing emotions, mirror them back to him as you perceive them. His reaction will tell you whether you're interpreting correctly.

If you've been listening at a thinking level and *don't* understand, tell him so and then probe. Summary statements combined with neutral questions are good for this. Here are a couple of examples:

The logic of that escapes me, Don. As I understand you, you're saying that you've got the strongest department in the industry, and yet you don't think they can get the job done. Please give me more of your thinking on this.

June, that sounds like a contradiction to me. A few minutes ago you advocated a price increase. Now you're saying that the market won't tolerate higher prices. Help me out of my confusion.

CAUTION

If you don't understand what's being said, don't blame the subordinate. Let her know you're confused—but don't accuse her of confusing you. Here's an illustration:

WRONG WAY.   Diane, it's impossible for anybody to follow you when you start talking about programming techniques. Can't you make your point in a logical, systematic way?

RIGHT WAY.   Diane, I'm not following you. Programming's a complicated subject . . . and I guess the only way I can understand it is to ask some questions. So, let me stop you and ask. . . .

Reward the Subordinate for His Participation

Psychological "rewards" encourage the subordinate to *stay* involved. They're a "payoff" that stimulates *further* participation. There are several ways to pay out psychological rewards:

- Express your appreciation and—if you can do it honestly—your approval ("Fine"; "I understand perfectly"; "That's a good idea"; "That makes sense to me").

- Listen with interest, and *show* it. An occasional nod of the head can help. So can brief assertions of interest ("Keep going," "Uh-huh," "Hmmmm"). Be sure to keep your eyes on the subordinate while he's talking. If you *look* distracted, he'll assume you *are*.
- Share your ideas without sounding as if you've already made up your mind. From his standpoint, an exchange of views with you is psychologically rewarding; it proves your interest and respect.
- Use reflective statements and summary statements. These, too show that you are interested.

Remember: rewards are important. Without them, the subordinate will sooner or later get the idea that he's talking to a brick wall, and he may stop talking.

Create on Advice-Seeking Climate

Resist the urge to give advice immediately This is hard to do; most superiors, aware of their power, give advice very readily. Most subordinates resent getting advice when they haven't asked for it; it seems like a power play by the boss to force his views when the subordinate isn't receptive. (You may say that you're only giving "advice," but, to the subordinate, it seems more like a command.)

One complicating factor is that most superiors offer unsolicited advice when the subordinate's receptivity is low. That is the very worst time, since the subordinate isn't prepared to consider it.

This doesn't mean that it's *always* wrong to give advice that hasn't been solicited. Unsolicited advice may be helpful in two situations: (1) when the subordinate is unable to analyze her own performance effectively, and (2) when her evaluation differs radically from yours. We'll talk about these situations later. For the time being, the best general rule is: Don't offer instantaneous, unasked-for advice. Instead, build a climate in which the subordinate, convinced of your interest and concern, *asks* for your advice.

How do you do this? How do you create an advice-seeking climate? Here are some guidelines:

1. Don't give advice during low receptivity. The subordinate either won't pay attention, or, if he does, he'll reject your advice immediately.

2. *Probe.* By drawing out the subordinate and getting him to amplify his thoughts, you'll get him to verbalize his uncertainties and doubts. Once he acknowledges that he's not sure about something, he'll find it easier to seek advice. Probing should help him realize, maybe for the first time, that he is uncertain, that he needs advice.

3.   When giving advice (at high receptivity), make sure the subordinate understands what she'll *get* by following it. She must understand *what's in it for her.* If she doesn't, why should she bother doing what you suggest?

4.   If, after you've made a serious attempt to build up receptivity, the subordinate still doesn't ask for your advice, *give it anyway*—factually and slowly. You can't wait forever for him to solicit it. But, again, make sure he understands the *benefit.* If you don't make that plain, your advice is likely to go over like a lead balloon.

Create a Problem-Solving Climate

You want to create a setting in which you and the subordinate can work together to solve his performance problems. You can't do this if you make *demands* on him. Demand-making happens when you tell a subordinate, whose receptivity is low, what to do, but *not* what he'll get from doing it. The subordinate usually sees this as an attempt to control and manipulate him. So resist the urge to "lay down the law." This is hard to do. It's very easy to begin an appraisal like this—and very damaging:

Look here, Vern, we both know that department of yours isn't delivering the goods . . . and something has to be done about it. Now, get this straight: I want to see a change . . . and I want to see it fast. We can't have this situation continue.

This states the problem (as *you* see it), but that's about all it does. If "we both know" that the department isn't delivering the goods, saying it out loud won't make things better.   This demand ignores the really significant questions: *Why* isn't the department delivering the goods? *How* can the situation be changed? Is it possible to change it "fast"?

It's especially easy to start making demands when a subordinate expresses opposition. Here's an example:

SUPERIOR.   I'm going to lay it on the line, Chuck. Ever since we made your operation a profit-center, I've been unhappy with the figures. Something must be out of control over there . . . otherwise your bottom-line numbers would look a lot better.

SUBORDINATE.   I don't buy that at all, Gene. When you take a look at the industry . . . and compare our figures with our best guesses about what competition's doing . . . I don't think our figures look so bad. In fact, I'm pretty proud of what we've done this past quarter.

SUPERIOR. Damn it, Chuck, I say the numbers look lousy . . . and I want to see some improvement. Don't tell me about competition. Just focus on your own operation and do something to improve it.

This sort of exchange is very common in performance appraisal—and very futile. The boss makes a demand before there's any agreement on what the problem is—in fact, before there's any agreement that there *is* a problem. This is Q1 (tell-and-do) appraisal.

In Q4 appraisal you want to (1) clearly define the problem so that both you and the subordinate agree on what it is, and (2) resolve the problem by (a) finding out *why* it exists, and (b) figuring out *how* to solve it. This is the only approach that can be depended upon to produce improvement.

Let's see how the preceding situation might have been handled in a Q4 way:

SUPERIOR. Chuck, now that we've profit-centered your operation, we've got to take a look at the bottom-line figures. How do you evaluate your profit performance so far?

SUBORDINATE. Not bad, Gene. Especially not when you look at the industry as a whole. If you compare us with what competition's doing . . . or what we *think* they're doing . . . the figures don't look bad. We're holding our own.

SUPERIOR. You feel you stack up pretty well against competitive profits . . . is that right?

SUBORDINATE. Yeah . . . so far as I can determine.

SUPERIOR. Well, leaving competition aside for a moment, how do you size up your numbers when you compare them to the objectives we set?

SUBORDINATE. That's a different story, Gene. We obviously haven't met our objectives . . . and I'm not happy about it.

SUPERIOR. Any clues to what the problem might be?

SUBORDINATE. I'm not really sure. When you compare our profits to our objectives, they look lousy. But, when you compare them to what competition seems to be doing, they look okay . . . or at least not bad. Maybe our objectives are unrealistic. Or, maybe I'm doing something wrong. To be perfectly honest, Gene, I'm not sure *what* the problem is.

SUPERIOR. Okay, Chuck . . . maybe you and I can come up with the answer in this appraisal.

This example is obviously abbreviated. But the *difference* between this approach (the nonblaming, information-seeking Q4 approach) and the Q1 approach (the accusing, now-you-hear-this approach) is clear.

Provide Reassurance—and Be Sure It's the Right Kind

Many people feel tense in an appraisal. To overcome this tension, most subordinates need some reassurance from the boss. All too often, they get the wrong kind of reassurance. Here's an example:

SUBORDINATE.   I've really been nervous about this appraisal.
SUPERIOR.   Don't worry about it.

Let's look closely at this brief exchange.

The superior (who probably thinks he's been reassuring) may actually come across as insensitive. The subordinate may think the boss is belittling his feelings in a Q1 way. The boss's words imply: "Don't be silly. You're making a mountain out of a molehill. You're blowing this out of proportion. You're getting needlessly worked up. Etcetera, etcetera." But the subordinate doesn't see it that way. His nervousness is real, and, from his standpoint, justified. And he doesn't want his feelings devalued.

The superior is wasting his time. Telling someone who feels worried that he should't worry almost never works. (If you doubt this, think back on the many times you've been told not to worry, and ask yourself if you stopped worrying as a result.) A subordinate who's worried is at low receptivity; his mind is closed to what you say because he's concentrating on his own feelings. Phrases like "Take it easy" or "Relax" or "Everything will be okay" go in one ear and out the other.

The subordinate may think that the superior is stifling him in a Q3 way. Instead of letting the subordinate vent his worry and "get it out of his system," the boss may seem to be glossing it over. When the subordinate hears an instant response like "Don't worry about it," he may interpret it as meaning: "Let's sweep your fears under the rug . . . let's pretend they don't exist . . . let's go on to other topics." But that's the whole problem: The subordinate isn't *ready* to go on to other topics, and he won't be ready until he gets real reassurance.

The result is that, with either Q1 or Q3 "reassurance," the subordinate will probably be *more* tense, *more* uncomfortable, because he's been "reassured" in the wrong way. His worry and anxiety will stay with him, bottled up inside where they'll simmer and stew and continue to drag down his receptivity.

How *should* reassurance be given? Here are two guidelines:

• *Vent and explore* the subordinate's feelings by probing. Use reflective statements to reduce interfering emotions. Then ask open-end questions to draw him out so he tells you why he's nervous. This will raise his receptivity.

• *After* exploring his feelings, give him honest reassurance. This will now come at *high* receptivity, so it will get through.

Here's an example:

SUPERIOR.   How ya doin', Bruce?

SUBORDINATE.   Not so hot.

SUPERIOR.   What's the problem?

SUBORDINATE.   I'm very uptight about this appraisal. *Very* uptight.

SUPERIOR.   What's got you so bothered?

SUBORDINATE.   Everything. My guts have been knotted up for a week. I've been snapping at people. I'm fidgety. And all because of this appraisal.

SUPERIOR.   I can see you're nervous. Tell me more. What's bugging you?

SUBORDINATE.   It's that contract we just lost. Everybody in the whole place is whispering about layoffs. And you know as well as I do that there's no better time to ax a guy than at an appraisal.

SUPERIOR.   I see. You're concerned you're going to get the ax. Why do you feel you're going to be laid off?

SUBORDINATE.   That's just it. I don't feel I *should* be. I think I've been doing a pretty good job. But this place is ablaze with rumors. And they make me very nervous.

SUPERIOR.   I can understand that. So let me tell you . . . right off the bat . . . that you have nothing to worry about. This is a performance appraisal. That means we're going to spend a lot of time talking about the *next* six months. And we wouldn't do that if you were about to be fired.

SUBORDINATE.   (Visibly relieved) Okay! That's what's been bugging me. Now that it's out of the way, let's get down to business.

Face Up to Disagreements, Resistances, and Negative Emotions

You can't reach understanding and commitment as long as you and your subordinate are on opposite sides. Negative emotions and resistance stand in the way of agreed-upon solutions and goals. You can't make them disappear by ignoring or suppressing them or pretending they're not there. The only way to get rid of resistance is to *face it* and *resolve it*. Unless you do, you're going to be confronted by continuing low receptivity. How, then, can you deal with resistance? Here are some guidelines:

• Bring the resistance into the open. Verbalize it. Admit it exists. You can't resolve a problem that nobody acknowledges.

- Don't blame ("Damn it, John, you're not giving me a chance to get through to you"). Just state the fact neutrally ("John, we seem to be at opposite poles on this, and I don't think we're getting any closer to agreement").
- *Probe.* Find out why there's opposition. Open-end questions and reflective statements are good for this. Here are two examples:

Marian, I can tell you're upset by what I just said. It would sure help us both if you told me why.

Jack, we obviously don't see eye-to-eye on this. What are your reasons for feeling as you do?

- Once the reasons are clear to both of you, generate alternative solutions. Involve the subordinate in this. ("Okay, Ellen, as I understand it, you think Carlton can't possibly function as your assistant. But you agree with me that your department needs more supervisory strength. If Carlton can't do the job, what would you suggest as an alternative?")
- Jointly evaluate the alternatives.
- Select the best one.

In dealing with resistance, keep the following points in mind. They'll help you make sense out of what might otherwise seem like pointless or ornery behavior.

1. In an appraisal, resistance is *normal.* After all, you are talking about things that many subordinates find threatening: change, giving up old habits, trying new ways of doing things. At the same time you are criticizing the subordinate's present way of doing things. (You may not consider it criticism, but she does. If you're not being critical of what she's been doing, why are you asking her to do it differently?) So it's only natural for subordinates to offer some resistance. What they're really trying to do is turn away the threat and offset the criticism.

2. A subordinate who doesn't *openly* resist doesn't necessarily *agree* with you. When he doesn't overtly resist, it's still reasonable to assume that he has reservations, but that he's afraid or unwilling to express them. Subordinates with strong Q2 security needs or strong Q3 social needs rarely *voice* disagreement; they *think* it.

3. Don't assume, then, that silence or conformity means agreement. Don't even assume that *enthusiastic* agreement means agreement. Some subordinates (those with strong Q3 needs for acceptance) will readily assent to what you say ("Sounds great to me") when they're actually

skeptical. The fact that their skepticism doesn't come to the surface doesn't mean it's not there. It *does* mean that you must *probe* to see if these ready assents are genuine or if they're a cover-up for doubt.

4. Resistance is easier to deal with when you understand the reasons behind it. When you meet opposition, ask yourself: (1) Is he resisting because what I'm asking him to do threatens his *security*? (2) Because he thinks it will endanger some of his *personal relationships*? (3) Because he's afraid he'll *lose face*? (4) Because he resents my trying to influence him? (5) Because he doesn't like being dependent on other people's advice? (6) Because he thinks my idea is no good? A subordinate may oppose you for several of these reasons.

5. It's important to involve the subordinate in discussing your ideas because the more she talks about them, the more likely she is to feel that they're partly hers. Familiarity with an idea helps to break down resistance; involvement fosters familiarity.

6. One reason it's important to space your ideas is that it's easier to overcome resistance to one idea at a time. Once a subordinate accepts one idea, he's more likely to accept the next one. So take each idea one by one or in small groups, probe for resistance, overcome it through discussion, and then move on to the next idea, building it on the preceding one.

7. One reason pauses are so important in an appraisal is that they let the subordinate think through an idea and thereby become less resistant to it. Anybody is likely to resist ideas if she feels pressured to accept them, and she's likely to feel pressured if they're presented in rapid-fire sequence, without pauses.

8. Opposition isn't always bad. It may mean that you're getting through, that the subordinate is thinking about what you've said (even though he doesn't agree with it), and that you have the makings of a lively dialogue.

9. Don't rely on logic to overcome resistance. Your logic may be flawless, but it's not likely to impress somebody who's resisting. If a subordinate accepts your logic, he must admit that something's wrong with *his*, and that's hard to do. As he sees it, accepting your logic is the same as saying, "I guess I've been stupid." Don't expect that to happen very often. Instead, abandon your reliance on logic and concentrate on probing. *The most serious mistake many superiors make in dealing with resistance is to counter with logic and argument.* Many times, this only intensifies the opposition.

10. Some superiors don't probe resistance because they're afraid they'll provoke further resistance. This is wrong. Good probing tends to *decrease* resistance. As she responds to the probes, the subordinate gets to vent her feelings; as she vents, the topic becomes less surrounded by heat and emotion. As the heat and emotion fade, the difference between you and the

subordinate is reduced to a difference about *facts* and *logic*. This difference can be dealt with objectively. But objective discussion can take place only *after* you've defused the topic, and you can't defuse it by logic, only by probing.

11.   Emotional resistance that *isn't* vented usually *increases*. When people get "uptight" and can't voice their feelings, the feelings intensify. This leads to three results—all bad. (1) People become heavily *subjective;* they become less able to think objectively, to step aside from the subject and view it unemotionally. (2) People begin to think in *stereotypes;* instead of seeing things in shades of gray, they see them in stark black-white, good-bad terms. And (3) people become *irrational;* they have trouble engaging in logical, coherent discussion. All of this makes problem-solving extremely difficult, maybe even impossible.

12.   It all comes down to this: A subordinate who is not allowed to vent, to talk about his feelings, begins to oversimplify and to see things in a personal light. His resistance hardens. He takes an "I'm right and you're wrong" stance. He becomes more stubborn, more unbudgeable, more inclined to see things in a "me versus you" light. *Only probing can prevent this.*

Remember: Total Agreement May Be Unattainable

Try to get as much agreement as you can, but don't try to eliminate all dissent. If you insist upon capitulation—"unconditional surrender"— you are likely to generate resentment, not growth. You want your people to do better work; you can achieve that without demanding that they become lackeys.

This is simple realism. For some subordinates, especially those with strong esteem and independence needs, it's important *not* to agree completely with the boss. They need to retain some small area of *dis*agreement; this is their way of "saving face," of proving that "I'm my own person." Where needs for esteem and independence are powerful, "unconditional surrender" is very unlikely.

Set Goals and Action-Plans Jointly

We've said it before, but it bears repeating: performance appraisal *should not be* (except when the subordinate cannot or will not get involved) a one-person show. Goals and action-plans should be set *jointly*.

The goals should be precise, measurable (if possible) and *challenging*. As we've shown, impossibly difficult goals discourage effort; "snap" goals don't produce growth. What's needed are goals sufficiently arduous to require *exertion*.

But what if your subordinate *cannot* be made a partner in setting these goals? What if joint goal-setting is out of the question? To answer that, let's go back to our definition of Q4 appraisal as appraisal that produces optimal results. And let's look closer at the word *optimal*.

THE OPTIMAL AND THE IDEAL

Optimal results are the best results obtainable *under a given set of circumstances*. They're rarely what you'd consider ideal results. They're almost never what you'd call "perfect." They're simply the best results you can hope to get from *this* subordinate at *this* time in *this* situation. When you think about optimal results, you don't ask: "What's the best outcome I can conceive of?" You ask: "What's the most I can get under these conditions?" Put another way, when you strive for optimal results, you're not necessarily dealing with things as you'd like them to be—you're dealing with things as they really are. You're dealing with hard—and sometimes unruly—realities. You're acknowledging, in effect, that you're working with people, not puppets.

To illustrate, let's ask this question: *Ideally*, what kind of results would you *like* to get out of every appraisal? Obviously, we can't answer that question in specific terms, because the specifics vary from organization to organization. But we can answer it in general terms. Almost surely, here are two things you'd *like* to get out of every appraisal.

1. Self-discovery

You'd like your subordinate to discover—for *himself*—how he's really doing on the job and how he can do better. You'd like to produce an "Aha" effect ("Aha! Now I get it!"). Instead of hitting him over the head ("Now listen to me while I tell you what the score is"), you'd like to make the light go on in *his* head.

2. Growth

You'd like your subordinate to show evidence that he's capable of further development on the job. You'd like to know—as a result of the appraisal—that he's able to take on more responsibility, or handle tougher assignments, or work more independently.

These are two things you'd *like* to see happen. They're ideal results. But—at this point—a whole series of "what-ifs" have to be asked:

- What if your subordinate *can't* or *won't* discover the truth for himself? What if the "Aha" never happens? What if the bulb never goes on?
- What if your subordinate doesn't *want* to grow? What if he prefers the security of staying in his present niche? What if he's afraid to grow? What if he prefers to shelter under your wing? What if he can't grow? What if he's got all he can do just to handle his present assignments?

In other words, what if the results you'd *like* to get and the results you *can* get are two different things? What if *ideal* and *optimal* never meet?

THE PERFORMANCE APPRAISAL DILEMMA

This leads to what we call the *performance appraisal dilemma*. The problem leading to the dilemma is this:

1. Even though ideal and optimal may never meet, you don't want to forget about the ideal. Far from it. In fact, you want to come as close to achieving it as possible. You want to produce optimal results that *approach* the ideal.
2. But, as we've just seen, in some cases there's going to be a wide gap between ideal and optimal—in spite of your best efforts. Some subordinates simply aren't going to achieve much (if anything) in the way of either self-discovery or growth.

So much for the problem. Now let's look at the dilemma. Strictly speaking, a *dilemma* is a situation in which you're forced to choose between two unsatisfactory alternatives. A dilemma is a *bind*. When you're appraising a subordinate who either can't or won't achieve self-discovery and growth, you're in a classic bind, because you're faced with two alternatives —*both unsatisfactory.*

1. You can acquiesce in the situation, shrug it off, and tell yourself that nothing can be done to get better results from this subordinate— he is what he is and that's that.
2. You can *impose* your own ideas, goals, and plans; you can say, in effect: "If you're not able or willing to think for yourself, you'll

have to accept *my* thinking; if you're not able to exercise autonomy on the job, you'll have to do things *my* way."

Either way, the choice is nothing to cheer about. But you have to choose one way or the other. Which horn of the dilemma, then, should you grab?

The Solution

The answer is: Grab the *second* alternative. If you can't generate self-discovery and growth, *impose your own decisions.* Insist that the subordinate accept the goals *you* set and the action-plans *you* develop. This isn't an ideal answer, not by a long shot. But it *is* the optimal answer, the answer best calculated to produce some improvement in performance. The alternative is to settle for things as they are.

The Self-Discovery and Growth Continuum

The solution to the performance appraisal dilemma can be depicted graphically, as shown in Figure 14.

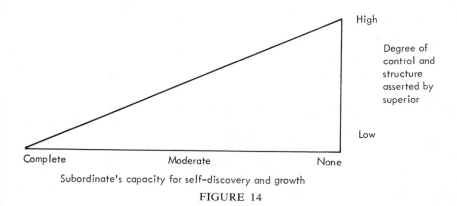

FIGURE 14

The diagonal line shows that where the subordinate demonstrates high capacity for self-discovery and growth, the need for you to exert tight control and impose your ideas is quite *low,* approaching (although rarely reaching) the vanishing point. But, where the subordinate shows little or no capacity for self-discovery and growth, you must exert considerable control during the appraisal, and you must impose many of your own ideas.

Let's sum up:

1. In Q4 appraisal, you want your subordinate to discover, *for himself*, as much as he can about how he's doing on the job and how he can do better. Instead of telling him, you want to *guide* him. Why? Because self-discovery is the kind of learning that's most likely to produce the understanding and commitment so vital to improved performance.

2. Unfortunately, some subordinates are less capable of self-discovery than others. For whatever reason, they can't see things for themselves. No matter how skillfully you guide them, they still don't "get it." And they're not likely to do much developing on their own, either.

3. How can you tell which subordinates have high potential for self-discovery and growth, which have low potential, and which are somewhere in-between? By experience and observation. If you know each of your people as an individual (and that's a big part of Q4 management), then you know which ones can figure things out for themselves, which ones can grow, and which ones can't.

4. In Q4 appraisal, then, the amount of control you exert is related to how much self-discovery and growth your subordinate can handle. When a subordinate has what it takes to discover things for himself and to exercise some autonomy, your job is largely one of guiding him (mainly by probing). When a subordinate can't or won't see the truth about his performance, and can't or won't function independently, you have to take a different tack and impose your own views. With many subordinates, of course, you do both: guiding toward self-discovery (as much as you can) and imposing your ideas (when you must).

5. Remember: don't impose your ideas too early in the appraisal, or you may cheat your subordinate out of the opportunity for self-discovery. Impose your ideas when it's obvious that no self-discovery is going to happen; if you don't, you're copping out on your responsibility. The best rule is: give each subordinate what he *needs*, and determine *what* he needs by getting to know him as an individual.

Conclusion

It boils down to this: When you do appraisal you can't be faulted for not getting ideal results, but you can be faulted for not getting optimal results. By definition, optimal results *are* achievable; they *can* be attained under the circumstances. It's up to you to obtain them. To do that, don't get hung up on the performance appraisal dilemma. Instead, if you must, impose your ideas and decisions. Do what's necessary for *this* subordinate at *this* time in *this* situation.

SUMMARY

1. To do Q4 appraisal, you must develop a win-win climate in which everybody—the subordinate, the organization, and you—benefits.

2. You cannot create a win-win climate unless the subordinate trusts you—is convinced that what you are doing is in her best interest. Trust cannot be created in an instant; it must be built up in day-by-day activities over a period of time.

3. To develop a win-win appraisal climate, do the following: (a) build a foundation of trust in your everyday contacts; (b) ask the subordinate to prepare his own evaluation before the appraisal; (c) take time to do the job right; (d) make it plain, at the start, that your ideas are not fixed and unchangeable; (e) get the subordinate to analyze his own performance; (f) listen at a thinking level; (g) reward the subordinate for his participation; (h) create an advice-seeking climate; (i) create a problem-solving climate; (j) give the right kind of reassurance; (k) face up to resistance and negative emotion; (l) remember that total agreement may be unattainable; and (m) set goals and action plans jointly.

4. Realistic growth will be more easily attainable if you keep the performance appraisal dilemma in mind. Not all subordinates are capable of the same degree of growth. The amount of "clout" you use in an appraisal should be inversely proportional to the subordinate's capacity for growth and self-discovery. Where that capacity is low, the clout should be high. Where that capacity is high, the clout should be low. If you impose your ideas on people who are able to discover the facts for themselves, you'll generate distrust, not trust. If you refuse to impose your ideas on people who cannot or will not see the facts for themselves, the appraisal will almost surely fail.

A LOOK AHEAD

Everything we've talked about so far depends upon preparation. You can't go into an appraisal "cold" and expect to get Q4 results. What *happens in* the appraisal will hinge on how well you've *prepared for* the appraisal. Our next chapter explains how to do Q4 preparation for Q4 appraisal.

13

Planning the Appraisal

Q4 appraisal begins well *before* the face-to-face meeting. It begins when both you and your subordinate, working independently, start to prepare. And this preparation must begin well in advance of the appraisal session.

Why? Because you cannot do effective appraisal off the "top of your head." You can't do Q4 appraisal "by ear." You can't "improvise" it. You can do it only if you have systematically prepared for it.

THE SCIENTIFIC APPROACH

When we say that Q4 appraisal begins prior to the appraisal session, we are saying something more: *Q4 appraisal requires a scientific approach.* The word *scientific* is misused a lot, and many things that aren't scientific at all get labeled "scientific." We are using the word in its literal sense. We mean exactly what we've said: Q4 appraisal follows a *scientific* format. Don't let the word mislead you into thinking that Q4 appraisal is cold and heartless. True enough, in common usage, "scientific" often suggests work that's austere, remote, and unfeeling. But, in practice, scientists—for all their objectivity—are deeply and wholeheartedly *involved* in their work. And that is characteristic of Q4 appraisal, too. In Q4 appraisal the superior strives for a clear-eyed, objective view of things, while, at the same time, he's deeply and wholeheartedly *involved*. Scientific appraisal is aware, sensitive, responsive.

Let us look more closely at what *scientific* implies. All scientists, no matter what their speciality, have one thing in common: the *way they approach their work*. Every scientist, from the astrophysicist to the zoologist, uses the same basic method, the same fundamental system, for solving problems (and all science is problem-solving). That applies just as well to performance appraisal as to pollen analysis.

Step 1: Recognizing the Problem

Every scientific project begins with the realization that "Something is going on and we're not sure why. We can *guess* at the explanation, but . . . given our present knowledge . . . we can't be *sure* of it." What started Isaac Newton on his fabulous scientific career was just this kind of puzzlement: according to legend, he knew that when apples fall from trees they always fall down, but he didn't know why. All he knew for sure was that nobody had ever seen an apple fall up.

A comparable situation confronts superiors every day: Joe seems to have everything it takes to be a stand-out salesperson, but he's not even coming close to meeting his sales objective. Why? Margie seems to be a good, hard-working illustrator, but she turns in every ad layout late and never meets her deadlines. Why? Ted has increased production at Plant #2 by 37%, and exceeded his quota for the year. Why? All science—and all Q4 appraisal—starts with awareness of two things: (1) something that needs explaining is going on, and (2) nobody knows for sure why it's going on.

Step 2: Observing Pertinent Facts

Once a scientist becomes aware that there *is* a problem he begins studying the facts surrounding it. He asks questions like: When does the problem occur? Under what circumstances? What other things happen at the same time? Before? After? What other occurrences does the problem seem related to?

Isaac Newton, for example, wasn't the first person to notice that apples fall down, but he went far beyond that observation and began to note *other* things that seemed related. For instance, he observed that *everything* that moves seems to move in a *prescribed* way. Apples don't rise up; they fall down. Planets don't go hurtling into space; they follow orbits. The tides don't move randomly; they follow a definite, predictable rhythm.

And on and on. One of Newton's great abilities was the ability to gather together, very patiently, facts that appeared to have some connection.

Connections—relationships—are important in preparing for appraisal, too. If Joe isn't meeting his assigned sales objective, you ought to examine, carefully, all the circumstances that seem *connected* to that fact. How many calls is Joe making each day? What is he saying and doing on those calls? How many new prospects is he digging up? What kind of competition is he encountering? Is anything wrong with product quality, with pricing, with delivery? And on and on. In science—and in performance appraisal—it's necessary to dig up as many facts as possible that appear related, in some way, to the problem.

Step 3: Formulating a Hypothesis

What the scientist needs next is a possible explanation of the problem—some notion that will (1) make all the observations hang together, and (2) provide a potential answer to the problem. So he formulates a *hypothesis;* he makes an educated guess that seems to fit all his observations and that seems to explain why whatever is happening is happening. The hypothesis is only tentative; it seems to make sense, to be "right," but nobody knows that for sure. It may later turn out that the hypothesis is all wet. At this stage, it's nothing more than an informed hunch.

Newton, for example, searching for some way to explain why apples fall down and why all things in motion follow certain paths instead of moving around haphazardly, came up with the hypothesis that there's an attraction between everything in the universe, and that this attraction holds these things in certain prescribed paths as they move. There's attraction between apples and the earth, between the earth and the sun, and on and on. He called this attraction—the force that pulls things together—*gravity.*

Hypothesis formation is essential to Q4 appraisal, too. In Joe's case, for instance, you might develop this hypothesis: Joe isn't meeting his sales objective because he's too lazy to make enough calls each day; the guy just isn't working hard enough. *At this point*, this is nothing more than an informed hunch, based on a review of all the available data, which include the fact that Joe averages fewer sales calls per day than any other salesperson in the region. It is not a proven fact: it is something to *test out*, just as Newton's notion of gravity had to be tested.

Step 4: Testing the Hypothesis

Once he has developed a hypothesis, a scientist has to devise a way to check it out—to determine whether it's fact or fiction. Newton did this by developing mathematical descriptions of how gravity works, descriptions that held up when checked against the real world; he made it possible to measure the effects of gravity. If it had proven impossible to demonstrate the operations of gravity, Newton would have had to revise or discard the hypothesis.

This is no different, essentially, from what happens in a Q4 appraisal session. One purpose of the appraisal is to find out whether or not the superior's hypothesis is valid. If it's not, it has to be discarded and replaced by one that is.

Now, let's recap three major points:

1. Effective performance appraisal follows the scientific method we've just described.
2. The first three steps of that method should be carried out before the appraisal session.
3. The fourth step should be carried out during and after the appraisal session.

Let's expand on these last two points:

- The time to *identify the problem* (which job goals is the subordinate meeting and which is he not meeting?) is *before* the appraisal.
- The time to *gather data related to the problem* (what are the facts that seem to be connected to his meeting, or not meeting, his goals?) is *before* the appraisal.
- The time to *formulate a hypothesis* (what makes all these facts hang together and explains the problem?) is *before* the appraisal.
- The time to *test out the hypothesis* (is it fact or fiction?) is *during* and *after* the appraisal. It's entirely possible that the hypothesis is wrong. Take the hypothesis about Joe, for instance. Joe may be making fewer sales calls than anyone else in the region not because he's lazy, but because his customers are separated by wide stretches of countryside so that Joe has to drive longer distances than his fellow salespeople. Maybe, given the nature of the territory, Joe should be given a smaller objective. Maybe he should make some of his calls by airplane, rather than by car. All of this has to be checked out.

But that's not all. Nowadays, more and more scientists work in teams; the stereotype of the isolated scientist working in solitude in his lonely laboratory accords less and less with the way things are really done. The same should be true of performance appraisal. Effective performance appraisal is the result of a two-person team, and both members of the team should be involved from the very beginning. That's why the subordinate, as well as you, should identify the problem, gather related data, and formulate hypotheses before the appraisal session. Then, during the appraisal (and, as we'll see, after) both of you should check out your own and one another's hypotheses.

So What?

One question remains to be answered: So what? What difference does it make if a systematic, scientific approach is used? The answer has two parts:

1.   The scientific approach is more likely to get *valid* results. It separates fact from fancy, and it uncovers real, not imaginary, explanations. That's why the results of the scientific method work. (Before Newton, a thinker named Descartes guessed that the planets are held in orbit as they circle the sun by an invisible and impalpable substance called *ether;* since every planet rested in ether, like an egg resting in an invisible cup, there was no way it could get out of orbit. If we still believed in Descartes' ether instead of Newton's gravity, the world would be a vastly different place, and satellite landings on Mars would be an impossibility.)

2.   The scientific approach is efficient. It doesn't completely eliminate false starts, hang-ups, and mistakes, but it does produce results more expeditiously than any other approach. The scientific approach cuts down on wasted time and energy, so it's the most economical approach to performance appraisal.

Content Planning and Process Planning

Actually, two kinds of preparation must be done: preparation of the *content*—the subject matter—of the appraisal, and preparation of the *process*—the interaction—of the appraisal. Content planning has to do with *what* will be discussed; process planning has to do with *how* it will be discussed.

The first section in this chapter describes a system that both you and your subordinate can use to prepare the content of a Q4 appraisal. The second section explains how you can prepare for the process—the interaction.

We don't claim that this system is the only one that works, but we do insist that unless you use this or some comparable system for *getting ready*, you're not going to do Q4 appraisal.

SECTION 1: PREPARING THE CONTENT

Why Bother?

Why go to all the trouble of planning the content of the appraisal? Why not go into the session "cold" and "play it by ear"? After all, appraisal takes enough time as it is. Do you really have to spend still *more* time preparing for it?

You sure do. To see why, let's look at what you and your subordinate can expect to get in return for the time and energy you spend preparing.

1. You'll get a more factual appraisal.

Q4 appraisal is concerned with what's really going on, not with what you or your subordinate "think" is going on. Unfortunately, most of the facts you need in order to determine what *is* going on aren't in your head. The records, the statistics, the dates, the *hard* data—these are usually buried in files or in computer memory banks. They must be dug out. The time to do the digging is *before* the appraisal session. If the two of you don't dig out the data, then all you'll be able to talk about in the appraisal will be vague recollections, top-of-the-head guesses, unsubstantiated opinions, and unfounded hunches. And you'll probably spend much of the appraisal *arguing*. Here's an example of what can happen:

SUPERIOR.   As I recall it, Lou, your costs jumped about 5% in August. That's bad.

SUBORDINATE.   Hold on, Dan. 5% *would* be bad ... but I was nowhere near 5%. The figure was more like 2.5 or 3%. And that's in line with the rest of the industry.

SUPERIOR.   Two point five or 3%? You've got to be kidding. I distinctly remember telling Jacobs how concerned I was when the figure jumped so high in one month. I never would have mentioned it to him if it had only been 2.5 or 3%. No ... 5% is more like it.

SUBORDINATE.   Dan ... I'd be willing to bet you're thinking about somebody else, not me. My figure was much closer to 3%. In fact, I'll go back to my office now ... if you want me to ... and try to dig out the August report. I'm sure I can prove it.

This is ridiculous, yet this sort of thing happens with discouraging frequency. There's no need to spin your wheels this way. The facts should be available at the *start* of the session. And they will be—if the two of you *prepare*.

2.   *You'll probably get a less emotional appraisal than you'd otherwise get.*

When both people come to an appraisal prepared with well-organized data, the appraisal starts on a more objective, a more businesslike, basis. Gut feelings, agitated emotions, and bad-tempered outbursts are likely to be more controlled when the discussion focuses on hard data, gathered by both parties. (But don't expect the appraisal to be free of emotion; even under the best circumstances, you'll almost surely have to contend with tension, anxiety, and perhaps touchiness on the part of the subordinate—and maybe on your own part, as well.)

3.   *You'll save time during the appraisal.*

As we've said, scientific preparation makes for efficient appraisal. There should be little or no need to go "looking" for records and data, and little reason to haggle about "what really happened." The information will be in your hands at the outset.

4.   *You'll have a track to run on during the appraisal.*

Instead of wondering "how to get started" or "what to talk about first," you'll have a *format* to follow. That format will be the *same format you followed in preappraisal preparation.*

It boils down to this: *efficient* appraisal requires preparation. Without it, the appraisal is virtually sure to be inefficient and ineffective.

A Caution

In preparing, you should do two things: (1) gather data that will be discussed and evaluated in the appraisal session; (2) formulate some tentative judgments about your subordinate's performance—judgments that will be confirmed, modified, or discarded when they're discussed. Do *not*, however, form hard-and-fast conclusions. It's premature—and very risky—to reach carved-in-rock conclusions during the preparation period. That should happen only in the appraisal *session*.

Four Important Points

Four things should be stressed before we get into the system itself:

1.   The system can be used no matter what formal system (or lack of system) your organization uses for setting goals. If your organization has a formal Management by Objectives program, our system can be incorporated into it. If you have no formal objective-setting program, our system can still be used. All we're trying to do is to describe an orderly and thorough way to prepare for an appraisal; this method will pay off in *any* organizational setting.

2.   This chapter assumes that you and your subordinate can agree on what his job goals have been for the period to be covered in the appraisal. If your organization has a formal goal-setting system in which specific goals have been written, you will have no problem. If not, you will have to develop a list of business and behavioral goals before you start the preappraisal planning.

3.   One point cannot be overemphasized: planning of the content must be done by *both* you *and* your subordinate. Make *sure* both of you prepare, and make sure both of you get plenty of time to do so. Schedule the appraisal well in advance. Don't spring any surprises ("Hey, Fred, I've got some spare time this afternoon. Whaddya say we take a crack at your annual appraisal?"). Make sure, too, that both of you follow a *written format*. This is the only way to guarantee that both of you zero in on the same topics, and that neither of you overlooks anything essential. Finally, make sure that both of you *write down* your findings. When you go into the appraisal session, both of you should have a written record of the points you want to cover.

4.   As the boss, your preparatory task is especially difficult because, ideally, you should prepare for the appraisal from *two* points of view: yours and the subordinate's. In other words, you should gather data and form conclusions that *you* think are justified, and you should also try to anticipate the data that your *subordinate* will use and the conclusions that *he'll* draw from the data. If you are going to be fully prepared for the appraisal session, you should ask, and try to answer, the following questions during the preparation period: Will my subordinate base his analyses on the same data I'm using, or is he likely to rely on different data? Will his interpretation of the data be pretty much the same as mine, or is he likely to draw different conclusions? If he is likely to use different data or arrive at different conclusions, what should I do to make sure that I'm able to discuss his views with him? Never assume that your subordinate's

thinking is going to parallel yours. The fact that he is following the same format doesn't mean that (a) he'll draw on the same sources of information as you, or (b) that he'll reach the same conclusions. Be prepared for disagreement.

AN OVERVIEW

Let's take a broad look at how Q4 content preparation is done. We'll then fill in the detail.

1. First, both you and your subordinate, working independently, should list the subordinate's job goals (business and behavioral) and gather all available data on his progress toward those goals. (If your organization does not do formal goal-setting—if you have never verbalized a *specific* set of job objectives to your subordinate—then start your preparation by asking yourself: "What do I think my subordinate should have accomplished on the job to date? What general achievements should he have pursued? What direction do I think he should have moved in?" Then, before you continue, tell your subordinate that these are the "goals" you intend to discuss during the appraisal. See if he wants to add any others. In this way, the two of you will come into the appraisal prepared to talk about the same general aims and purposes.)

2. After examining the data determine, tentatively, which goals have been met and which haven't. In a few cases it may be impossible to make even a tentative judgment. So you may end up with as many as three groups of goals: (1) achieved, (2) not achieved, (3) can't tell (uncertain).

3. Next, analyze each achieved goal, using four criteria: (a) the *goal itself*, (was it too easy?); (b) the *subordinate* (what did he do to achieve the goal, and what credit does he deserve?); (c) the *superior* (what did you contribute, and did you actually "carry" the subordinate?); (d) the *situation* (was it a windfall?).

4. After this, determine what *benefits* the subordinate, the organization, and you have derived, or will derive, from the achievement. What difference does it make that the goal was met?

5. Up to this point, you've been focusing on the past. Now shift your attention to the future. Ask yourself: Has anything happened to change my subordinate's job duties or business objectives from now on? Will the nature of his work be significantly different in the future from what it's been up to now? The answer to this question will obviously influence your thinking about what the subordinate should do to perform even more effectively and get optimal results in the future.

6. Next, in the light of your analysis of his past performance and of what you know about the future requirements of the subordinate's job, list the things he should do to get optimal results from here on out. What should he continue to do? What should he change?

7. Next, analyze the goals that *were not* achieved, using the same four criteria but taking a different slant on each: (a) the *goal itself* (was it too tough?); (b) the *subordinate* (what didn't he do that he should have done?); (c) the *superior* (what did you fail to do that you should have done?); (d) the *situation* (did circumstances beyond the control of either of you make it impossible to achieve the goal?).

8. After this determine (a) the consequences of the failure (how does it hurt the subordinate, the organization, and you?); and (b) what should be done to overcome the problems that account for the goal not being met.

9. Now, once again, shift your focus from past to future. Ask yourself: What, if anything, will be different about my subordinate's job from now on? What new demands will be made on him? What old demands will be eliminated?

10. In the light of all this, list the actions your subordinate should take to optimize future results.

11. Now move on to the goals that you're not sure about. Determine why you are not sure (is the goal itself too vague, or do you simply lack performance data?). Figure out what should be done about it.

That's it. When you've done it, you'll have a solid grasp of the subject matter of the appraisal. You'll have tentative answers to three questions:

1. How well is the subordinate doing?
2. Why?
3. What should be done about it?

Your subordinate, of course, will have his own answers to these questions. They may not agree with yours (in fact, the data on which he bases his answers may not agree with yours), but at least the two of you will have something to *start with*.

So much for the overview. Let's get into the details. In Figure 15, we've produced a chart that shows each of the steps, and their sequence, in our content-preparation system. The rest of this section explains each item on the chart.

How this Section is Organized

To explain our system, we talk about each item separately. To help you follow our explanations, we reprint segments of the chart, and then focus

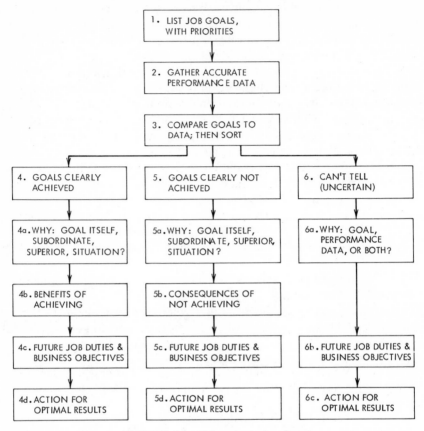

FIGURE 15.   Q4 content planning.

on the boxes in those segments. Our explanations are addressed to "you"—the superior—but remember that the subordinate should do exactly the same kind of analysis and evaluation. Let's get started.

Preliminary Evaluation

The first six boxes on our chart refer to things that must be done before you do a detailed analysis of goals and performance. These preliminaries have two purposes: (1) to give you an overall view of your subordinate's performance, and (2) to help you organize your thinking about the appraisal. Detailed analyses should be done only after this preliminary analysis. Let's look at the first six boxes again in Figure 16.

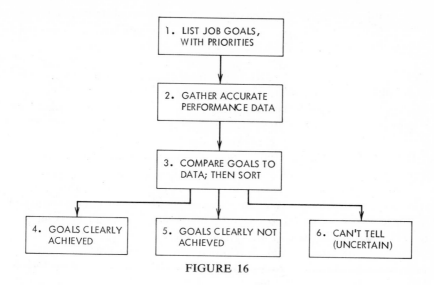

FIGURE 16

Box 1.   *List job goals, with priorities*

Your organization may not use the word *goals*. It may use *objectives, standards, targets, quotas, assignments,* or some other word. The word doesn't matter; what matters is that you evaluate performance against *criteria*. It doesn't help much to tell a subordinate that he's doing a good job or a bad job. The critical question is: good or bad compared to *what?*

Let's distinguish, again, between *business* job goals and *behavioral* job goals. In all likelihood, you'll want to analyze your subordinate's performance against both kinds.

- *Business* job goals are objective. They're concerned with impersonal achievements. They're fairly precise and relatively easy to measure.
- *Behavioral* job goals are concerned with the relationships that influence the attainment of business job goals. They're usually less precise than business job goals, and they may be measurable only in a gross way.

To begin preparing, then, ask two sets of questions:

1. What are my subordinate's present *business* job goals? What objective, impersonal standards have been assigned to him that he should have met by this time?

2. What are his present *behavioral* job goals? What improvements in personal behavior or interpersonal relationships have been assigned to him that he should have achieved by now?

This shouldn't be either difficult or time consuming. The subordinate's goals should have been clearly spelled out, in writing, in his previous appraisal. If those goals have since been changed, or new ones added, you should have a record of that fact. So listing the job goals ought to be fairly easy.

Don't merely list the job goals, however; whenever possible, list them in order of *priority*. This will help you to put first things first when you get to the appraisal session. (All too often, appraisals bog down because secondary goals—"You were supposed to get the water cooler fixed and it still leaks"—are discussed ahead of major goals—"You were supposed to realize a cost decrease of 4.5%, and you're only at 2%").

The topic of priorities raises an interesting question: What if you and your subordinate come to the appraisal session with *different* lists of priorities? The answer is: this shouldn't happen. The two of you should *not* come to the appraisal with goals listed in different order of priority because the whole matter of priorities should have been settled in the previous appraisal. If every appraisal ends, as it should, with you and the subordinate agreeing on (a) what his new job goals are and (b) what their order of importance is, and if the two of you get together periodically between appraisals to review his progress, then at the *next* appraisal there should be no question about what the goals are or how important or urgent they are.

Box 2. *Gather performance data*

Now collect any information that measures or indicates how close the subordinate has come to achieving each goal.

- For *business* job goals you should have fairly precise, and hopefully quantitative, measures. Here you'll rely largely on accounting reports, budget figures, computer print-outs, and so on. Where you don't have such measures, you may have a problem on your hands; we'll discuss this shortly.
- For *behavioral* job goals you'll probably have far less precise measures. Here you'll rely largely on your personal observation, and reports and comments from other knowledgeable and concerned people (the reliability determined separately in each case).

Box 3. *Compare goals to data, then sort*

Now, take each goal, one at a time, and compare it with the data you've gathered. This will enable you to sort the goals into three groups: (1) those that have clearly been achieved, (2) those that have clearly not been achieved, and (3) those about which you can't tell for sure. Don't forget: this is a preliminary breakdown; there's nothing final about it, and there won't be until you've discussed it with your subordinate in the appraisal session. Don't worry about *why* a goal has or hasn't been achieved; that will come a little later. Right now, the only thing you want to do is examine the data and determine, tentatively, whether a given goal belongs in Box 4, Box 5, or Box 6. Let's look closer at each box.

Box 4. *Goals clearly achieved*

In your judgment, there seems to be little or no doubt about these goals; they've been achieved, and you've got good evidence of it. Here are two examples:

Joe's business job goal was to achieve a 12% increase in sales in the Northwest district in the last six months of the year. Computer reports plainly show that the sales increase is not 12%, but 18%.

Joe's behavioral job goal was to "see to it that you and Snyder start working together without argument, so that no more reports of feuding reach the home office." No reports of feuding between Joe and Snyder have been received in the home office during the past six months.

Clearly, in both cases, the goals have been achieved.

But let's complicate things a little. Let's suppose that you are Joe's boss, and that you don't think Joe deserves credit for either achievement. Why not? Because (1) the 18% sales increase was, in your judgment, a windfall (your major competitor went out of business), and Joe just "fell into it"; and (2) the fact that there have been no reports of squabbles between Joe and Snyder is entirely due, as you see it, to Snyder; Joe is as belligerent and as combative as he's always been, but Snyder, who is very eager to be promoted and who knows that a continuation of his feud with Joe will hurt his chances, refuses to get drawn into a fight. What should you do? Put both goals in Box 4 anyway. At this point, the *only* thing you're concerned about is achievement, and the goals *have* been achieved. The circumstances under which they have been achieved will be considered later.

Box 5. *Goals clearly not achieved*

As far as you can determine, there's no argument about these goals, either: they have *not* been achieved. Two examples:

Joan's business job goal was to reduce turnover in her department by one-third; there has been no decrease in turnover.

Joan's behavioral job goal was to "start speaking up in department-head meetings, so that the interests of your department are represented and defended"; unfortunately, at every meeting, Joan continues to sit in a corner and say nothing, with the result that her department's interests are rarely discussed or considered. A number of people in her department are openly grumbling about this.

There could be extenuating circumstances, of course. Joan may have good reasons for not achieving these goals. Don't worry about that now. Simply consider the fact that, as far as you can see, the goals have not been attained, and put them in Box 5.

Box 6. *Can't tell*

You may find, after examining all the available performance data, that you are uncertain whether the goal has been achieved or not. This is especially likely to happen if the goal is vague, if the data are meager, or if the goal involves a heavily subjective element. Here's an example:

Paul is head of the public-relations department. One of his business goals is: "Develop an improved format for our annual report." As a result, Paul has completely redesigned the annual report: the size has been changed, the arrangement of contents is different, and the copy is written in a simpler style. Reaction from company executives and stockholders has been mixed. One vice-president of the company recently said that "We've outclassed every one of our competitors with this report"; a stockholder wrote a letter saying "This handsomely designed report made me proud to be a shareholder." On the other hand, a member of the company's executive committee called the report a "monstrosity," and another stockholder wrote in to complain about the "silly, simple-minded style in which the report is written." A tabulation of reactions shows that about half the comments are decidedly favorable, and the other half are decidedly unfavorable.

So the question is: Has Paul met his goal? Has he "developed an improved format"? This goal might well be assigned to Box 6. (This is a good example of what happens when a goal uses vague language. The word *improved* should never have been used. Instead, the goal should have been phrased something like this:

Develop a new format for our annual report that (a) produces fewer complaints from stockholders that the style is longwinded and difficult to follow, (b) looks different from anything our competitors have done in the past, so that we're no longer accused by stockholders of being "copy-cats," and (c) brings fewer complaints from stockholders that it looks drab, colorless, and monotonous.

Even this version leaves room for uncertainty about whether the goal has been achieved, but it's a definite improvement—because it's much more specific.)

So much for the preliminary evaluation. Up to now you've listed the subordinate's job goals in priority order, you've gathered all available performance data, you've compared the goals and the data, and you've sorted the goals into "achieved," "not achieved," and "can't tell" groups. Now let's look at the heart of the preparation process: *evaluating performance.*

Evaluating Performance

This part of the content preparation is concerned with three basic questions:

1. What are the *reasons* the goals have been met, or not met, or that you're not sure one way or the other?
2. What *difference* does it make that the goals were or were not met?
3. What, if anything, should be *done* about it?

Put another way, this part of the preparation looks at the past (at the factors that affected performance), the present (the impact of the performance), and the future (what should be done to improve performance). Before getting into the details, let's look at the next relevant portion of our chart, Figure 17 (next page).

Box 4a.   *Why: goal itself, subordinate, superior, situation?*

For each goal that has, in your judgment, clearly been met, you now want to determine *why.* Was it attained because of something the subordinate did, or something you did; because of something in the goal itself, or because of external factors for which the subordinate deserves no credit at

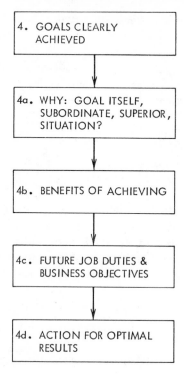

4. GOALS CLEARLY
   ACHIEVED

4a. WHY: GOAL ITSELF,
    SUBORDINATE, SUPERIOR,
    SITUATION?

4b. BENEFITS OF ACHIEVING

4c. FUTURE JOB DUTIES &
    BUSINESS OBJECTIVES

4d. ACTION FOR OPTIMAL
    RESULTS

FIGURE 17

all (or does he deserve special credit for achieving the goal in spite of external factors)?

Before we get into the details of this step, let's dispose of a question that may be perplexing you: Why bother to analyze *achieved* goals at all? If a goal has been met, it's been met; wouldn't it make good sense, then, to leave well enough alone and not worry about *why* or *how* it's been met? The answer, obviously, is no, for two good reasons:

1. A subordinate should understand why she met a particular goal; it's important to her growth. Don't make the mistake, when goals have been achieved, of cutting short the appraisal with a compliment. This is unfair to the subordinate; it cheats her of a chance to discover something about herself. To develop her fullest potential, she needs insight into her strengths as well as her weaknesses. If she is doing something right, she should know what it is so that she can *keep on* doing it. If she is mystified by her performance, if she is not clear on *why* she's getting good results,

she may tamper with behavior that should be left alone. An example from sports may make this clearer:

Dorothy is a weekend golfer. She shoots consistently low scores but doesn't have any idea why; all she knows is that she must be doing something right. One reason for her success is that she grips her clubs properly. Not realizing this, Dorothy says to herself one day: "Maybe if I tried something different I'd shoot even better scores. Maybe I'll try gripping the clubs a new way." She does, and her performance worsens. What she obviously needed was someone to tell her that her grip was *already* sound and should *not* be changed. Maybe Dorothy was doing other things that needed changing (and certainly she should have been told about them), but she should have *continued* gripping the clubs as she always did. Moral: *Success demands analysis as much as failure.*

2.   What looks like successful performance by the subordinate may not be successful performance at all; it may even be bad performance. But you will never know that unless you analyze the reasons why the goal was achieved. This example will illustrate what we mean:

Dwight, a district sales manager, was assigned this goal: Increase sales in the South River district by 5% during the year. At the end of the year, sales had increased by 14%. Was this an example of successful performance? Absolutely not. In fact, throughout the year Dwight mismanaged his district; among other things, he spent far too little time in the field with his salespeople, spent hours in the office each week talking with his stockbroker about personal investments, and hired three new salespeople who proved to be incompetent yet were still on the job at the end of the year. How, then, did the district realize a sales increase of 14%? Through a windfall. Halfway through the year, a major manufacturer moved into the area and started placing huge orders with one of Dwight's salespeople. This was *not* new business; the same customer had previously placed orders with one of the company's salespeople in another district. In other words, the business was *transferred* from another district to Dwight's district; while Dwight's sales figures jumped dramatically, the company failed to realize any net increase in sales to this customer. But that's not all. Careful analysis of Dwight's performance reveals that, if he had done his job properly, he would have attained his projected 5% increase *in addition* to his windfall increase of 14%. Actually, his district should have shown a 19% increase for the year. Thanks to his ineffective performance, what looks like success is actually much, much less than that.

For both these reasons—because a subordinate is more likely to grow if he understands the reasons for his success, and because poor performance is sometimes hidden beneath the *appearance* of success—it is important to find out why goals have been achieved. So let's look at the possible underlying reasons.

THE GOAL ITSELF

Before you start congratulating the subordinate for her performance, take
a hard look at the goal. Was it so vague ("Do a job that'll make us all
proud") that almost *any* performance would have sufficed to meet it?
Was it a "snap"—a goal so easy that failure to meet it would have been
more of an achievement than meeting it? Either way, you'll want to discuss
the matter in the appraisal.

THE SUBORDINATE

Next, determine what the subordinate contributed to the achievement of
the goal. What part of the achievement can be attributed to her effort?
Did she do anything "extra" or noteworthy that deserves special attention?
Here are a few examples:

GOAL.   Open a minimum of 12 new target accounts by December 31.
SUBORDINATE'S ACCOMPLISHMENT.   She opened 14 new target accounts by November 15, in spite of increased competition in the territory.

GOAL.   Oversee installation of a new EDP system and have it fully operable by
October 31.
SUBORDINATE'S ACCOMPLISHMENT.   He had the new system operable two months
ahead of the deadline, and he overcame a number of unforeseeable problems in
doing so.

Knowing what the subordinate did is only part of the story; equally
important is knowing *how* he managed to do it. What skills or attitudes
were responsible for the achievement? (In Appendix B, we've listed and
explained a large number of skills and attitudes that might help in achieving
a goal.) If you do this analysis thoroughly, you should be able to say something
like this (to yourself) about each achieved job goal:

One of Walt's top-priority goals was to increase production at Sunnybrook by 4%
while holding cost increases down to $\frac{1}{2}$ of 1% ... and, according to my figures,
he did that and more. The data I've got show that he realized a 5.5% increase
without any cost increase at all. That's quite an achievement ... and I think I
know at least three things that enabled him to do it. First of all, his suggestion that
we install those new presses made a very sizable difference in output, and his plan
for trading in the old presses and depreciating the new equipment enabled us to
do it without showing a cost increase. Second ... he got Morrison into shape for
the first time in years—Morrison's finally acting like a real plant manager, and
that's due to the coaching Walt has been doing with him. And ... third ... Walt's
idea for by-passing the reduction operation has enabled us to produce 13 additional
units each day ... and he did quite a job of selling that idea to the people over in

Industrial Engineering. So . . . as I see it . . . two changes in production technology and one change in the human factor have made all the difference.

Of course, all of this thinking is tentative. You'll want to explore and test it out during the appraisal session.

THE SUPERIOR

In examining your own contribution to the achievement of the goal, you need answers to two sets of questions:

1. Did I do the subordinate's work for him? Did I carry the burden while he coasted?
2. Did he achieve the goal in spite of me? Can he honestly say that I hindered rather than supported his efforts?

Either way, be careful. Don't inflate your own contribution, and don't claim credit for what's really a debit. Superiors sometimes insist on doing for a subordinate what the subordinate is perfectly capable of doing for himself. Then they complain that "I had to do it all" and that "If it weren't for me, nothing would have been done." In fact, all that they've really done is to intrude upon the subordinate and stifle his development. They've preempted his responsibility and made it their own. This is nothing to take credit for; if anything, it's a serious managerial debit.

On the other hand, if you *have* hindered your subordinate by failing to give her support, admit it. And be willing to give her full credit for achieving the goal in spite of your neglect. (Appendix B lists and explains a number of ways in which a superior can help or hinder a subordinate.)

THE SITUATION

This part of the analysis should help you answer two questions:

1. Was the achievement the result of a windfall?
2. Did outside circumstances make the goal even tougher than anticipated, so that the subordinate deserves special credit for achieving it?

Here are two examples to illustrate the kind of thing you should be looking for:

Brad, a district manager, was assigned this goal: Increase sales of fuel oil in your district by 20%. He achieved a 30% increase, but this was hardly remarkable, since the winter turned out to be the coldest in history, and fuel-oil use throughout the area increased by 50%.

Stu, a district manager for the same company in another part of the country, was also given a goal of achieving a 20% sales increase. He achieved exactly that, in spite of the fact that recorded temperatures were the highest in history, and the use of fuel oil in the area dropped by 30%.

As these examples show, an analysis of the situation is critically important. Without it, Brad would get credit for doing a better job than Stu; with it, Stu's achievement is considerably more impressive than Brad's.

A Tough Decision.   Your analysis up to this point may force you to conclude that one or more of the goals you had considered "clearly achieved" should not be credited to efforts by the subordinate. You may conclude: "Sure, the *goal* was achieved . . . but it wasn't achieved by the subordinate, and, since this is his appraisal, I can't give him credit for something he didn't do." Obviously, if you make this decision, you'd better be fully prepared to defend it.

Box 4b.   *Benefits from achievement*

If you conclude (a) that the goal was clearly achieved and (b) that the subordinate deserves the major share of the credit, then ask yourself: "What difference does it make? Who benefits from this achievement? In what way?" Work out the benefits, as you see them, to the subordinate, to yourself, and to the organization.

Benefit to the Subordinate.   Let's recall our formula $J + N \rightarrow B \rightarrow P$ (link *job goals* to *needs*—tangible and intangible—so that the *benefit* of pursuing the job goals becomes clear to the subordinate, who then *performs* in a committed way.) The point of the formula is this: you cannot separate *motivated* performance from *benefits*. People do committed work when they understand "what's in it for me" and when they *want* "what's in it."

You are now at the point at which you should link *job goals* with *tangible* and *intangible needs*. The idea is to show how achieving the job goals produced benefits to the subordinate. But why? Why bother to worry about the benefits now that the goal has been achieved? After all, benefits are supposed to motivate performance. But, in this case, the performance has already happened. Why dwell on something that doesn't matter any more?

That's exactly the point: it *does* matter. In fact, it matters a great deal. By showing the subordinate that his performance has, indeed, paid off, you are intensifying the trust between you and the subordinate, and *that* is immensely important as far as future performance is concerned. In effect, you are saying: "Look . . . at our last appraisal, we agreed that if you achieved this goal, these payoffs were likely to happen. Well . . . you *have* achieved the goal . . . and the payoffs *have* happened. You . . . I . . . the organization . . . we've all benefited as the result of your efforts." In other words, what was formerly a *projection* has now been *confirmed;* benefits that were merely forecast have actually *occurred* (or at least comparable benefits have occurred). This is profoundly important, and it should be driven home to the subordinate during the appraisal session.

Benefits to You and the Organization.   Now determine what you and the organization will get out of the subordinate's achievement. He deserves to know. Be specific: "Because you landed these three accounts, we're projecting a $750,000 increase in volume next year"; "Thanks to your negotiating an end to the Longhorn strike, we were able to hold our losses to $2,000,000"; "By restructuring that entire level of jobs, you helped us avert some very serious labor unrest. Without your efforts, I don't think we could have kept that plant open." And let him know how *you've* benefited from his accomplishment: "Jack, watching you maneuver to land that account taught me several things about selling that I never knew before. Let me tell you what they are . . .". If you withhold this information from a subordinate, you're not being candid.

Box 4c.   *Future job duties and business objectives*

At this point the focus of the analysis shifts. Up to now you've been examining the past. Now you want to start looking at the future, to ask yourself: "What lessons can my subordinate draw from his past performance that will help him continue to do well . . . or even better . . . in his future performance?" But before you can answer that question, you must answer an even more basic question: "What will my subordinate's future performance *require* of him? Will he be expected to continue doing pretty much what he has been doing? Or will he be called upon to do different things? Have his job duties changed? Will his business objectives be different?" A few examples will illustrate the possibilities:

Phyllis, whose appraisal you are now preparing, has, up to now, been specializing in market analysis work. Next month, she'll transfer to the field and begin doing direct selling. Your analysis of her past performance has focused on a number of skills (statistical analysis, design of interview formats, preparation of market reports with special emphasis on graphing and charting) that don't have very much to do with her future performance. On the other hand, her future performance will require a number of skills (territory planning, prospecting, making sales presentations, servicing accounts) that she hasn't had a chance to practice in the past. Obviously, the actions Phyllis will have to take in order to optimize her results as a salesperson will be considerably different from the actions that would have been needed to optimize results if she had continued as a market analyst.

Ben, whom you are now preparing to appraise, was hired a year ago as an accounting trainee. He has spent the past year working at a number of jobs in the accounting department and learning the ropes. Next week he'll be promoted to cost accountant and begin supervising a section of three people. Obviously, many of your observations about his performance during the past year will apply to his performance during the coming year. But many of them won't. Therefore, before you can think intelligently about what actions he should take to optimize future performance you will have to ask yourself: "What will be required of him in his new situation? How will his new job resemble the old? How will it differ?"

You are getting ready to appraise Mitch, your production supervisor. During the past year Mitch was instructed to concentrate on productivity and not to worry too much about product quality; units, not quality, counted. During the coming year, due to severely increased competition, Mitch will be instructed to focus on quality; output will be less important. This is a change in *business objectives*, and, obviously, it will require actions by Mitch different from those he's been practicing.

Box 4d.   *Action for optimal results*

Now, in the light of all you've done up to this point, ask yourself: "What should my subordinate do to get optimal results during the period following the appraisal? What should she continue to do as she has been? What should she do differently? *How* should she do it differently?"

As far as *achieved* goals are concerned, you may feel that little or nothing should be done differently. But not necessarily. The fact that your subordinate has achieved *satisfactory* results (results that were good enough to satisfy the goal) doesn't mean that she's achieved *optimal* results (the best results achievable under the circumstances). And it's optimal results—not merely satisfactory ones—that you are interested in. The question now is: What can be done to get optimal results next time? (Don't overlook the possibility that some action may be required of *you* before results can be optimized.)

Goals not Achieved

So much for goals that have clearly been achieved. Let's look now at that part of our chart dealing with "goals not achieved," Figure 18, and then explain the boxes.

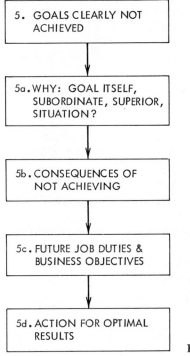

5. GOALS CLEARLY NOT ACHIEVED

5a. WHY: GOAL ITSELF, SUBORDINATE, SUPERIOR, SITUATION?

5b. CONSEQUENCES OF NOT ACHIEVING

5c. FUTURE JOB DUTIES & BUSINESS OBJECTIVES

5d. ACTION FOR OPTIMAL RESULTS

FIGURE 18

Box 5a. *Why: goal itself, subordinate, superior, or situation?*

The question is: What reasons or combination of reasons kept the subordinate from achieving the goal?

THE GOAL ITSELF

Did the subordinate fail to meet the goal because of some flaw in the goal itself? Flawed goals usually fall into one of four groups (a) unrealistic goals—goals that cannot be achieved under existing circumstances; (b) incomprehensible goals—goals that cannot be understood by the subordinate; (c) vague goals—goals so general that nobody can know for sure whether they've been achieved or not; (d) incomplete goals—goals that aren't comprehensive, so that no one knows what all the elements of the goal are. Let's examine each category.

Unrealistic. Was the goal of the get-out-there-and-run-a-mile-in-three-minutes variety? Was it a pipe dream, an indulgence in wishful thinking? Was it so implausible that it didn't deserve to be taken seriously?

Incomprehensible. Was it impossible for the subordinate to understand? Did you phrase it in a jargon that only you understood? Did you word it so confusedly that it didn't make sense? Did you misuse words, so that you meant one thing while he thought you meant something else?

Vague. Was the goal so general that any achievement might be considered as meeting it ("Do a good job"; "Give it your best"; "Don't let me down")? If so, is it possible that *you* think the goal hasn't been met ("I asked you to do your best and you didn't do it") while he thinks it has ("Oh yes I did")?

Incomplete. Did the goal lack comprehensiveness? Were important elements (costs, deadlines, etc.) left out of the goal, so that, once again, you may think it hasn't been met ("I think it's terrible that your costs have risen 5% in six months") while he may think it has ("You never said a word about costs when you assigned that goal to me")?

THE SUBORDINATE

Part of the reason the goal wasn't met may lie with the *subordinate*. Let's look at some possibilities.

Maybe the job goal wasn't reached because the subordinate lacks skill, know-how, or experience. The problem is not one of attitude; it's one of capacity or ability. But just knowing that he lacks skill isn't good enough. Before performance can be improved, both the subordinate and you must know exactly what the deficiency is. The critical questions are: *Precisely why* can't he do the job? *Where* is he hung-up? In *which* areas is he weak? *What* skills does he lack? *Where* is his knowledge inadequate? Answer these questions (tentatively) at this point.

At this early point you may not know the *exact* reason for the subordinate's failure. You may have nothing more than a hunch, an "educated guess," about why he's having problems. If so, you'll have to *test it out* during the appraisal. For the present, do the best you can to pinpoint the areas in which he is having trouble; wherever possible, support your conclusions with evidence. *But don't get locked into your conclusions.* You may have to change them later if you discover new facts.

It's also possible that the job goal wasn't achieved because the subordinate didn't *really try* to achieve it, even though he had the necessary know-how and experience. The problem is not lack of ability but lack of *motivation*, *drive*, *interest*, *desire*. Or it may be a lack of confidence, a refusal to believe that he can do the job. Primarily, these are all matters of *attitude*, of the way a subordinate feels about his job goals, about himself, or about both. (Appendix B will help you understand what subordinate factors may have interfered with goal achievement.)

THE SUPERIOR

This part of the analysis hits home. It forces you to consider the possibility that *you* are part of the subordinate's problem. It forces you to acknowledge that maybe *you are* getting in her way, inhibiting her, constraining her, squelching her. Obviously, its a lot tougher to look objectively at yourself than at other people, and a lot easier to manufacture alibis for your own behavior. This analysis demands scrupulous objectivity: the ability to stand back and look at your *own* performance as if it were somebody else's. It requires *taking the role of your subordinate*—asking yourself how your behavior looks from *her* viewpoint. This is hard to do, but you *must* do it if the appraisal isn't to turn into a fraud in which the subordinate is made to assume responsibility for things she didn't do.

Generally, your weakness, if any, will lie in one of five management areas: planning, organizing, leading, motivating, controlling. (All of these are covered in detail in Appendix B.)

THE SITUATION

Do this part of the analysis *cautiously*. It's all too easy to use the situation as a cop-out—to tell yourself: "It's not my subordinate's fault that he didn't reach the job goal, and it's not my fault either. It's the fault of circumstances beyond the control of either of us." This may be true, but be careful; it may be a convenient Q3 rationalization, an alibi to get everyone off the hook and spare everyone any unpleasantness. The best way to do this analysis is skeptically. Don't settle for any explanation without hard evidence. For example, if you think the job goal wasn't reached because of competitive conditions, support your conclusion with data. Who were the competitors? What were the conditions? Did these same conditions exist elsewhere? Did they have the same bad results? Was there anything you or your subordinate could have done to alleviate or eliminate these conditions?

A list of items to consider when analyzing situational factors is in Appendix B. On all these be sure to ask: Is this a *significant* explanation for the failure to achieve the job goal? Granted that the situation existed, did it really hinder the achievement of *this* particular goal?

Box 5b.   *Consequences of not achieving*

Now ask yourself: "What difference does it make that my subordinate did not achieve this goal?" If the answer is "None at all," then the goal was trivial, and never should have been assigned in the first place. But probably the failure to reach the goal *does* make a difference, and that difference should be spelled out.

The idea is not to threaten or berate the subordinate; the idea is to make sure he discusses and understands three things: what he lost as a result of not meeting the goals, what you lost, and what the organization lost. Many appraisals are ineffective because the subordinate leaves them knowing full well where and how he failed, but thinking to himself: "It really doesn't matter." In Q4 appraisal the subordinate leaves knowing that it *does* matter, and understanding why. This is indispensable to his future development.

Box 5c.   *Future job duties and business objectives*

Once again, make sure you've thought through any changes in the subordinate's job duties or business objectives that will require a different kind of performance from him in the future.

Box 5d.   *Action for optimal results*

You will probably have to spend a lot of time and thought on this box. Obviously, the goals you are now analyzing have not been optimized; they haven't been achieved at all. What should be done about it? What changes need to be effected—either in the goals themselves, in the subordinate's performance, or in your own performance?

Can't Tell

You are now ready to analyze the third group of goals—those whose achievement you are unsure about. Let's look at the applicable portion of the chart, Figure 19; then we'll examine the boxes.

Box 6a. *Why: goal, performance data, or both?*

If you can't tell whether a goal has been achieved or not, there are at least two possible explanations: (1) something is wrong with the goal itself, or (2) the performance data are inadequate. Let's look at each.

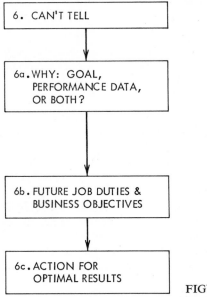

FIGURE 19

THE GOAL ITSELF

The problem may be that the goal was so unrealistic, incomprehensible, vague, or incomplete that nobody could tell if and when it was achieved. If so, you are going to have to be candid about it during the appraisal. You might come to the following conclusion: "I've looked at that goal from every angle, and, to be perfectly frank, I don't know whether the subordinate has achieved it or not, and I don't think I ever will. The problem is that the goal is so vague (or so unclear, or so unrealistic, or so incomplete) that I'm not really sure *what* he was supposed to achieve. The fact is that, last year, when we set that goal, we didn't do a very good job of it. This year we've got to make sure that we do a more effective job of goal-setting." If the goal itself is defective, you may perhaps focus your discussion with the subordinate not on his performance, but on the *goal-setting process.*

THE PERFORMANCE DATA

The goal may be sound enough, but the data on performance may be inadequate (incomplete records, garbled statistics, inaccurate computer reports, etc.). If this is the problem, you'd better start digging for the information you need. If a serious search fails to turn it up, then you'd better do something about your record-keeping system (or nonsystem).

There's another possibility, however. Whether or not the goal has been achieved may hinge upon a highly subjective judgment, and you may feel unable to make that judgment, one way or the other. We gave one example earlier in this chapter. Here's another:

Suppose that you are a Vice-President of Corporate Finance and that, in *last* year's appraisal, you said the following to Leonard Brooks, the controller of your company: "Len, I've been getting some negative feedback about your reports to the Finance Committee. A few people seem to feel they're pretty dull stuff. So let's just say that one of your goals during the coming year will be to improve the quality of these reports. I'm darned sure you can do it if you concentrate on it." As a result, during the intervening year, Len's reports have been briefer and, because he's added a number of charts and graphs, they've seemed more interesting. But now members of the committee are complaining that the reports are hard to follow, a complaint you haven't heard before. The question you now have to resolve is this: Did Len meet his goal or didn't he? The goal was "to improve the quality of these reports." Has he or hasn't he? On the one hand, nobody complains anymore that the reports are too long or too dull, but some people are complaining that they're hard to follow. Is this an improvement? Your conclusion may well be: "I don't know." If it is, you'll have to discuss the matter during the appraisal; maybe the best answer that the two of you will be able to come up with is: "The reports have improved in certain respects and declined in others."

This example helps us make two points:

1. It isn't *always* possible to come up with a clear-cut, yes-no decision about whether a goal has been achieved. On occasion, you may have to settle for a yes-*and*-no decision.
2. This is less likely to happen when the goal is highly *specific*. The situation in our example might have been avoided if, instead of being told to "improve the quality of these reports," Len had been told to "shorten your reports and make them more interesting, while keeping them as informative and understandable as in the past." If this had been the goal, you could plainly say that Len has failed to meet it.

Box 6b.   *Future job duties and business objectives*

Be sure you've got these clearly in mind and use your understanding in the next step.

Box 6c. *Action for optimal results*

Even though you are not sure whether these goals have been achieved, you should have some specific ideas about how the process of setting goals and gathering performance data can be improved.

Where Are You Now?

Once you and your subordinate have separately considered all the pertinent items on the chart, you can both say that you're ready with the *content* for the appraisal, *provided* that you've answered the relevant questions with *data*, not with top-of-the-head guesses. You should now have a sizable amount of *written* information to use in the appraisal: records, statistics, notes, and so on. You should also have, *in writing*, a list of questions that you weren't able to answer on your own, but that you hope to get answered during the appraisal.

SECTION 2: PREPARING THE PROCESS

The Need for Process Planning

So far, we have talked only about planning the content of the appraisal. If you are going to take a thoroughly scientific approach, however, you have to plan *process* as well. In other words, you have to plan the inter-action: the way in which you intend to present the content, the way in which you expect your subordinate to present his version of the content, the resistances you expect to encounter, the way you plan on handling them, and so on. Without process planning, the best content planning in the world may produce poor results.

How to Do It

To do Q4 process planning, you need to know two things:

1. The Q4 appraisal format (we described this in Chapter 5).
2. The behavior (Q1, Q2, Q3, or Q4) that your subordinate is most likely to display during the appraisal (you know this from your daily experience).

By putting these together you should be able to answer this question: What is likely to happen between my subordinate and me during the appraisal, and what should I do about it so that we can follow the Q4 format and get optimal, Q4 results? (We talk about "what you should do about it" in detail in Chapters 14 through 17.)

To illustrate how this is done, let's look at the Q4 format once again, and list some of the questions you should ask—and answer—*prior to* the appraisal session. (Keep in mind that your answers will be hypotheses, nothing more.)

Step 1.   *Arouse interest and test receptivity*

Be Appropriately Sociable.   How much sociability, and what kind, is appropriate with this subordinate?

Explain How the Appraisal Can Be Expected to Pay Off for the Subordinate.   How can I develop benefits that really mean something to him? How can I make sure he sees what's in it for him? Which of his tangible and personal needs will this appraisal help to fill? How?

Probe to Learn How the Subordinate Feels About Proceeding.   What response do I expect? What is her initial feeling about the appraisal likely to be?

Size Up the Subordinate's Receptivity by Observing His Behavior.   What is that behavior likely to be? Q1—cocky and blustery? Q2—watchful and apprehensive? Q3—talky and disorganized? Q4—businesslike and ready to collaborate?

Step 2.   *Raise receptivity and get the subordinate's self-evaluation*

Probe to Raise the Subordinate's Receptivity If It's Low.   What kind of probes should I use? How should I word them?

Promote a Candid, Realistic Self-Evaluation.   Is this likely to be a problem? Instead of candor and realism, am I likely to get Q1 boasting, or Q2 reticence, or Q3 overoptimism? What can I do about it?

Step 3.   *Present your own evaluation*

Assess the Subordinate's Self-Evaluation.   How can I make sure my assessment is open-minded and fair? Is she likely to say anything that will lower my receptivity and reduce my objectivity?

Confirm Where You Agree.   What am I likely to agree with? What am I likely to disagree with?

Where You Disagree, Give Your Own Views.   How should I do this? How can I disagree with this subordinate without arousing antagonism or hurt feelings? How can I express differences without starting a fight or making him clam up?

Present Your Views a Few at a Time.   What is the most logical way to group my views? How fast or how slow should I go when presenting ideas to this subordinate?

After Presenting Each Part of Your Evaluation, Check Subordinate's Understanding and Reaction.   How can I do this without making him think I consider him stupid?

Summarize the Agreements and Disagreements Between You.   How can I make sure that she really hears this summary? What will I do if she resists, picks an argument, or ignores what I'm saying?

Step 4.   *Vent emotions and resolve disagreements*

Encourage Venting of Interfering Emotions.   What emotions do I expect? Do I anticipate Q1 anger? Q2 sullenness? Q3 exhilaration? What is the best way to vent whatever feelings I expect to encounter?

Conduct a Give-and-Take Discussion to Settle Any Disagreements.   How can I generate give-and-take with this subordinate? How can I make sure we have a genuine, business-oriented discussion instead of a Q1 shouting match or a series of Q2 nods and shrugs or Q3 chit-chat that ignores the whole problem?

Step 5.   *Work out the final resolution*

Develop Goals and Action Plans.   How can I involve the subordinate in this? Where do I expect him to fall on the self-discovery continuum? What should I do about it?

Make the Benefits Explicit.   How do I do this? How do I make $J + N \rightarrow B \rightarrow P$ "come alive" for this subordinate?

Check the Subordinate's Understanding and Commitment; Set Up a Review. How can I make sure the understanding and commitment are real? Will she withhold full commitment? Or will she agree to anything I say? Will she voice her reservations, or suppress them? What can I do about it?

A Candid Admission

We candidly admit that you may find it impossible to answer all these questions. But they should be asked anyway. The idea is to force yourself to anticipate likely process hang-ups, so that you can plan tentative action for overcoming them. Let's emphasize the words "likely" and "tentative." You can't know for sure what problems you are going to encounter, but you can make an informed guess as to what problems you're *likely* to encounter. And you shouldn't plan fixed action, but you should plan *tentative* action. Unless you anticipate likely problems and plan tentative responses, you may find yourself doing a lot of on-the-spot improvising during the appraisal. And that's not the way to get optimal results.

There is one other reason why it's so important for you to do process planning: your subordinate, especially if he's "savvy," is going to be doing it from *his* end. He probably won't do as systematic a job of it as we are recommending you do (and we *don't* suggest that you have him do systematic process planning), but it's a safe bet that, on his own, without urging from you, he'll try to anticipate how you'll behave during the appraisal, and he'll try to figure out the best way to cope with your behavior. Make no mistake about it: your "sharper" subordinates will do all they can to foresee problems that might arise during the appraisal and to plan action to deal with those problems. There is no need to ask them to do it; they'll do it anyway. So it's important that *you* be prepared, too.

Synergism

"Synergism" is a fancy, but handy, word for what happens when two people achieve more by working together than they could possibly achieve on their own. If you and your subordinate follow the scientific approach, you have a good chance of synergizing in the appraisal session. To see why, consider the following:

1. Going into the appraisal neither one of you has all the answers. You've got some strong hunches, some educated guesses, some informed suppositions, but nothing more. By yourselves, the best either one of you can come up with is hypotheses.

2. If you have done a good job of process planning, the interaction during the appraisal session should be constructive and productive. The two of you should, with little wasted effort, be able to test out your hypotheses, discard or modify those that aren't sound, and confirm those that are.

3. This should pave the way for action planning based neither on make-believe nor wishful thinking, but on *fact*. And that, of course, is the only kind of action planning that can produce optimal results.

The upshot? A synergistic appraisal in which the whole is greater than the sum of its parts. That's what Q4 appraisal is all about.

SUMMARY

1. To do Q4 appraisal you must apply the same methods that scientists use in their work.

2. This scientific approach is a four-step process: (a) recognition of the problem, (b) observation of pertinent facts, (c) formulation of a hypothesis, and (d) testing the hypothesis. The first three of these steps should be done prior to the appraisal session.

3. This preappraisal preparation should focus on both content and process.

4. Q4 performance appraisal cannot be done unless both you and your subordinate plan the content of the appraisal. This preparation should be systematic; it should follow a written format that is the same for both of you.

5. If both of you prepare content adequately, the appraisal will almost surely be (a) more factual, (b) less emotional, (c) shorter, and (d) more systematic and efficient.

6. Whichever system you use, you and your subordinate should do four things in planning content: (a) organize your thinking about the appraisal; (b) decide tentatively which job goals have been achieved, which ones haven't, and which ones you're unsure about; (c) analyze the reasons for the performance in each case; (d) decide tentatively on the action required to optimize future results.

7. In doing this, search for evidence. Don't settle for hunches; if you can, dig out data to confirm or deny your suppositions.

8. Write down whatever you find out, and also write down any questions that need to be explored in the appraisal session.

9. As the superior, you'll want to go one step further and prepare the process of the appraisal. Process planning is concerned with this question: What's likely to happen between my subordinate and me during the ap-

praisal, and what should I do about it, so that we can follow the Q4 format and get optimal Q4 results?

10.   To answer this question, take the Q4 appraisal format and ask yourself, at each step, what behavior (Q1, Q2, Q3, or Q4) your subordinate is likely to display at that point, and how you should handle it.

11.   If you do effective planning of both process and content, the chances are good that you'll do a synergistic appraisal.

A LOOK AHEAD

Once you've done a scientific job of planning, you are ready for the appraisal itself. The question now is: How can I *tie together* all the diagnoses and all the prescriptions in this book to do optimal, synergistic Q4 appraisal? We're about to answer it. Our next four chapters integrate everything we've talked about so far, from developing Q4 benefits to creating a win-win climate. They explain how all the insights and skills we've discussed can be woven together to do *individualized* appraisal: appraisal suited to real people in real situations.

14

The Q4 Appraisal
STRATEGY FOR Q1 SUBORDINATE BEHAVIOR

People differ. That's a recurring theme of this book. They have different needs and they behave in different ways. Obviously, then, if you are going to do Q4 appraisal, you must adapt the basic appraisal format to fit the different needs and the different behaviors of each of your subordinates.

Q4 appraisal is tailor-made. A tailor may use one basic coat pattern for all of his customers: for the men, for the women, for the heavy-set, for the thin, for the short, for the tall, and on and on. But, if he's going to stay in business, he'll have to *alter* that pattern in every instance. He'll have to customize each coat by adapting and modifying his basic pattern.

That is what happens in Q4 appraisal, too. Each appraisal follows a basic pattern (our Q4 format), but each is customized to fit the specific subordinate. The pattern is always altered, always adapted and modified, so that it's "suited" to *that* subordinate.

This chapter describes the first of four fundamental ways to customize the Q4 format. Of course, each of these fundamental ways must itself be adapted to fit the needs of a particular subordinate. We can only set out general guidelines; cutting and trimming and stitching them to get a perfect fit is something *you* must do. This chapter contains some pointers for customizing the Q4 format to fit Q1 subordinate behavior. Q4 strategies for Q2, Q3, and Q4 subordinate behavior are found in our next three chapters.

Note that we've mentioned only Q1 (or Q2, Q3, or Q4) subordinate *behavior*. We have said nothing about Q1 (or Q2, Q3, or Q4) *subordinates*. This has been true throughout this book. It continues to be true in the chapters on Q4 strategies, and in all our later chapters. The reason is simple: very early in this book, we cautioned against labeling *people* and urged that only *behavior* be labeled.

We repeat this caution now because it's so important, as you read the chapters on Q4 strategies, to remember that these strategies apply to *behavior*, not people. The behavior, of course, is manifested by people, but that doesn't mean you're going to find a one-to-one correspondence between behavior and people. For instance, don't expect every subordinate who manifests a considerable amount of Q1 behavior to manifest *nothing but* Q1 behavior. Don't expect every subordinate who manifests strong esteem and independence needs to manifest *only* esteem and independence needs. Remember that people are complex, intricate, and often surprising creatures; remember that behavior can shift from quadrant to quadrant; remember that people may manifest numerous needs in an appraisal, including some (the so-called noninteractional needs) that we've mentioned but haven't actually considered in this book.

Bear in mind, then, that nothing in this chapter is about Q1 *subordinates*. In fact, we think the very phrase is a misnomer because it grossly oversimplifies reality. That is why we've refused to use it in this book. This chapter is about Q1 subordinate *behavior*. It's about what you should do when you're face-to-face with a subordinate who's behaving in a Q1 way. The same applies to our next chapters, too.

Q1 BEHAVIOR: A REMINDER

Before getting into the Q4 strategy for Q1 subordinate behavior, let's pause to remind ourselves what that behavior is all about. Underlying most Q1 behavior are strong personal needs for *esteem* and *independence*. This means that, during the appraisal, you should:

- Let the subordinate know, by your behavior, that he has your esteem and respect.
- Let him know that you're not trying to "crowd" him—that you want him to exert some independent thought, some self-management, some autonomy.

General Guidelines

To make sure you don't neglect the subordinate's esteem and independence needs, keep these general guidelines in mind:

1. Stress benefits that deal with esteem and independence.
2. Vent angry emotions; probe flat assertions.
3. Deal with his concerns and opinions first.
4. Keep your Q4 cool.
5. Display the strength of your convictions without making flat assertions.
6. Rely heavily on open-end questions, summary statements, and reflective statements.
7. Be prepared to shift your approach if the subordinate's behavior shifts to another quadrant.

Let's see how these guidelines can be implemented by looking at some of the major steps in the Q4 strategy for Q1 subordinate behavior.

THE Q4 STRATEGY FOR Q1 BEHAVIOR

Arouse Interest and Test Receptivity

BE BUSINESSLIKE YET WARM; HOLD DOWN THE SMALL TALK

This subordinate (like most people with strong esteem needs) respects strength and directness. If you waste time on chit-chat, he may think you're too "soft" to come to grips with the real issue: his performance. Once he gets that idea, he may try to "take over" the appraisal for his own purposes. So finish the initial amenities promptly and get down to business. He'll see this as a *display of strength.*

FIT THE PURPOSE AND BENEFITS TO THE SUBORDINATE'S PERSONAL NEEDS FOR ESTEEM AND INDEPENDENCE

Explain how the appraisal can help her gain new admiration and respect, or greater status and prestige. Explain how it can make her more autonomous, or give her more control over her own future. Stress greater freedom, less supervision, more influence.

OFFER BENEFITS THAT FIT THE SUBORDINATE'S TANGIBLE NEEDS, IF YOU CAN

You may not be able to offer a tangible reward. (Remember: when it comes to tangible rewards, demand exceeds supply.) But, if you can, make the tangible reward fit his tangible needs. For instance, if he wants a promotion and you can offer him one, that's ideal. The offer should motivate him to do the job necessary to get the promoton. But if he wants a promotion and you offer him a lateral transfer, the offer may fall flat. So, if possible, tie in the tangible reward with his tangible need. If you can't, you may have to rely on *in*tangibles to motivate him.

EXPECT EARLY DISAGREEMENTS, NEGATIVE EMOTIONS, FLAT ASSERTIONS

People with strong esteem and independence needs are likely, at first, to disagree ("I'll show him I've got a mind of my own"), to be negative ("He's not going to shove any of this stuff down *my* throat"), and to "come on strong" with flat assertions ("I know what the score is, and I'm going to let him know that I know"). Don't be surprised by any of this. Anticipate it and be ready to deal with it. *Don't ignore it.* This behavior is a sign of low receptivity; if you plow ahead without coming to grips with it, you may end up talking to yourself.

Raise Receptivity and Get the Subordinate's Self-Evaluation

DEAL WITH THE SUBORDINATE'S CONCERNS FIRST (OPEN-END QUESTIONS)

If receptivity is low (and with *this* subordinate it probably will be), start raising it before you do anything else. Set your own concerns aside and deal with hers first. Respond to her response with an open-end question or questions ("Tell me why you feel that way"; "Why do you say that?"). An open-end probe is the ideal response to esteem and independence needs. It says, in effect, "I respect your views and want to hear more about them. I'm going to defer to you and let *you* talk. You can say whatever's on your mind; I wan't squelch you." This is what someone with strong esteem and independence needs *wants* to hear. That's why it will help spin up receptivity.

SUMMARIZE THE MULTIPLE FLAT ASSERTIONS; LET THE SUBORDINATE
DESIGNATE WHERE TO START (SUMMARY STATEMENTS)

This subordinate is likely to make not one but several flat assertions. Deal with these by summarizing them and then asking the subordinate which one he'd like to discuss first. Don't try to juggle all the flat assertions at the same time; take them one by one. But let him tell you which one comes first. This will keep him involved, it will help his esteem need, and it will tell you which objection he considers most important. By the time you dispose of one or two of the objections, he may shrug off the remaining ones.

VENT HIS NEGATIVE EMOTIONS AND KEEP YOUR Q4 COOL

The subordinate may deliberately try to provoke you just to see if you can take it ("Let's see if this guy can stand a little needling"). Or he may resist you just to exert some independence ("He may be the boss, but I'll show him he can't push me around"). In any event, don't let him aggravate you. Keep cool; be patient; continue probing. If you blow your top, you'll only convince him that (1) you can't take it, or (2) you don't respect his opinion enough to discuss it rationally. Either way, you'll drive down receptivity.

AS A LAST RESORT, FOCUS ON PROCESS HANG-UPS; DON'T BLAME OR CHALLENGE

A *process hang-up* is anything that keeps you and your subordinate from having a receptive Q4 discussion. If you've tried everything we've suggested and still can't raise receptivity, try to get the process hang-up out in the open where the two of you can talk about it and resolve it. ("Joe, you seem so convinced of your position that I'm beginning to wonder if there's any room for any real two-way discussion. What do you think?") Admit that there *is* a problem and that it has you stymied. Whatever his answer, probe and discuss it. Don't pretend the problem doesn't exist. That will only make things worse. And don't blame him for the process hang-up. Just acknowledge that there *is* one. You're looking for a resolution, not a villain.

ASK FOR AND THEN LISTEN CAREFULLY TO THE SUBORDINATE'S SELF-EVALUATION; CHECK YOUR UNDERSTANDING (SUMMARY STATEMENT)

This is harder than it sounds. You may find it hard to listen carefully because you're busy with your own thoughts ("Boy, am I going to lay it on the line the minute this guy shuts up. I'm really going to tell him a thing or two"). As long as you're preoccupied with what you're going to say next, you won't really hear what he's saying. So the first thing to do is spin up your own receptivity. Force yourself to listen carefully and analytically. When your subordinate has finished, summarize his ideas and ask him if he agrees with your summary. ("As I understand it, you think . . . Have I got it right?") The fact that you've listened closely and are able to summarize his ideas will be a strong boost to his self-esteem.

Be sure not to *rush* your subordinate through his self-evaluation. People with strong esteem and independence needs don't like to feel "pushed" or "crowded." Let him present *all* his views; probe those that you don't fully understand. Don't give him the idea that the self-evaluation is a mere formality, to be gotten through as quickly as possible. It isn't. It's a vital part of Q4 appraisal. Give him time to do it right. *And give him a chance to shine.*

Present Your Own Evaluation

DO IT WITH CONVICTION BUT WITHOUT FLAT ASSERTIONS

When you present your views, be careful not to make flat assertions (dogmatic, unqualified statements: "I couldn't disagree more"; "I don't buy anything you've said"; "That's completely one-sided"). This subordinate makes plenty of flat assertions herself (that's typical of Q1 behavior). If you make them, you'll only encourage her to respond in kind. Before you know it, you'll find yourself in a verbal shooting match, with one flat assertion hitting another, like this:

YOU.   Your analysis doesn't make sense.
SHE.   Doesn't make sense? Sure it does. I'm right and you know it.
YOU.   You're being stubborn. You're not right. You're dead wrong.
SHE.   Dead wrong? You just haven't been listening, that's all.

Don't squabble. Don't make flat assertions.

SUPPORT YOUR EVALUATION WITH FACTS AND DETAILS

This subordinate prides herself on her "toughmindedness," her respect for "hard facts," her skepticism and her hardnosed approach to things ("Nobody can pull the wool over *my* eyes"). So, if you want to make a persuasive case, back up your views with records, details, and statistics (if they're available). This shouldn't be hard to do; you dug out the facts in preappraisal. Now *use* them.

Vent Emotions and Resolve Disagreements

VENT EMOTIONS (REFLECTIVE STATEMENTS)

You and the subordinate are almost sure to disagree about something. And chances are that he's going to be unhappy about it. He may resent the fact that you haven't "bought" his evaluation; he may feel your evaluation is unfair; he may feel you are trying to impose your views on him. In any event, you can expect some displeasure. *Get it into the open.* A reflective statement should help ("You seem angry").

As always, stay cool. Venting is never fun. While your subordinate is speaking his piece and getting some hostility "out of his system," you may start to feel exasperated. He may say things that strike you as unfair, unreasoning, or just plain stubborn. Don't show your annoyance.

ASK THE SUBORDINATE TO SUMMARIZE THE MAJOR DISAGREEMENTS (OPEN-END QUESTIONS)

Venting gets disagreements out into the open, but it doesn't resolve them. The resolution has to come *after* the venting, after the air has cleared and heated emotions have cooled off. So, once your subordinate's emotions have vented, and once you've explored their causes, try to resolve your differences. Get him to summarize the disagreements ("How do you see the differences between us?"). Make sure the *subordinate* does the summarizing. This bolsters his self-esteem and, at the same time, shows him that you are not afraid to let him say what the disagreements are all about.

DON'T EXPECT 100% AGREEMENT, JUST UNDERSTANDING

Subordinates with strong esteem and independence needs often refuse, almost on principle, to go along with the boss all the way. They need to maintain some margin of difference as *proof* of their independence. They want to be able to say, after the appraisal: "I didn't knuckle under. I didn't cave in. I preserved my integrity." So don't be surprised if, after a rational, businesslike discussion, the two of you still don't see eye-to-eye on everything. Get all the agreement you can, but don't expect "unconditional surrender." However, even if you don't fully agree, make sure you fully *understand* one another.

Work Out the Final Resolution

KEEP AN OPEN MIND (THE SUBORDINATE'S GOALS AND SOLUTIONS MAY BE BETTER THAN YOURS)

Now the focus shifts from what has been happening to what is going to happen. From here on out, the question is: What job goals should the subordinate aim at between now and the next appraisal, and what should he do to achieve them? (As for *business* job goals, these may already be set, or they may not be set until some time in the future; that all depends upon your organization's policy. But when it comes to *behavioral* job goals, now is almost surely the time to discuss them.) Start by asking (to whatever extent policy permits) what the subordinate thinks her new goals and action plans should be. Listen carefully. Don't be misled by her brash manner; beneath the bluster, she may have some solid ideas. In fact, her thinking may beat yours. So keep *your* receptivity high.

IF THE SUBORDINATE'S SUGGESTIONS ARE OKAY, SAY SO

Don't prolong the discussion if you're satisfied with what you've heard. If all or part of the subordinate's ideas are sound, tell her.

IF NOT, PRESENT YOURS, WITH FACTS AND DETAILS (NO FLAT ASSERTIONS)

Don't present your ideas as if the subordinate's all wrong and you're all right ("I can't buy anything you've said; let me set you straight"). Flat assertions will only drive her receptivity down, at a time when it must be *up*. She *must* hear and consider your views, so don't present them in a right-wrong, smart-stupid way.

ASK THE SUBORDINATE TO COMPARE THE TWO SETS OF ACTION PLANS AND COME UP WITH THE "BEST" IN EACH

We've said it many times: Q4 appraisal is *collaborative*. Now prove that you believe it. All the collaboration up to this point won't mean much if you don't let the subordinate evaluate the two sets of action plans. Let him stack your ideas against his, and let *him* say which are best (or let him suggest some blending). This demonstrates that you are not trying to shove your ideas down his throat. (We're assuming that the subordinate is *able* to do the necessary analysis and self-discovery. If not, you'll have to impose your ideas.)

REACH A FINAL RESOLUTION THROUGH GIVE-AND-TAKE

Discuss both proposals and thrash out the differences. If the two of you cannot agree on certain points, you'll probably end up going with *your* ideas. But, in choosing yours over hers, let her know that you've carefully considered her ideas, that you respect them, and that there are good reasons for rejecting them. *Then explain the reasons.* Don't give her the idea that you're deciding in favor of your own views just because they *are* your own.

GET THE SUBORDINATE TO SPELL OUT THE BENEFITS

If the appraisal has really worked, the subordinate should be able to list the benefits that she'll realize from pursuing the new goals. So ask her to do so ("As you see it, what will you get out of this?"; "What, in your view, is the payoff to you if you achieve these goals?"). If she can't answer, something's wrong, and you'll either have to discuss the benefits some more, or accept the fact that she's *not* committed to the goals.

NOW SPELL OUT THE BENEFITS AS YOU SEE THEM

If you can offer tangible rewards, do so. If you can't, at least offer intangible rewards. Be sure they're rewards that will gratify his Q1 needs for position, rank, power, status, influence, recognition, acclaim, freedom, autonomy, elbowroom, special attention, and so forth.

RECAP

Everything we've recommended in this chapter will help you carry out the guidelines we listed at the beginning. Let's review them.

1.   Stress benefits that deal with esteem and independence.

When you discuss "what's in it" for the subordinate, make sure that "what's in it" will gratify his need to be important, to get attention, to move ahead, or to exert more autonomy.

2.   Vent angry emotions; probe flat assertions.

Expect anger and resistance; that is how this subordinate manifests her esteem and independence needs. Don't dismiss her flat assertions out of hand, no matter how outrageous they sound; try to find out what truth, if any, lies at their core.

3.   Deal with his concerns and opinions first.

What better way to manifest your respect for him and to give him elbowroom, than to defer to him by giving his interests and ideas precedence in time?

4.   Keep your Q4 cool.

If you blow your stack, he'll figure that he's "getting to you" and that you can't take it. If he thinks you are "soft," your esteem will mean less to him. People with strong esteem needs want respect from "strong" people—and, as they see it, one sign of strength is unflappability.

5.   Display the strength of your convictions without making flat assertions.

State your views confidently but not dogmatically. Flat assertions made by the boss usually come across as put-downs or coercion. Either way, they'll probably backfire when directed toward subordinates with strong esteem and independence needs.

6.   Rely heavily on open-end questions, summary statements, and reflective statements.

Why? Because *open-end questions* give him a chance to shine by speaking his piece in full, and they prove to him that you are not afraid to give him a chance to say what he wants to say. Because *summary statements* prove to him that you've been listening attentively, thus demonstrating your esteem for his thinking. Because *reflective statements* show that you take his feelings seriously, that you recognize them and are tough enough to acknowledge them.

7.   Be prepared to shift your approach if the subordinate's behavior shifts to another quadrant.

We can't say it often or strongly enough: real people in real appraisals behave in complex ways. Don't expect Q1 behavior to *stay* Q1 behavior. It may, or it may not. In fact, if you do all the things we've recommended in this chapter, you'll probably see a *diminution* of the subordinate's esteem and independence needs. As the intensity of these needs decreases, you are likely to see your subordinate display more Q4 behavior, and you'll have to modify your own behavior accordingly. Of course, it's also possible that something in the interaction may cause the subordinate to shift to other kinds of behavior (a lapse into Q2 sullenness, a chatty Q3 mask, and so forth). Don't let *any* kind of behavior change catch you off guard.

SUMMARY

Instead of summarizing each of the points in this chapter, we'll close by outlining, step-by-step, the Q4 strategy for Q1 subordinate behavior. If you want a quick breakdown of the strategy, the outline below provides it. If you want more information on the major steps in the strategy, you'll find it earlier in this chapter. (And if you want a "sample" of how the Q4 strategy for Q1 behavior might actually work, you'll find it in Appendix A, where we've printed the "transcript" of a mock Q4–Q1 appraisal.)

Q4 Strategy for Q1 Subordinate Behavior

1. AROUSE INTEREST AND TEST RECEPTIVITY

    Be appropriately sociable

    - Show businesslike warmth; minimize small talk.

    Arouse interest

    - State purpose and benefit with conviction.
    - Make the purpose and benefits fit the subordinate's intangible needs (stand out, control own future, etc.).
    - Offer benefits that fit subordinate's tangible needs, if you can (status, position, title, recognition, etc.).

    Probe

    - Probe the subordinate's reaction and willingness to proceed (open-end).

    Size up behavior and receptivity

    - Expect early disagreements, negative emotions, flat assertions.

2. RAISE RECEPTIVITY AND GET THE SUBORDINATE'S SELF-EVALUATION

    Raise receptivity

    - Deal with the subordinate's concerns first (open-end).
    - Vent negative emotions (reflective).
    - Summarize multiple disagreements and flat assertions; let the subordinate designate where to start.
    - Keep you Q4 cool.
    - As a last resort, focus on process hang-ups; don't blame or challenge.

    Get the subordinate's self-evaluation

    - Ask for it (open-end).
    - Probe for "facts" as the subordinate sees them (open-end).

Listen carefully; summarize his evaluation; check your under-standing (summary).
• Don't disagree or state your own views prematurely.

3. PRESENT YOUR OWN EVALUATION

- Confirm where you agree with the subordinate's evaluation.
- Present yours with conviction but without flat assertions.
- Support it with facts and details.
- Contrast your disagreements.
- Ask for feedback (open-end).
- Summarize both evaluations; don't expect 100% agreement.
- Focus on process hang-ups, if necessary.

4. VENT EMOTIONS AND RESOLVE DISAGREEMENTS

Encourage venting of emotions caused by disagreements

- Vent emotions (reflective).
- Explore their causes (open-end).
- Summarize the subordinate's position (summary).
- Keep your Q4 cool.

Resolve disagreements

- Ask the subordinate to summarize the major disagreements (open-end).
- Ask her to analyze the causes of performance problems as she sees them (open-end).
- Use summary statements to achieve understanding of both positions.
- Don't expect 100% agreement, just understanding.

5. WORK OUT THE FINAL SOLUTION

Develop goals and action plans

- Keep an open mind (the subordinate's goals and solutions may be better than yours, or, through discussion, the two of you may come up with ideas that synergize.
- By probing (open-end), get the subordinate to suggest goals and solutions.
- Probe each recommendation for details (closed-end, fact-finding).
- Summarize your understanding.
- If his goals and plans are acceptable, say so.

- If not, present yours; back them with facts and details (no flat assertions).
- Ask the subordinate to compare the two sets and come up with the "best" in each.
- Suggest final goals and plans, incorporating your "best" thinking and his.
- Reach final resolution through give-and-take.

Make the benefits explicit

- Get the subordinate to spell out the benefits (open-end: "What's in it for you?").
- Present benefits (for her tangible and intangible needs—status, recognition, superiority, etc.).

Check for understanding and commitment

- Ask the subordinate to summarize (open-end).
- Don't expect 100% agreement, only high commitment.

Set up a review procedure

A LOOK AHEAD

We look next at the Q4 strategy for Q2 subordinate behavior. It is not, by any means, a repetition of this chapter. The strategy differs because Q2 behavior differs from Q1. We'll see that difference almost from the outset.

15

The Q4 Appraisal

STRATEGY FOR Q2 SUBORDINATE BEHAVIOR

In this chapter, we look at ways to adapt the Q4 format to Q2 subordinate behavior. Once again, we hit the main points first, then conclude with a step-by-step outline of the strategy.

Q2 BEHAVIOR: A REMINDER

Let's remind ourselves of the underlying motivation of Q2 behavior. Beneath most Q2 behavior is a strong need for *security*. This means that during the appraisal there is one thing you must *not* do and one thing you *must*.

- You must *not* do anything to arouse or augment the subordinate's fears. Threats, snide remarks, sarcasm, belligerence, put-downs—any of these is likely to stir apprehension.
- You *must* bolster his willingness to participate (it's a safe bet that if he had a choice, he'd prefer *not* to go through with the appraisal). It's up to you to get him to unwind, to untense, to become receptive, to collaborate. This chapter offers some tips on how to do this.

General Guidelines

To help you respond to this subordinate's security needs, keep these general guidelines in mind:

1. Stress benefits that deal with security.
2. Be patient; slow your pace.
3. Show genuine interest.
4. Guide firmly but gently.
5. Establish trust.
6. Stress open-end questions, pauses, and brief assertions of interest.
7. Be prepared to shift your behavior if the subordinate's behavior shifts.

Now let's look at some ways to implement these guidelines.

THE Q4 STRATEGY FOR Q2 SUBORDINATE BEHAVIOR

Arouse Interest and Test Receptivity

DON'T BE TOO FRIENDLY, PERSONAL, OR INTENSE; SLOW DOWN

This subordinate is already tense and apprehensive. If you are too friendly or personal, you may make him more anxious, or even suspicious ("I wonder why he's being so nice to me"). He feels most comfortable with people who are courteous and affable, but not overwhelming. He feels awkward with people who expect him to be talkative or exuberant. So take it easy. Be friendly in a quiet, restrained way. Slow your pace. Don't "come on too strong." Be low-key; don't be lackadaisical, just somewhat subdued.

EXPLAIN THE PURPOSE OF THE APPRAISAL IN A "LOW RISK" WAY

Don't add to the subordinate's anxiety by telling her that "a lot is at stake" or that "today's the big day." Don't give her the idea that you're putting her on the griddle, that she's facing a severe test, that everything hinges on what happens in the next couple of hours. Don't overdramatize; be matter-of-fact. One good idea is to talk about "us," not "you" ("This appraisal should help all of us overcome some problems and get even better results in the future").

INTEGRATE THE PURPOSE WITH BENEFITS THAT FIT THE SUBORDINATE'S INTANGIBLE NEEDS

This subordinate isn't interested in risk, adventure, or excitement. He doesn't want to be a hero, attract a lot of attention, or make organizational waves. He wants stability—a calm, dependable environment in which he can do his job with a minimum of stress. Keep this in mind when laying out benefits.

OFFER BENEFITS, IF YOU CAN, THAT FIT HER TANGIBLE NEEDS

She'll welcome anything that makes her more secure, that makes her life less unpredictable. So, if you're able, offer tangible rewards like fringe benefits, assured tenure, firm policies and guidelines to lean on, and so on. Concentrate on reducing the chancy, haphazard aspects of her job.

EXPECT NEUTRAL, ALOOF, NONCOMMITTAL BEHAVIOR

You'll probably find receptivity quite low. If you ask, "How does all this strike you," he may answer, "Okay, I guess" or "Whatever you say" or something equally noncommittal. These answers really mean: "I'm not about to stick my neck out by telling you what I think." In other words, he's not ready to collaborate openly and candidly; he's not ready to share ideas and disclose his real thoughts. So you must raise his receptivity. Only then will it make sense to proceed with the evaluative part of the appraisal.

Raise Receptivity and Get the Subordinate's Self-Evaluation

DON'T TALK TOO MUCH; SLOW DOWN; DON'T INTERROGATE

This is a closed-mouth subordinate. If you show him that you want to do most of the talking, he'll be happy to let you. This will get him off the hook; he won't have a *chance* to say much. So don't talk too much; use plenty of pauses; let him get involved. To do this, slow your pace; you cannot have a brisk, snappy dialogue with this subordinate. What you can have is a somewhat slow-moving, subdued dialogue. There's nothing wrong with that, as long as he *is* involved and *is* sharing his thoughts. Finally, don't interrogate. Nothing will "turn him off" faster than third-degree treatment. Remember: you want to *remove* the aura of threat, not add to it.

REASSURE HER WITH REFLECTIVE STATEMENTS

This subordinate needs plenty of reassurance. So give it to her, but make it the right kind. If she expresses fear or anxiety, don't shunt her feelings aside with a glib "Don't worry about it." She'll think you're not taking her seriously, or that you don't consider her fears important. Use a reflective statement ("I can tell you're bothered"; "It's obvious that you're deeply worried"). Let her know that her tension and uneasiness are *getting through* to you. This doesn't mean you agree with her feelings, only that you recognize them. And that's reassuring.

USE MULTIPLE PROBES (OPEN-END) TO UNCOVER HIDDEN CONCERNS AND DOUBTS

Don't expect one probe to do the job. It's a safe bet that you'll have to use a number of probes before you know what's really bothering her, and why her receptivity isn't higher. This takes patience, but there's no other way to spin up Q2 low receptivity.

AS A LAST RESORT, FOCUS ON PROCESS HANG-UPS, BUT DON'T BLAME OR CHALLENGE

If, after doing your best, you can't get the subordinate to open up, confront the fact. Admit the problem but don't be critical; don't suggest that he's done something wrong. Just acknowledge that there is an obstacle ("Ed, I get the impression that you'd rather not talk about this . . ."; "Dora, I get the feeling you'd prefer for me to drop the whole matter . . ."). Pause, let the subordinate respond, and then probe and discuss the response. The obstacle, whatever it is, must be overcome before you proceed. (Whatever you do, don't taunt the subordinate about his silence: "What's the matter . . . are you afraid to say what you really think?" "How come you're not responding? Have you got laryngitis?" Smart cracks like these can only turn a chilly appraisal into an icy one.)

SHOW YOU'RE LISTENING

Once the subordinate begins his self-evaluation, keep him going with brief assertions and neutral phrases and questions. He'll probably keep his evaluation brief; he's not likely to fill in with many details or illustrations. So neutral phrases and questions are especially useful ("Fill me in on that last point"; "Give me a couple more examples"; "Tell me more about that").

USE CLOSED-END PROBES TO GET SPECIFICS; EXPLAIN WHY FIRST

The best probe for pinning down details is the closed-end question ("Do you think 5% makes more sense than 4.5%?" "Should we try it in late Spring or early Fall?" "Is the lower figure acceptable to you?"). But there is one problem: people with strong security needs don't like being pinned down because they don't want to risk committing themselves. They'd rather stay neutral, but that's difficult to do in response to closed-end questions. So, when you use closed-end probes with this subordinate (as you must from time to time), *explain why first*. Tie your explanation to his personal need for security and predictability: "Fred, I'm going to ask you a couple of very specific questions, because your answers will help both of us avoid this kind of unforeseen situation in the future"; "Bea, I know you're as eager as I am to cut down on these emergency situations, so let me ask you a couple of very direct questions that'll help us do just that"; "Jack, if you'll give me specific answers to a few questions, I think we can figure out a way to get this problem off your back."

Present Your Own Evaluation

IN PRESENTING YOUR EVALUATION, SLOW DOWN, DON'T PRESSURE, BLAME, OR MAKE FLAT ASSERTIONS

Restrain yourself. Don't rush through your evaluation, don't make sweeping generalizations, don't censure or accuse. Make a measured, careful, deliberate presentation. Don't overstate or understate. Come across as *helpful*, not threatening.

INVITE FEEDBACK AFTER EACH POINT

If you bunch your ideas, the subordinate will think you're "putting the screws to him." But if you voice *one* idea and then invite his comments, he'll know that you're not trying to squeeze him. So present one idea at a time, ask for feedback with an open-end question ("How does that sound to you?") and then *pause* so that he can gather his thoughts and respond.

DON'T BE FOOLED BY SURFACE AGREEMENT

At first, you're likely to get nothing but agreement. In fact, if you follow each point with only *one* open-end probe, you may get the idea that he agrees 100%. Here's a typical example:

SUPERIOR. It seems to me that we were too conservative when we set this objective. In view of what's happened, I think that if we had set it at 6% instead of 4%, we would have achieved the 6% without any trouble. What do you think?

SUBORDINATE. (Slowly) Yeah . . . I guess that's right.

SUPERIOR. Fine. Glad to hear you agree. Let's go on.

If you play this game, asking only *one* open-end question and then dropping the subject, you may never hear a word of dissent. The only way out of this trap is to probe *in depth:*

SUPERIOR. Fred, I feel that we may have missed the boat last year when we set that objective at 4%. Knowing what we know now, I think we should've set it at 6%. Hitting 6% would've been possible. What do you think?

SUBORDINATE. (Slowly) Yeah . . . I guess you're right.

SUPERIOR. You sound hesitant. What are your doubts?

SUBORDINATE. (In an off-handed manner, without conviction.) None. None at all. If you say 6%, I'll buy it.

SUPERIOR. Fred, you don't sound convinced. I could be wrong about the 6% . . . maybe I'm being too optimistic. What do you think?

SUBORDINATE. (Slowly) Well . . . I'm not sure about the 6%.

SUPERIOR. Go on.

SUBORDINATE. Well . . . it's just that we had so darned much trouble reaching 4%. To tell you the truth, Dan, for a few months I was scared to death we weren't going to reach the 4% figure. It was a real struggle.

SUPERIOR. I see. Reaching 4% was really tough . . . right?

SUBORDINATE. Right. It really was. I don't see how we could ever have hit 6%. Maybe 4.50%. 4.75% at the outside. But not 6%.

At this point, you may be thinking: "Nobody in the world has the time or energy to do that kind of probing on every point." There are two answers to this: (1) You don't have to do this on *every* point; do it on *critical* points, or on any point where you get halfhearted agreement. (2)

The alternative to in-depth probing is to settle for an appraisal marked by evasion, equivocation, and downright misstatement of fact. Unless you really *don't* want to know what your subordinate thinks, you must do this kind of probing.

Vent Emotions and Resolve Disagreements

BE READY FOR WITHDRAWAL AND MOODINESS

If you've been critical of the subordinate's performance, she may withdraw (shutting up and saying nothing) and sulk (implying, without actually saying, that you're being harsh). Don't try to josh her into a good mood ("Cheer up. It's not as bad as all that"). Treat her mood seriously by giving her a chance to discuss it ("I can see you're concerned"; "You seem reluctant to talk about this"). Don't let her bottle up her feelings; they'll only poison the appraisal. Vent them.

DON'T INTERPRET WITHDRAWAL AS AGREEMENT

Don't kid yourself that silence is golden. In *this* case, silence is *troublesome;* it probably means that your subordinate is suppressing something you should know. So find out if the silence means "I agree" or if it means "I think you're crazy but I don't dare say so." Do this by probing.

HAVE THE SUBORDINATE ANALYZE DISCREPANCIES

Ask him if he can resolve the differences between his evaluation and yours. Be careful; don't let him cave in and say that he's all wrong and you're right. And don't let him put you off ("I'm really not sure"; "I'd like to think about that for a few days"). Try to find out what he really thinks. This will take some delicate (don't make him think you're hounding him) but persistent probing. Naturally, you'll want to add your own ideas after patiently probing his.

Work Out the Final Resolution

GUIDE GENTLY BUT FIRMLY

During this phase it's crucial to keep the subordinate involved. Don't let her lapse into silence. Keep her in the middle of things by consistent probing. Don't sound impatient ("Come on now, stop beating around the bush . . .") or coercive ("I want an end to all this hemming and hawing.

Just tell me what you think in plain English"). Be firm, even-mannered, controlled.

People with strong security needs don't like change: it's disruptive, unsettling, maybe even frightening. But performance can only be improved if change occurs. How are you going to get your subordinate to commit herself to change when she prefers to avoid change? By setting goals that can be achieved incrementally—first one step, then the next, then another, and so on. Work out plans that can be carried out in the same gradual, piecemeal way. The cliche that "Every journey of a thousand miles begins with a single step" is worth remembering. In fact, don't even *mention* a journey of a thousand miles. Just talk about the individual steps. The more grandiose the journey, the less likely she is to undertake it.

WHERE POSSIBLE, SET UP TWO ALTERNATIVES SO THE SUBORDINATE CAN SELECT ONE

If he feels pressured to accept one and only one plan, his old insecurity and apprehension may revive ("The boss is really pushing hard. I'm being shoved into a corner. I'd better go along quietly or I'll be in big trouble"). Why not give him a choice (if that's feasible)? Simply say: "Charlie, there seem to be two good ways to approach this goal . . . which sounds best to you?" or "Ted, from my point of view, Plan A and Plan B both make good sense. Which do you prefer?"

ASK THE SUBORDINATE TO SUMMARIZE; DON'T EXPECT TOO MUCH

The summary may be halting and incomplete, but it's still important that he do it. Don't pre-empt him; don't say to yourself, "I can do a better and faster summary than he can, so I won't even bother to ask him." *Keep him involved.*

SUMMARIZE THE GOALS AND PLANS; STATE YOUR OWN COMMITMENT

After his summary, make your own. Express your own conviction and commitment. Let him know that you're on his side, that you believe in the goals, that you think the plans make sense, and that you feel confident the goals are attainable. If *you* sound doubtful or unenthusiastic, you're sure to trigger doubt, worry, and indecision in the subordinate.

RECAP

The pointers we've just discussed will help you carry out the guidelines we listed at the start of the chapter. Let's take another look at them.

1. *Stress benefits that deal with security.*

When you explain "what's in it" for the subordinate, make sure that "what's in it" *won't* arouse apprehension and fear and *will* make her feel reasonably safe and assured.

2. *Be patient; slow your pace.*

Take your time. Don't be hurried or eager to get it over with. Don't fidget or show exasperation if the subordinate is slow to respond or evasive. Remember: you want to draw him out of his shell. The reason he's inside the shell in the first place is that he's seeking protection. As long as he feels threatened or under attack, he's going to stay inside. He'll emerge only when he's reasonably sure that he won't get hurt. It's up to you to reassure him. You can do it only if your approach is low-key and restrained.

3. *Show genuine interest.*

Don't be misled by the subordinate's slow, halting manner. In all likelihood, she's got some thoughts that you *should* be interested in—that are *worth* hearing. Their *style* may be drab and unexciting, but that doesn't mean the *content* is. So stay interested; probe; find out what she really thinks and feels. Chances are you'll be amply repaid for your efforts.

4. *Guide firmly but gently.*

This subordinate may never say it out loud, but he wants (and needs) guidance; guidance makes him feel more secure. So guide him, but do it without shoving. Give him all the leadership he requires, but don't be noisy about it.

5. *Establish trust*

This is indispensable in *any* appraisal. But it's immensely important with a subordinate who has strong security needs. If you give her any reason to doubt your motives, you may never get a candid remark out of her.

6. *Stress open-end questions, pauses, brief assertions of interest.*

Why? Because *open-end questions* indicate that you're really interested in what he thinks—that you want to hear the whole story. Because *pauses* prove that you're not trying to crowd him or push him—that you are willing to move along at a relaxed, measured pace. Because *brief assertions of interest* encourage him to keep on talking—to do more than simply offer terse, one-sentence responses.

7. *Be prepared to shift your behavior if the subordinate's behavior shifts.*

As we said in our last chapter, people can be surprising. This subordinate may, in certain circumstances, become more intensely or less intensely Q2 in his behavior; he may even, if sufficiently provoked, lash out (Q1 behavior), or, if sufficiently relaxed, meander (Q3 behavior). Or you may get him to manifest some open, businesslike Q4 behavior. Whatever he does, *don't* be surprised. Be ready for shifts, and modify your own behavior accordingly. Stay loose.

SUMMARY

Let's close this chapter, as we did the last, with a step-by-step outline of the Q4 strategy for Q2 subordinate behavior.

Q4 Strategy for Q2 Subordinate Behavior

1. AROUSE INTEREST AND TEST RECEPTIVITY

   Be appropriately sociable

   • Don't be too friendly or personal; slow your pace; be less intense.

   Arouse interest

   • Present the purpose in a "low risk" way; avoid words like "evaluate," "criticize," "new," and so on.
   • Integrate the purpose with benefits that fit the subordinate's intangible needs (low risk, safe, secure, etc.).
   • Offer benefits, if any, that fit his tangible needs (fringe benefits, tenure, structure, etc.).

Probe

- Probe the subordinate's reactions and willingness to proceed (open-end and pause).

Size up behavior and receptivity

- Expect neutrality and aloofness.

2. RAISE RECEPTIVITY AND GET THE SUBORDINATE'S SELF-EVALUATION

Raise receptivity

- Get the subordinate willing to share ideas (open-end and pause).
- Don't talk too much; slow down; don't interrogate: explain the reason for your questions.
- Encourage her to keep talking (brief assertions and neutral phrases; deemphasize leading questions and closed probes).
- Reassure with reflective statements ("I can see you're concerned," not "Don't worry about it").
- Use multiple probes (open-end) to uncover hidden fears and doubts.
- Build trust.
- As a last resort, focus on process hang-ups; don't blame or challenge ("I get the feeling you're reluctant to go ahead . . ." pause).

Get the subordinate's self-evaluation (while raising receptivity)

- Ask for his evaluation (open-end and pause).
- Show you're listening (brief assertions and neutral phrases).
- Acknowledge and encourage his evaluation (summary).
- Use closed-end probes to get specifics; explain why first.
- Don't prematurely offer your evaluation or disagree.

3. PRESENT YOUR OWN EVALUATION

- Confirm where you agree with his evaluation.
- Present yours; slow down; don't pressure, blame, or make flat assertions.
- Don't bunch ideas.
- Invite feedback after each point (open-end and pause).
- Contrast your differences.
- Don't be fooled by surface agreement.
- Focus on process hang-ups if necessary.

4. VENT EMOTIONS AND RESOLVE DISAGREEMENTS

Encourage venting of emotions caused by disagreements

- Be ready for withdrawal and moodiness; probe with reflective statements ("I can see you're concerned"; "You seem reluctant to discuss this"; etc.).
- Don't interpret silence or withdrawal as agreement.

Resolve disagreements

- Use multiple probes (open-end) to bring hidden disagreements to the surface; suggest that she has doubts.
- Ask her to summarize disagreements (don't expect too much).
- Have her analyze the disagreements; guide gently but firmly.
- Make sure both positions are understood before proceeding.
- Don't let surface agreement fool you.

5. WORK OUT THE FINAL RESOLUTION

Develop goals and action plans

- Guide gently but firmly.
- Ask the subordinate to suggest goals and plans (open-end and pause); briefly summarize them.
- Add your own ideas; back up with facts; don't overwhelm.
- Use leading or closed-end (yes-no) questions to establish details of goals and plans.
- Where possible, break goals and plans into small, progressive steps.
- Where possible, set up two alternatives so the subordinate can select one.
- Invite feedback; probe for hidden doubts (open-end and pause) or suggest that the subordinate has doubts.

Make the benefits explicit

- Get the subordinate to state the benefits (open-end and pause— "What do you feel you'll gain?" . . . pause).
- Present benefits (for intangible and tangible needs—safety, certainty, less worry, tenure, etc.).

Check for understanding and commitment

- Ask the subordinate to summarize; don't expect too much.
- Summarize goals and plans; state your own commitment.

- Ask him to express any doubts or lack of commitment (open-end and pause).

A LOOK AHEAD

Our next chapter looks at the Q4 strategy for Q3 behavior. Once again, it's decidedly different from either this chapter or the preceding one. Q3 subordinate behavior offers a whole new set of problems and challenges. Let's look at how you can overcome them.

16

The Q4 Appraisal
STRATEGY FOR Q3 SUBORDINATE BEHAVIOR

How do you tailor our Q4 appraisal format to fit subordinate behavior that's mainly Q3? We're ready to get the answer.

Q3 BEHAVIOR: A REMINDER

Let's start by reminding ourselves of the needs that underlie Q3 behavior. In general, Q3 behavior can be accounted for by strong *social* needs, joined to *security* and *esteem* needs. The key needs are social; when they are satisfied, the subordinate feels both more secure and more esteemed. This means that during the appraisal you must:

- Never forget how important *acceptance* is to the subordinate. If you create an accepting climate, he'll be less concerned about himself and freer to concentrate on the appraisal.
- Make sure you are not "soft" about it, however. This subordinate needs (and actually *wants*) guidance and structure. Don't "go along" with him; *lead* him. Provide control, direction, and system.

General Guidelines

1. Stress benefits dealing with social acceptance, security, and esteem.
2. Socialize without getting sucked into the Q3 whirlpool.

261

3. Focus on business while allowing some meandering.
4. Guide firmly; make specific suggestions.
5. Probe the subordinate's enthusiasm and easy yeses; solicit his under- lying doubts.
6. Rely heavily on closed-end questions, summary statements, and re- flective statements.
7. Be prepared to shift your behavior if the subordinate's behavior changes.

Now let's look at some ways to implement these guidelines.

THE Q4 STRATEGY FOR Q3 SUBORDINATE BEHAVIOR

Arouse Interest and Test Receptivity

EXPECT TO SPEND MORE TIME (AT FIRST) SOCIALIZING

This subordinate needs plenty of signals that you like and accept him. So you'll have to spend more time (initially) socializing with this subordinate than with any other; you can't afford to be all briskness and efficiency. Take time to chat briefly and informally.

DON'T GET SUCKED INTO THE "Q3 WHIRLPOOL"

There's a risk here. If you are too unhurried, too unbusinesslike, you'll set a bad tone for the appraisal. Be *appropriately*, not indiscriminately, sociable. Don't get caught in a whirling eddy of conversation. Keep the sociability under *control*.

PRESENT THE PURPOSE OF THE APPRAISAL AND ITS BENEFITS CONCISELY

Don't encourage talkiness. Not with *this* subordinate. She'll be talky enough without help from you. Set an example of *compactness* early in the appraisal. Say what should be said, but say it in the fewest words. Compress your thinking.

INTEGRATE THE PURPOSE WITH BENEFITS THAT FIT THE SUBORDINATE'S PERSONAL NEEDS

This subordinate wants to belong, to be "one of the gang," a "nice guy," a "team player." Make the purpose of the appraisal fit these personal needs. ("If we succeed here today, you'll be able to get even better results next year, and have even higher morale in your department"; "If you can achieve this, you'll make a real contribution to the company and earn the gratitude of a lot of people").

OFFER BENEFITS, IF ANY, THAT FIT HER TANGIBLE NEEDS

If a tangible reward is available, and if this subordinate is a suitable candidate for it, offer it. You'll probably find that what she wants is closely related to her social needs ("I'd sure like to get into outside marketing so I could do public-contact work every day; this being tied down to a desk is driving me crazy"; "I'd really like the assistant manager's job so I could spend more time moving around and working with people; I get sick and tired of being shut in an office all day by myself").

EXPECT MEANDERING, GENERALIZATIONS, EASY "YESES", SURFACE ENTHUSIASM

This subordinate talks a lot and meanders off the subject because that's his way of ingratiating himself; he's vague because he doesn't want to be pinned down to a position he might have to defend (and argue about); he agrees readily and enthusiastically because he wants to go along, to be "in" rather than "out." But this doesn't mean he's receptive. Receptivity is willingness to listen and consider and collaborate; it's willingness to be candid and analytic, and, if necessary, to *dis*agree. So in spite of the subordinate's easygoing manner, you've got a case of *low* receptivity on your hands.

Raise Receptivity and Get the Subordinate's Self-Evaluation

PROBE HER ENTHUSIASM AND AGREEABLENESS; SUGGEST THAT SHE HAS DOUBTS

Find out if she's as enthusiastic about the appraisal as she claims. She's probably not. ("Ellen, you sound completely enthusiastic about this. But . . . as a rule . . . most people have a few qualms about being appraised. How about you? What doubts do *you* have?")

VENT OVERLY POSITIVE EMOTIONS

Positive emotions can interfere with the appraisal just as much as negative ones. If the subordinate wants to express elation, let him ("I can tell you're excited . . .''; "You sure do seem enthusiastic . . ."). Once he's expressed his high spirits, he'll almost surely subside into a more restrained, business-like mood.

CONTROL MEANDERING

This is vital. If you can't get the subordinate to *focus* his attention, you can't control the appraisal. Do this by using closed-end probes. Of course, there's no guarantee that they'll make him stick to the subject. A really talky subordinate can give longwinded answers to any questions, even closed-end questions. Here's an example:

SUPERIOR.   Do you think we'd have been better off if we had projected a 2% increase?

SUBORDINATE.   That's a darned good question . . . a darned good question. Let me answer you by going back to something that happened a few years ago. Give me a minute or two to describe this situation, and I think you'll begin to see why I'm so intrigued by the question you just asked. About three or four years ago, when Ken Alberts had your job . . .

What do you do in a situation like this? Three things: (1) interrupt; (2) explain why you're interrupting; and (3) restate the original closed-end question. For example:

Sam . . . we seem to be straying off the path. A direct answer to the question I just asked would really help both of us. *Do* you think we'd have been better off if we had projected a 2% increase?

You may have to do this several times. Don't give up. Keep on asking closed-end questions until the subordinate gets the idea that this is an *appraisal*, not a gabfest.

AS A LAST RESORT, FOCUS ON THE PROCESS HANG-UP; DON'T BLAME OR CHALLENGE

If you are at the end of your rope and can't bring order and coherence to the appraisal, lay that fact on the line and try to resolve it. Be careful not to blame the subordinate ("Doggone it, Stan, you've been yakking for ten minutes now and we haven't made a bit of progress"). He'll interpret any censure as evidence that "The boss is unhappy with me"; this will drive his receptivity lower. Instead, make a neutral statement of fact

("Stan, I have the feeling that we're trying to cover too many bases at one time, and I'm afraid we're not covering any of them very effectively. Can we shift gears and zero-in on just one topic?"). This should help turn things around. But don't expect it to have a permanent effect. At any moment, the subordinate may start meandering again. If he does, be ready.

ALLOW SOME MEANDERING; DON'T LOSE DIRECTION; GUIDE FIRMLY

Like it or not, you'll have to tolerate some meandering. If you don't permit some detours, you'll only create a tense situation. So let her wander off once in a while if she wants, but keep the meandering to a *minimum*. Again, closed-end questions are your best help.

SUMMARIZE FREQUENTLY TO KEEP IMPORTANT MATTERS IN FOCUS

One good way to stay on track is to boil down what the subordinate says to the fewest possible words; in this way, he may get the message that, in spite of all his talking, he's not really saying much. For example, try something like: "Let me see if I can restate what you've been saying . . ." and then summarize in *one short sentence*. After you do this a few times, he may start to see that there's not much substance behind all his wind. In any event, it'll help keep the appraisal zeroed-in on topics that matter.

Present Your Own Evaluation

BE CONCISE; DON'T CONFUSE THE SUBORDINATE WITH NEEDLESS DETAIL

It's impossible to define "needless detail" precisely. You have to decide what's needed and what's not. In general, any details that aren't required to *prove* a point or to make your evaluation *stand up* are "needless." Why? Because, with this subordinate, they won't serve any purpose. They'll only confuse or bore him. Remember: this subordinate is more concerned about his *relationship* with you than about evidence and documentation. When you talk, he's really listening for signs that you like him. He doesn't require massive substantiation; he requires acceptance. So don't bother with superfluous facts.

CONTRAST YOUR DIFFERENCES

This is touchy. This subordinate doesn't like to hear about disagreements. So, in contrasting his views and yours, don't sound as if you're rejecting *him*, and don't sound as if your differences are *personal*. Here are examples of the wrong way to begin: "Doggone it, Dan, it really bothers me that you don't see this the way I do." "Julie, I don't see how you could take such a short-sighted view of things; let me list all the areas where you and I are miles apart." Make it plain that, as far as you're concerned, the differences are *temporary* and can be *reconciled:* "Jeff, let me list the areas where we presently disagree . . . so we can come back to them later and try to resolve the differences." Don't imply blame or disapproval.

Vent Emotions and Resolve Disagreements

BE READY FOR EASY YESES; THEY MAY HIDE DISAGREEMENT

Don't accept these easy yeses as the real thing just so you can save yourself the trouble of resolving the disagreements buried beneath them. Assume that each yes hides a no. This could be wrong; some of these yeses may be genuine. But the opposite assumption is safer. Start with the premise that beneath each yes is a dissent. Then test out the premise.

GUIDE THE SUBORDINATE FIRMLY THROUGH AN ANALYSIS OF THE CAUSES OF PERFORMANCE DISCREPANCY

Get him to scrutinize his own performance. If you do a good job of this, you should resolve many of your differences. Start out something like this: "Larry, it's obvious that our two evaluations don't agree at every point. I think we can reconcile a number of these differences by taking another close look at your performance and by reexamining the data you came up with in preappraisal. So let me start by asking you this: In the light of everything we've said so far, do you see anything either of us failed to do that might have hindered your performance?" Then keep on probing. The result should be an evaluation that's more thorough and more objective than his initial evaluation. Don't be surprised, however, if you have to make strong suggestions as to how the differences can be resolved.

Work Out the Final Resolution

ASK THE SUBORDINATE TO SUGGEST GOALS AND PLANS; TIE DOWN SPECIFICS WITH CLOSED PROBES

Try something like this: "Barbara, I know you've got some good ideas about where we ought to go from here. So tell me what you think. First of all, what do you think your weekly call ratio should be between January and July?" Make sure each question requires an *explicit* answer.

PRESENT YOUR OWN GOALS AND PLANS, IF DIFFERENT, AND COMPARE
THE TWO SETS

This is your last chance to produce some specific conclusions. If you
haven't been able to pin down your subordinate, you yourself must recommend detailed goals and plans. Be definite; cite particulars; make your
recommendations terse and to-the-point. Then compare yours and his.

ASK THE SUBORDINATE TO SUMMARIZE; EXPECT AN OVERLY GENERAL
SUMMARY AND SURFACE ENTHUSIASM

Be careful. Since the appraisal is almost over, the subordinate may figure
that it's time to relax and chat. Make sure he sticks to business. And don't
be lulled by his surface enthusiasm. Don't settle for good intentions ("I'll
do my best"). Get a specific commitment ("I'll start the reorganization
program on Monday"; "I'll talk to Kelly this week for sure"). If you can't
get him to do an effective summary, summarize the specifics for him.

RECAP

Let's take another look at our general guidelines in the light of the tips
we've just covered:

1. *Stress benefits dealing with social acceptance, security, and esteem.*

Remember: when this subordinate feels he's accepted, then he feels more
secure and more esteemed. So you can fill all three needs, in part, by focusing on the social needs. He isn't especially interested in being a big-shot;
he doesn't want to be left alone. He wants to know that "what's in it" for
him is continued, or increased, acceptance by as many people as possible.

2. *Socialize without getting sucked into the Q3 whirlpool.*

There are two ways to do any appraisal: you can either be a *weather vane*,
shifting with every breeze from the subordinate, or a *compass*, steadily
pointing in one direction. When you appraise someone with strong social
needs, it's very easy to become a weather vane, chatting when he wants
to chat, telling a story in response to one of his stories, wandering off the
main path whenever he starts to stray. Don't let this happen. Take the
compass approach; point yourself toward true north (better performance
results) and make sure *he* follows you.

3. *Focus on business while allowing some meandering.*

The trick is to be genial and accepting and *also* efficient and businesslike. The way to do this is to focus on *business* matters in a *congenial* way. While you'll have to allow some meandering, the greatest part of the appraisal, by far, should zero in on business, but it should do so in an *accepting* manner.

4. *Guide firmly: make specific suggestions.*

This subordinate wants and needs guidance. See that he gets it. Remember: with this subordinate "guidance" means *structured* leadership—leadership that helps him see the *specific* path to follow. His intentions are good, but what he needs are clear plans for following through on his intentions. You'll have to help him discern those clear plans.

5. *Probe the subordinate's enthusiasm and easy yeses; solicit her underlying doubts.*

Don't accept her declarations at face value. Explore them. She's human, after all; she's bound to have some reservations about the appraisal. But she'd rather keep them to herself than express them and maybe "hurt" you. Only diligent probing can overcome this.

6. *Rely heavily on closed-end questions, summary statements, and reflective statements.*

Why? Because *closed-end questions* control meandering. Because *summary statements* help separate the wheat from the chaff. Because *reflective statements* help vent positive emotions and clear the air for business.

7. *Be prepared to shift your behavior if the subordinate's behavior changes.*

Don't be lulled by "nice guy" behavior. It *can* change. Be ready for that if it happens.

SUMMARY

Let's wind up this chapter with a step-by-step outline of the Q4 strategy for Q3 subordinate behavior.

Q4 Strategy for Q3 Subordinate Behavior

1. AROUSE INTEREST AND TEST RECEPTIVITY

   Be appropriately sociable

   - Expect to spend more time (at first) socializing; show sincere warmth.
   - Don't get sucked into a "Q3 whirlpool."

   Arouse interest

   - Present the purpose and benefit concisely.
   - Integrate the purpose with benefits that fit the subordinate's intangible needs (popularity, contact with others, acceptance, etc.).
   - Offer benefits, if any, that fit the subordinate's tangible needs.

   Probe

   - Probe his willingness to proceed (closed-end, yes-no).

   Size up behavior and receptivity

   - Expect meandering, generalizations, easy "yeses," surface enthusiasm.

2. RAISE RECEPTIVITY AND GET THE SUBORDINATE'S SELF-EVALUATION

   Raise receptivity

   - Probe surface enthusiasm and ready agreement; suggest that the subordinate has doubts.
   - Vent overly positive emotions (reflective).
   - Control meandering (closed-end).
   - Reassure with reflective statements ("I know you're concerned that I might disapprove . . . let's focus on that . . .") followed by fact-finding questions.
   - As a last resort, focus on process hang-ups; don't blame or challenge ("We seem to be going in too many directions . . . can we pull this together?").

   Get the subordinate's self-evaluation (while raising receptivity)

   - Ask for her evaluation (start with open-end probes, then focus with neutral and closed-end probes).
   - Allow some meandering; don't lose direction; guide firmly (closed-end).
   - Use frequent summaries to focus relevant topics.
   - Summarize all relevant aspects of the subordinate's evaluation.

3. PRESENT YOUR OWN EVALUATION

- Confirm where you agree with the subordinate's evaluation.
- Be concise; don't confuse him with needless detail.
- Contrast your differences.
- Don't bunch ideas.
- Invite feedback after each point (closed-end, yes-no probes; suggest that the subordinate has doubts).
- Don't let surface agreement fool you.

4. VENT EMOTIONS AND RESOLVE DISAGREEMENTS

Encourage venting of overly positive emotions

- Be ready for overly positive emotions.
- Vent them with reflective statements ("I can see you're happy about this"; "You're really elated, aren't you?").

Resolve disagreements

- Be ready for easy "yeses" which may hide disagreement.
- Ask the subordinate to summarize the disagreements.
- Probe for hidden differences (suggest that there are disagreements, then probe with closed probes; focus on specifics).
- Summarize disagreements.
- Firmly guide her (closed-end probes) through an analysis of the differences.
- Make sure both positions surface and are understood *before* proceeding.
- Don't be fooled by surface agreement.

5. WORK OUT THE FINAL RESOLUTION

Develop goals and action plans

- Guide firmly; develop specifics.
- Ask the subordinate to suggest goals and plans; tie down specifics with closed probes (what, where, when, who, how much, etc.).
- Summarize the essential elements in his suggestions.
- Present your own, if different, and compare the two sets.
- Ask for specific reactions.
- Suggest final goals and plans, expect surface agreement.
- Probe for hidden doubts (closed-end).

Make the benefits explicit

- Get the subordinate to state the benefits ("What do you think you'll gain?"); expect overstatement.
- Probe (closed-end probes) to assure accurate understanding of benefits.
- Present benefits (for tangible and intangible needs—popularity, acceptance, contact with others, etc.).

Check for understanding and commitment

- Ask the subordinate to summarize; expect an overly general summary or surface enthusiasm.
- Don't be lulled by surface enthusiasm; probe for specific commitment.
- Summarize your own understanding of final specific goals and plans.
- Set a review procedure.

A LOOK AHEAD

We're finally ready to look at the Q4 strategy for Q4 subordinate behavior. We do that in our next chapter.

17

The Q4 Appraisal

STRATEGY FOR Q4 SUBORDINATE BEHAVIOR

This chapter tells how to tailor the Q4 appraisal format to fit a subordinate whose behavior is mainly Q4. We'll be brief because we've covered many of the major points elsewhere in the book.

Q4 BEHAVIOR: A REMINDER

Needs for *independence* and *self-realization* underlie Q4 behavior. This means that during an appraisal you must:

- Give your subordinate optimal autonomy. Expect him to exert more initiative than most. He likes taking the lead. So he'll probably need *less* guidance from you than other subordinates will. If he's able to carry the ball without much help, let him. How much freedom you can give, and how much structure he needs, is up to you. Chances are that you'll want to leave plenty of slack in the reins. If you don't, he may force the issue.
- Be prepared for a demanding appraisal. This subordinate expects you to back up your ideas, help him develop himself, and deliver on your promises. If you can't produce evidence to support your evaluation, if

you can't stretch and challenge him, and if you can't show him how your ideas can help him realize himself, you may find yourself in hot water.

General Guidelines

1. Stress benefits dealing with self-realization and independence.
2. Be businesslike and to-the-point, yet avoid flat assertions.
3. Expect full involvement by the subordinate; stay flexible.
4. Use the full range of probes, especially open-end questions and summary statements.
5. Be prepared to shift your strategy if the subordinate's behavior changes.

Now let's look at some of the details.

THE Q4 STRATEGY FOR Q4 SUBORDINATE BEHAVIOR

Arouse Interest and Test Receptivity

STATE A BUSINESSLIKE PURPOSE

A simple, very brief, exchange of civilities is all that's needed. Explain what the appraisal should produce for the subordinate, for the organization, and for yourself: "Carl, if we are successful here today, we should come up with goals and plans for the next half-year that will help you prepare for a possible move to the management committee, that will accelerate company growth, and that will make this division more productive and profitable than it's been since I took over."

USE BENEFITS LIKE: "INNOVATIVE," "NEW," "BETTER"

In explaining the benefits, emphasize the opportunity to try something new or to improve something old, to experiment or innovate, to take on larger responsibility, to participate in a "breakthrough" or to set the pace for competition, and so forth.

EXPECT RECEPTIVITY TO BE HIGH

You'll probably have to spend less time raising the receptivity of this subordinate than of any other. He's probably been looking forward to the appraisal and should be ready to collaborate wholeheartedly. But don't take anything for granted; *test* his receptivity.

Raise Receptivity and Get the Subordinate's Self-Evaluation

ASK FOR THE SUBORDINATE'S SELF-EVALUATION

Since receptivity is likely to be high, you can probably move right into the self-evaluation. Be ready to hear some things you may not like. Expect candor, directness, and full disclosure. This subordinate won't pull punches. So be prepared to take it. But don't expect her to tell you everything you need to know unless you do some probing. Full disclosure rarely happens without give-and-take. So dig for details.

Present Your Own Evaluation

CONFIRM WHERE YOU AGREE AND EXPLAIN WHERE YOU DISAGREE

You don't have to be cautious about it. With this subordinate, you can say what's on your mind in plain English. There's nothing wrong with telling him: "I don't buy this" or "I disagree with you on that."

AVOID FLAT ASSERTIONS

Being straightforward does not mean using flat assertions. "I disagree" is a simple statement of fact. But "You're all wet" or "That's crazy" or "That's the most cockeyed thing I've heard yet" are flat assertions. Be candid, but don't be dogmatic. If you are, you'll only drive down his receptivity ("Why should I knock myself out in this appraisal? He's not even giving me a chance to get through to him").

BE FACTUAL

This subordinate respects facts. He feels comfortable with them because they can be tested and verified. He feels less comfortable with vague, overblown versions of what's been going on. So zero in on what can be validated and substantiated.

Vent Emotions and Resolve Disagreements

ASK THE SUBORDINATE TO EVALUATE THE DIFFERENCES BETWEEN YOU

You'll probably find that she's fairly objective and unemotional. She'll be less defensive, less touchy, than your other subordinates. But that doesn't mean that you won't have to vent any negative feelings. After all, she's human; she may feel hurt or angry or upset over your analysis.

LISTEN CAREFULLY; THEN OFFER YOUR OWN VIEWS

If you do listen carefully, you may change your mind about the differences between you. There is a good chance that the subordinate will marshal solid facts and strong arguments in behalf of her views. If she does, you may want to modify your own. If you don't, then present your views of the differences between you. Again, be direct and be factual.

Work Out the Final Resolution

CONTRAST THE DIFFERENCES

Resolve them and ask the subordinate to summarize. If his behavior is heavily Q4, he'll probably do as much probing at this point as you. The resolution will be worked out through give-and-take and, quite possibly, through Q4 argument. By "Q4 argument" we mean a debate that's free of belligerence and rancor—a debate that's not intended to produce a "winner" and a "loser" but only the *best resolution of your differences*. During this debate, there's a good chance that *both* of you will moderate your positions. That's fine, as long as the end-result is an *optimal* resolution.

RECAP

Let's take one more look at the guidelines with which we started this chapter.

1. *Stress benefits dealing with self-realization and independence.*

Make sure that "what's in it" for the subordinate is a chance to fulfill his potential and assert more autonomy. He wants to become whatever he's got it in him to become. It's up to you to show him how.

2. *Be businesslike and to-the-point, yet avoid flat assertions.*

There is no reason whatever to "play games" with this subordinate. He respects solid, workmanlike appraisal, so be solid in your facts and work-manlike in your approach. Be direct; don't be dogmatic.

3. *Expect full involvement by the subordinate; stay flexible.*

Don't expect him to take a passive role. He's sure to speak out, challenge, question, and if necessary, debate. Keep your own ideas and conclusions flexible, so that what results is synergistic Q4-Q4 interaction.

4. *Use the full range of probes, especially open-end questions and summary statements.*

You'll probably need all kinds of probes, but open-end and summary should prove particularly useful. Why? Because *open-end* questions are the best way to find out what this subordinate thinks and feels, and whatever he thinks and feels is worth hearing. Because *summary statements* are a good way to test your understanding—to make sure that what you've heard and what he means are one and the same.

5. *Be prepared to shift your strategy if the subordinate's behavior changes.*

Don't expect even *this* subordinate to be a paragon. She's a human being. Her behavior can change. Don't let yourself be caught off guard.

SUMMARY

Let's close this chapter by outlining, step by step, the Q4 strategy for Q4 subordinate behavior.

1.   Arouse Interest and Test Receptivity

- State a businesslike purpose.
- Use benefits like: "innovative," "new," "better."
- Probe the subordinate's interest in proceeding.

2.   Raise Receptivity and Get the Subordinate's Self-Evaluation

- Ask for the subordinate's self-evaluation.
- Use appropriate probes to gather information and check understanding.

3.   Present Your Own Evaluation

- Confirm agreements.
- Avoid flat assertions.

- Present and contrast differences.
- Be factual.

4. Vent Emotions and Resolve Disagreements

- Summarize disagreements.
- Ask for the subordinate's reactions and evaluation of differences.
- Explore the causes.
- Offer your own opinions.

5. Work Out the Final Resolution

- Get the subordinate's goals, solutions, plans.
- Offer your own.
- Contrast the differences.
- Resolve the differences and ask the subordinate to summarize.
- Set up a review procedure.

A LOOK AHEAD

We've seen how one format—the Q4 appraisal format—can be adapted to fit any kind of subordinate behavior. That leaves us with one major topic still to be explored: the review session. We do that in our next chapter.

18

Q4 Review

The last step in the Q4 appraisal format is both a review and a preview.
In this step you and the subordinate look back at what he has been doing
since the appraisal session (which probably happened 3 to 6 months
earlier) and you look ahead at what he's going to be doing from now on.
This means that Q4 appraisal never really ends. Each review is more than
a review; it's a prelude to *future* action. So when we talk about the "final"
phase of performance appraisal, we don't mean that it "stops cold" at
that point. Appraisal never stops, because your organization can't afford
to let the growth and development of its people stop.

This is a short chapter, because so much of what happens in a Q4 review
is a briefer repeat of what happened in the Q4 appraisal session. A short
description, then, is all that's needed.

Q4 REVIEW

Prepare

Before the review session, collect data on how well your subordinate is
achieving the job goals you agreed on in the appraisal. Review performance
records. Check your own observations. Determine if he's on target or off,
and by how much. Have him do the same.

Before you object that this is too time-consuming, we'd better repeat something we said in talking about preappraisal: preparing prior to the session, whether it be a regular appraisal session or a review, is far more efficient than coming into the session unprepared and then stumbling around in a hurried search for data. The Q4 approach does take time, but, in cost-benefit terms, it's by far the *least* costly approach.

State Purpose and Benefits

Start the review by explaining its dual purpose: (1) to find out what problems the *subordinate* is having with the plan of action and to develop strategies for overcoming them, and (2) to find out if the *plan* is workable, and to revise it if it's not. In other words, the review focuses on *both* the subordinate *and* the plan of action. If the plan isn't working the fault may lie with the plan, with the subordinate, with you, with the situation, or with a combination of these causes. As always, stress the benefit of the review to the subordinate, and make it plain that you want him to be open and candid with you. (Don't "cop-out" by revising goals downward just to make them easier. This is Q3 surrender or Q2 withdrawal; it has no place in a Q4 review.)

Reconnect

Ask the subordinate to summarize the priorities and the plan of action established in the previous appraisal. Make sure both of you still agree on what the priorities are and on what the subordinate was supposed to do. If there's any disagreement, clear it up by referring to the written record of the last session.

Probe

Next, ask the subordinate how he thinks he's doing. Probe for specifics. For example, if you are a sales manager, you'd want answers to questions like: Is he on schedule in meeting his quota? How many sales calls has he been making? Does the number correspond to the number you agreed on in the appraisal? What happened during his calls on the three target accounts you established? What were the results? Why? What plans has he made for follow-up on these calls?

Don't sound inquisitorial; this isn't a third-degree. And don't ask the questions in a blaming way. For example: say you are a sales manager, and you and your salesperson agreed in the earlier appraisal that he'd increase his daily calls from seven to eleven; so far, he's only increased them from seven to nine. The fault may be his: he may be goofing off, or spending too much time on each call, or otherwise mismanaging his territory. But the fault may also lie in the action plan. Maybe eleven calls each day is unrealistic, maybe nine is the optimal number. This has to be explored, patiently and open-mindedly. You can't do that if you assume that whatever is wrong is the subordinate's fault.

State Your Views

Having heard what your subordinate thinks about her progress, offer your own thinking. Back up your opinions with examples from observation and with recorded data. Give a complete picture. Where praise is merited, praise; where you *yourself* are responsible for problems, admit it.

Compare

Now ask the subordinate to compare the two analyses. Probe to make sure the comparison is candid. Then discuss it and try to agree on what (if anything) should be done differently. The two of you may hammer out improvements in the action plan, change or modify the job goals, or realign priorities. The whole idea is to come up with an up-to-date plan that fits *today's* realities—and *tomorrow's* anticipated realities.

Revise

Finally, agree on a new review date. Like its predecessor, today's action plan is not a document for the ages. It's a *working tool*, that's all. If subsequent experience proves that it doesn't work, then it, too, will have to be revised.

ELIMINATING SURPRISES

One great value of periodic review sessions is that, if they are properly done, they virtually eliminate surprises from the next appraisal session. If reviews do what they are supposed to do, your subordinate can't say, at the next appraisal, "Gee . . . I had no idea you weren't satisfied" or "This comes as a real shock; I thought I was doing great." If you *do* get these reactions during the appraisal, they're a pretty good sign that you've pulled your punches (Q3) or gone through the motions (Q2) in the review sessions.

CONCLUSION

A few chapters back, we said that Q4 appraisal is scientific appraisal. This chapter on review proves it.

A couple of centuries ago David Hume, an English thinker who helped develop the modern scientific method, made a point that every superior ought to keep in mind. So far as we know, he said, the sun has risen every morning in the past. But that doesn't *guarantee* that it will rise tomorrow morning. If you want to know *for sure* that the sun will rise tomorrow morning, you'll have to wait until tomorrow morning and then observe it. What has happened in the past can never give you scientific certainty about what is going to happen next. That can only come through observation of what actually does happen.

What has this got to do with performance appraisal? Everything. The fact that you and your subordinate agree that you've developed sound goals and plans doesn't *guarantee* anything. If you want to know *for sure* whether the goals and plans are working out, you have to observe them *in action*. That is what the review session is for. It enables you to take stock of what's actually going on.

We make this point because it's very easy—and very tempting—to forget about the review session, to assume that everything must be going well and that there is really no need to do a review. Don't get caught in this trap. This is the *non*scientific way. The scientific way is to *take nothing for granted*.

A LOOK AHEAD

The time has come to tie all the ideas in this book together, to attempt one final summary of Q4 appraisal. We do that in our next chapter.

19

The Q4 Appraisal

A SUMMARY

Now that we've explained how to do Q4 appraisal, it might help to summarize our major points in a few short, easy-to-remember rules. We'll list 10 major points, then comment on each. In so doing we'll touch upon and tie together all the major themes of this book.

1. Do systematic preappraisal.
2. Start with firm, but not fixed, ideas.
3. Get your subordinate to collaborate.
4. Take enough time.
5. Be supportive.
6. Expect problems.
7. Don't expect total agreement.
8. Aim at realistic growth.
9. Set goals that stretch the subordinate.
10. Review.

Let's examine each point, and, at the same time, summarize the basic ideas of this book.

DO SYSTEMATIC PREAPPRAISAL

We'll say it one last time: unless you and your subordinate do systematic preappraisal, you can't do Q4 appraisal. There is no other way to appraise performance scientifically.

Why bother to appraise performance scientifically? Because the scientific approach is more *efficient*. It costs less in time and frustration. It pays off.

The scientific approach to doing anything—from appraising performance to analyzing pollutants—consists of four steps: (a) recognizing that a problem exists and determining what that problem is; (b) observing facts that seem to be related to the problem; (c) formulating a hypothesis, an educated guess about the causes of the problem; and (d) testing the hypothesis to see whether it's a valid explanation or a phony one. The *first three* steps should be carried out—by *both* you and your subordinate—*before* the face-to-face appraisal.

Nothing is easier than to find reasons for *not* doing preappraisal, or for doing "quickie" preappraisal. Any superior can come up with plenty of alibis: "We're too busy on crash projects right now; we can't take the time to do all that preappraisal research"; "It isn't necessary; both of us carry the necessary facts in our heads"; "There's no need to make a big deal out of it; in 10 or 15 minutes before the appraisal, I can cram in all the facts I have to remember"; and so on. But when we talk about scientific preappraisal, we're not talking about "cramming" for 10 or 15 minutes. We're talking about systematic study and research that may take several *hours* of your time and of your subordinate's.

If you are still skeptical about this, take another look at the charts and procedures covered in our preappraisal planning chapter. Then ask yourself two questions: Would I really prefer to go into an appraisal session *without* having done this analysis? Can I go through these procedures in a *serious* way in 10 or 15 minutes? The answer to both questions must be: "No . . . not if I want the appraisal to pay off."

There is another question, however, that must be answered before you decide that you can dispense with scientific preappraisal: "Do I really have *anything* more important to do than help this subordinate turn in the best possible performance?" If the answer is *no* (and it *should* be no, because as a superior, your primary responsibility is to see to it that your subordinate does do the best possible job), then there is no good reason for not doing systematic preappraisal.

START WITH FIRM, BUT NOT FIXED, IDEAS

If you do systematic preappraisal, you should come into the appraisal session with firm, but not fixed, ideas. Let's examine both phrases: *firm* and *not fixed*.

Firm. A firm idea is an idea based on solid evidence. One reason for doing systematic preappraisal is that it helps you uncover solid evidence about your subordinate's performance. So you should have good *reasons* for holding whatever ideas you start out with in the appraisal session.

Not fixed. A firm idea is not an unchangeable idea. It's an idea which, although based on solid evidence, will be changed if it's disproved by other evidence. Begin every appraisal with hypotheses, not fixed ideas. Subject the hypotheses to testing; check them out, see if you've overlooked contradictory evidence, see if you've misinterpreted the original evidence.

This insistence upon checking out ideas and discarding those that don't stand up under examination is what we mean by Q4 openness. When we call Q4 behavior open, we mean that it is open to *all* the facts, not just convenient ones. And it is open to all the facts even if they prove the superior wrong. In Q4 appraisal the superior says: "Look, what really counts is learning the truth about my subordinate's performance. Whether I'm right or wrong is not at issue. What *is* at issue is how effectively my subordinate is performing, and how I can help her perform more effectively."

GET YOUR SUBORDINATE TO COLLABORATE

Throughout this book, we've insisted repeatedly that Q4 appraisal is synergistic collaboration. We mean this literally. The precise definition of *collaborate* is *to work together.* It comes from a couple of old Latin words meaning *to labor together.* So synergistic collaboration isn't just casual cooperation; it isn't just any work. It is working *hard* toward the same goal—and doing it in a way that produces *better* results than you or your subordinate could produce on your own.

To do Q4 appraisal, then, you must do several things:

1. *Get your subordinate to do thorough preappraisal research.*

There's no reason why he shouldn't work as hard at this as you. If it makes sense for you to spend several hours getting ready for the appraisal, it makes sense for him, too.

2. *Keep him involved during the appraisal session.*

Never let him sit on his hands and "just listen." Find out what he knows; get him to voice his opinions; encourage him to debate with you if he thinks you're wrong. Make him work and work hard.

3. *Listen at a thinking level.*

Don't expect him to collaborate with you unless you pay attention to what he says and give it serious consideration.

4. *Master the concept of receptivity.*

If you can't recognize low receptivity, if you don't know how to spin it up, if you don't know how to keep it high once it's been spun up, you can't get him involved. If you can't manage low receptivity, you can't do Q4 appraisal.

5. *Become a skilled prober.*

Getting a subordinate to work hard during an appraisal requires hard work on your part. Probing is hard work. It demands diligent (and tiring) listening, it demands close attention to the subordinate's behavior and intelligent interpretation of that behavior, and it demands careful planning and phrasing of every question and every statement. Unless you can do all of this, you can't do Q4 appraisal because you can't get your subordinate to collaborate.

To summarize: If you and your subordinate collaborate, if you work hard toward the same goals, and if you do it in the way we've recommended in this book, the two of you should *synergize:* produce something extra, something special, that you could not have produced without collaboration.

TAKE ENOUGH TIME

We've said that preappraisal is time consuming. Now we'll add that the appraisal session is also time consuming. Unless you take the time to do the job right, you can't do Q4 appraisal. This is hard for many superiors to accept. They keep thinking that there must be some short cut, some more direct route to Q4 results than the one we've laid out. There isn't. Like it or not, Q4 appraisal takes time, frequently several hours.
This means three things:

1. If you can't devote several hours to the appraisal because you are really under severe pressure to get something else done, reschedule the appraisal. Don't squeeze it in between a panic and an emergency.
2. Don't try to do something else at the same time. When we talk about the appraisal taking several hours, we mean several *uninterrupted*

hours. Don't even *think* about doing an appraisal if you expect intrusions from your secretary, phone calls, or recurring crises.

3.   Don't let on, during the appraisal, that you are eager to get it done with. Nothing will discourage collaboration more than some sign of impatience from you. Don't fidget. Don't look restless. Make it plain to the subordinate that you have *nothing more important to do* than this appraisal.

BE SUPPORTIVE

Before she collaborates, a subordinate must believe that "nothing I say will be used against me." She must believe that you have her best interests at heart. She must, in brief, *trust* you.

We won't repeat what we said earlier about building a trustful, win-win climate. We'll only say this: it's foolish to expect a subordinate to work hard during an appraisal if the only reward she can expect is a bawling out or disinterest or platitudes. Again and again, we've seen that the question that keeps recurring to people is: "What's in it for me?" And that is the question any subordinate is going to ask herself *before* she starts to level with you: "If I tell him what I really think . . . if I cooperate . . . if I candidly share my ideas . . . what will I get out of it?"

Because she *is* asking these questions, there are two things *you* must do:

1.   Master the $J + N{\rightarrow}B{\rightarrow}P$ concept, and *use* it. State the benefit *early* in the appraisal, and keep it in the forefront *throughout*. Don't let your subordinate lose sight of "What's in it for me."

2.   Master the trust-building skills we described earlier. Let the subordinate know that: "We're on the same side. I want you to get what you want out of this appraisal. I want it to work to your benefit. I want all of us—you, me, the organization—to come out winners."

EXPECT PROBLEMS

Few things are rarer than a problem-free appraisal. Maybe someday you'll do a Q4 appraisal that goes off without a hitch, but it's much more likely that you'll encounter *some* trouble, *some* hang-ups, in *every* appraisal.

Why? Because you are appraising the performance of human beings. And, as we said early in this book, human beings are sensitive to, and anxious about, any evaluation or criticism of their performance. Furthermore, because they're human, their performance probably leaves something to be desired. So here's the situation:

1.   If you are doing candid Q4 appraisal, you'll probably *have to* make some negative points about the subordinate's performance during the appraisal.
2.   If he is being candid in return, he'll probably voice some disagreement or displeasure. If he is not being candid, he'll probably suppress his real feelings and pretend that he agrees. Either way, *you've got problems.*

DON'T EXPECT TOTAL AGREEMENT

Everything we've just said implies two things:

1.   Expect some argument or some game playing in any appraisal. Learn how to deal with these responses (through probing)—but don't kid yourself that you can always eliminate them. Sometimes you can; sometimes you can't. Sometimes you can resolve all argument and dissolve all deception; sometimes you have to accept a certain residue that just won't go away.
2.   Don't insist upon total capitulation or "unconditional surrender." This is the Q1 way; it has no place in Q4 appraisal. Reconcile yourself to the fact that you may have to "live with" a certain amount of disagreement and disgruntlement. (Whether or not living with it is a good decision, and whether or not it would be better to hire somebody else, are matters for you to decide.) All we're saying is that many successful appraisals end without absolute agreement.

AIM AT REALISTIC GROWTH

One of the most important judgments you have to make during the appraisal is where your subordinate belongs on the *self-discovery continuum*. In fact, everything you do during the appraisal should be conditioned by two factors:

1.   The subordinate's behavior. We've described at length the different ways in which the basic Q4 format can be tailored to fit different subordinate behaviors. Very early in the appraisal, you must size up the subordi-

nate's behavior and adapt the basic Q4 strategy to it. At any time during the appraisal, you must be prepared for shifts in the subordinate's behavior, and modify yours accordingly.

2.   At the same time, you must ask yourself: "If I do the necessary guiding and probing, does this subordinate have what it takes to figure out her performance problems for herself? Can she do the necessary thinking and analyzing? Is she able to develop insight into her shortcomings?" If the answers are all no, then you'll have no choice but to *tell* her what she can't discover on her own.

It comes down to this: Q4 appraisal takes each subordinate for what she is. It recognizes that some subordinates don't have the intellectual skills needed to puzzle out certain matters, some have "blind spots" that prevent their seeing certain truths, some are too stubborn or too afraid to do a good job of examining their own performance. So, when all is said and done, you may have to lay it on the line and say: "Here's the way it is . . . and here's the way it must be." If you do this with every subordinate, that's Q1 appraisal. But if you do it only after you've accumulated convincing evidence that it is necessary, it's Q4 behavior. That's what we mean by Q4 *flexibility:* behavior that responds to the evidence at hand.

SET GOALS THAT STRETCH THE SUBORDINATE

Your job is to help your organization grow. *Grow* doesn't necessarily mean get bigger. It may mean *do things better* or *increase profits* or *outclass competition* or something else besides increase in size. But however your organization defines growth, it is not likely to get it unless its people *stretch.*

When a subordinate stretches, he taps unused potential. He does things better than before, maybe even better than he thought he could. Stretching is the use of dormant, and perhaps unrecognized, ability.

The goals that come out of Q4 appraisal should require stretching. You can't do Q4 appraisal unless you keep in mind everything we said earlier about goals and motivation. Only *challenging* goals stretch (why bother exerting yourself for a goal that isn't challenging?). And only those goals that are optimally difficult are challenging. To repeat what we've already said at length: extremely difficult goals discourage effort; snap goals discourage effort. Goals that require realistic exertion stretch.

But that is not all. Stretching requires more than challenging goals; it requires *relevant* goals. This brings us back to $J + N \rightarrow B \rightarrow P$. The only way to show that a goal is relevant is to tie it to the subordinate's needs.

When the subordinate asks himself: "Why should I work hard to meet this goal?" the answer should be: "Because if I do, I'll get something that *I* want as well as something that's good for the organization."

This doesn't mean that the subordinate's needs should govern what the goal will be. Not once in this book have we suggested anything like that. The organization's needs must govern what the goal will be. But the organization's needs, expressed as job goals, must be related to the subordinate's needs. That's where you and your Q4 skills come in. It's up to you to do the relating.

REVIEW

Strictly speaking, a subordinate should *always* know how he is doing on the job. That is why periodic reviews are so important. They *keep* the subordinate posted on his progress. As such, they are one of management's most important control tools. Properly done, they eliminate surprise from the appraisal session.

So resist the temptation to skip reviews. Nothing is easier to put off, or to omit entirely. Don't do it. If you do, you may find yesterday's goals becoming today's irrelevancies.

CONCLUSION

Q4 appraisal is hard work. That is why no one has yet written (or will write) a book titled "Six Easy Steps to Q4 Appraisal" or "A Quickie Guide to Q4 Appraisal." As we've said throughout, there are no short cuts to effective performance appraisal. The Q4 way is hard work. *At the very least,* to do Q4 appraisal you must first learn:

1. How to size up behavior—your own and each of your subordinates'.
2. How to motivate performance by tying job goals to your subordinate's tangible and intangible needs.
3. How to set job goals—business and behavioral—that get subordinates to stretch.
4. How to size up receptivity, and how to spin it up if low.
5. How to probe.
6. How to listen.
7. How to generate dialogue.
8. How to make your ideas understandable and persuasive.
9. How to build trust.

10. How to plan the content and process of the appraisal.
11. How to use the basic Q4 appraisal format during the appraisal.
12. How to tailor the format to fit the behavior of each of your subordinates.

None of this is easy. But none of it is impossible, either. In fact, every skill on this list can be *learned*. None of these skills is inborn or inherent. None of them depends upon having a special "gift" or "talent." Every one of them can be learned. Once learned, every one of them can be mastered. Once mastered, they'll produce better results for your organization, for your subordinates, and for you yourself.*

Q4 appraisal is hard work, but it's worth it.

A SUGGESTION

Now that you have come this far, you will probably be both entertained and instructed if you *go back* to Chapter 3 and respond, once again, to the questionnaire in that chapter. When you first rated yourself against the items in the questionnaire, you did so without having read our chapters on benefits, receptivity, probing, communication, goal-setting, trust-building, or appraisal. Now that you have read these chapters, you may find that you see yourself—as an appraiser—differently than you saw yourself at the start of the book. The surest way to find out is to rate yourself against the questionnaire one more time. By comparing the "before" and "after" ratings, you'll be able to tell if your self-perception has changed during the reading of this book, and how much. You'll probably find (at least we suspect you will) that your view of yourself is now more realistic and less Q4. If it is, the way to change that view into one that is both realistic *and* Q4 is to practice the skills we've described in this book. (See Appendix C for a way to start this practice.) In any event, a retake of the questionnaire should be enlightening; it's sure to be interesting. We urge you to try it.

A LOOK AHEAD

We have said that Q4 appraisal starts and ends with benefits, so it makes sense that a book about Q4 appraisal should start and end the same way. We began this book by talking about the benefits of effective performance appraisal; in our final chapter, we take one last look at these benefits in the light of everything we have said since the first chapter.

---

* For information about a proven way to learn—and begin mastering—Q4 appraisal skills, see Appendix C.

20

The Q4 Benefit Package

We began this book by pointing out that appraisal has evolved over 60 centuries from a technique for computing material value (as practiced by the Sumerians) to a technique for computing and then *increasing* human value (as practiced by modern organizations). The Sumerians appraised in order to find out what things were worth; we appraise in order to find out what performance is worth and how to make it worth *more*. That is the ultimate benefit of Q4 appraisal: it enhances people's value—to themselves, to you, to your organization.

In enhancing people's value, Q4 appraisal delivers a number of other benefits. Taken together, these make up what we call the *Q4 benefit package*. In this, our final chapter, we look at the components of that package.

Benefit 1. *Q4 appraisal puts the subordinate face-to-face with reality*

It gets him to look at his overall performance—the good aspects, the bad, the average ones. It doesn't overemphasize negatives (as Q1 appraisal does) or positives (as Q3 appraisal does). It doesn't ignore issues (as Q2 appraisal does). It presents a full, thorough, candid picture.

For this reason Q4 appraisal rarely makes the subordinate feel comfortable, at ease, or contented. To the contrary, it often makes him feel tense and uncomfortable. Why? Because looking at reality is frequently a painful, or at least discomfiting, experience. It's no fun to see your performance as it's *really* been, and to become aware of what it *might* have been. It's no picnic to realize that you need to *change,* and that the change is going to be hard work. It's no pleasure to discover that because of your performance, you've lost out on benefits that could have been yours. Yet this awareness, unpleasant as it is, is a prerequisite to growth and development.

Q4 appraisal, then, generates *constructive tension*—the kind of tension that leads to a resolve to *do something* to eliminate the tension. It stimulates *creative discontent*—the kind of discontent that produces a determination to *change* the situation. Make no mistake about it: a Q4 appraisal is more likely to produce self-dissatisfaction than self-congratulation. But that is good. Self-dissatisfaction frequently leads to improvement. Self-congratulation frequently leads to stagnation.

Benefit 2.   *Q4 appraisal treats each subordinate as an individual*

In an era when many people feel like "numbers on a keypunch card" (and resent it), Q4 appraisal insists on treating each subordinate as an individual, with her own needs, concerns, and aspirations. There is nothing mechanical about a Q4 appraisal; although we've talked in this book about "formats" and "formulas," we've repeatedly insisted that these must always be adapted and modified to fit the person being appraised. Q4 appraisal is flexible and responsive, because only flexibility and responsiveness can take account of the idiosyncracies, mannerisms, habits, preoccupations, worries, doubts, and fears of individual subordinates in individual situations.

This means that even though a subordinate comes out of a Q4 appraisal feeling constructively tense, she'll also come out of it feeling deeply satisfied that her individuality has been respected. Whatever else may have happened during the appraisal, at least it was directed to *her* as a special, unique person.

Benefit 3.   *Q4 appraisal respects the integrity of each subordinate*

Let's not kid ourselves: *any* knowledge and *any* skill can be used manipulatively. Any or all of the techniques and insights taught in this book can be used in a Q1 way: to exploit, take advantage of, undermine the subordinate. But that is not the Q4 way.

Q4 appraisal is respectful appraisal. Even if the subordinate's performance has been bad, the subordinate *himself* is treated with dignity and consideration. Nobody ever leaves a Q4 appraisal feeling "used." If he does, it hasn't been a Q4 appraisal.

The whole purpose of the techniques and insights taught in this book is (a) to help the subordinate benefit from his job and (b) to help the organization benefit from his performance. As long as both aims are kept in mind, as long as benefit to the organization is linked to benefit to the subordinate, the appraisal will be respectful, not manipulative.

Q4 appraisal respects the integrity of the subordinate in another way: it never tries to *remake* him in the image of what the superior *thinks* he should be. In fact, it doesn't try to remake the *subordinate* at all. The aim of Q4 appraisal is to *improve performance,* not to change people. It may, indeed, help people to mature and grow. But it doesn't try to force growth on anybody. That's the whole point of the self-discovery continuum. The continuum recognizes that different individuals have different capacities to change and grow. The Q4 approach seeks optimal realization of each person's capacity. It does not try to ramrod change. And that is what respect for the integrity of the subordinate is all about.

Benefit 4.   *Q4 appraisal is efficient*

In the short run, it's true, Q4 appraisal may take more time than other types. But, in the long run, Q4 appraisal promotes efficiency. How? (1) By developing some subordinates (not all) who become capable of discovering their performance deficiencies for themselves; as a result, they become more self-directed and less dependent on you. (2) By promoting candor, thereby eliminating many of the communication barriers and much of the game playing that waste so much time and money. (3) By providing clearer, more realistic goals, so that effort is directed at sensible, achievable targets, instead of being squandered.

Benefit 5.   *Q4 appraisal produces synergism*

In plain English, *synergism* simply means that by collaborating, people get better results for a given amount of effort than they'd get if they expended the *same* amount of effort but didn't collaborate. In other words, in synergism, *collaboration makes a difference*—and the difference is always a plus. That is why we've stressed the fact that Q4 appraisal is collaborative . . . or, as we put it in our last chapter, *synergistic collaboration.* Collaboration is more than a mere process; it's a way of getting a *dividend,* a *bonus.*

Why does Q4 collaboration produce synergism? Because two people who collaborate spur one another to greater achievement. The cross-fertilization of ideas, the rubbing together of viewpoints, the pyramiding of one idea on top of another, all of this requires people *working together*. This is what happens in Q4 appraisal.

Benefit 6.   *Q4 appraisal improves the organizational climate*

How does it do this? By impressing upon subordinates that they *count for something*. One of the messages that comes across to subordinates in Q4 appraisal is: "My ideas matter. I *can* get through to the boss . . . I *can* have some impact around here. I'm not a cipher . . . not a nonentity. I'm somebody who's listened to—who's actually encouraged to speak out and contribute." This message, regularly reinforced in periodic appraisals and in review sessions, does much to create a climate in which a broad range of human resources is tapped and used.

Benefit 7.   *Q4 appraisal enhances people's value—to themselves, to you, to the organization*

This is the ultimate benefit in the Q4 benefit package. By stimulating optimal performance toward optimal goals, Q4 appraisal actually makes the work that people do *worth more*. And that is what your job, in the last analysis, is all about. Every superior has one overriding goal: to get optimal results from people—to see to it that people produce the value they are capable of producing. By itself, of course, Q4 appraisal can't do this. But *without* Q4 appraisal, it is very unlikely that your other managerial efforts can do it either. Q4 appraisal is an indispensable ingredient in the managerial mix.

If you still remain to be convinced, try it—and see for yourself.

Transcript of
a Q4 Appraisal

The following is a "transcript" of a *fictitious* appraisal between a superior using a Q4 strategy and a subordinate using mostly a Q1 strategy. The transcript has two purposes: (1) to tie together many of the recommendations in the book and to show you how these recommendations might actually "sound" in an appraisal, and (2) to give you an example longer than any we included in the text of what a Q4 strategy is like. To help you connect the transcript with the points we discussed in the text, we've provided a running commentary.

Two points about the transcript should be made clear: (1) It is not complete; a full transcript would be much longer. As we said in the text, Q4 appraisals sometimes run several hours. While the transcript is by no means complete, however, we think it provides a good idea of what is likely to happen in Q4 appraisal and how it might sound. (2) We have tried to make the appraisal realistic, so the behavior is not "pure" Q4. The commentary makes the shifts in behavior clear. We have not tried nor have we wanted to create a perfect "hero." We have tried to portray two genuine human beings.

The superior in the appraisal, Ed, is President of Transcon Corporation; the subordinate, Harry, is Vice-President of Sales.

ED.   How's it going, Harry?

At the outset Ed is setting an appropriately sociable tone.

HARRY.   Busier than Hell . . . and I imagine that's a busy place. Lew Emerson's flying in this morning . . . got a meeting scheduled for one o'clock. Should be a knock-down, drag-out battle.

Harry's gruff, self-important manner is typical of Q1 behavior. People with strong esteem needs often make it a point to say how busy they are, and they often see their relations with others in terms of "battle."

ED.   (Interestedly) Sounds as if you expect some fur to fly . . . huh?

HARRY.   (With considerable self-assurance; he's obviously a man who knows his authority.) Only if Lew insists on it. The guy's (this is said with a tincture of fondness) so doggoned stubborn that we usually end up screaming at one another. And today . . . I suspect . . . he'll probably throw a real tantrum.

Notice the lack of insight. According to Harry, it's *Lew's* fault that they end up screaming at one another. There's no suggestion that Harry himself may be part of the problem.

ED.   Why? What's coming up today?

Up to now Ed has shown interest by using two probes to get information from Harry. This is a good way to deal with strong esteem needs.

HARRY.   Today he's got to explain why sales in the South-Central region have plummeted so badly. And . . . if I know Lew . . . he'll rave and rant and try to obscure the whole issue.

ED.   Sounds like you're gonna have your hands full. (He smiles) Good luck. Speaking for myself, I'd rather have a drink with Lew . . . any day . . . than a business discussion. (The smile disappears. His manner changes as he shifts gears. It becomes more brisk, and he takes on a let's-get-down-to-business note.) Well . . . since you'll be tied up with Lew this afternoon, we'd better get on with the appraisal.

This is the point at which the "appropriate sociability" comes to an end. Ed is obviously in control, steering the discussion in the direction he wants it to go.

HARRY.   (Confidently. He is obviously not worried about what's coming.) Let's get on with it.

The brisk, cocksure response is typically Q1.

ED. Harry, I know you want to make Transcon number one in sales in the industry . . . and I know you want to become the industry's marketing pacesetter. I think today's appraisal should move you closer to both goals.

> This is a clear-cut statement of benefit. Ed has phrased "what's in it" in terms that are sure to appeal to Harry's tangible and intangible needs: to be recognized as number one, to be a pacesetter for the entire industry, and so forth.

HARRY. (Matter-of-factly) Sounds good. In fact, we're well on our way to the number one spot. Things look great.

> Notice the build-up, the insistence that things *already* "look great." This is typical Q1 self-congratulation.

ED. (He pulls several sheets of paper from the folder on the desk and arranges them in front of him on the desk. At the same time, Harry pulls several sheets from *his* folder, and arranges them on his lap. He looks comfortable and unruffled as Ed starts to speak.) That's what we're here to talk about. Harry, we've both had a chance to do some preliminary analysis . . . so why don't you start by telling me what you've come up with on your appraisal form? Then I'll do the same . . . and then we can compare our evaluations.

> A good Q4 beginning. Ed asks Harry for his self-evaluation, giving him an opportunity to present his views first.

HARRY. Better yet, Ed . . . in the interest of expediting things . . . why don't we forget about the form and just *talk* about our analyses? A lot of the stuff on this form is irrelevant anyway, and it'll just slow us down.

> This is a standard Q1 comeback. The implication is that Harry knows a "better way" to conduct the appraisal than the one Ed has proposed. This is a subtle put-down of Ed, and a not-so-subtle way of saying that "I'm too busy to take the time to do it your way." It's also a sign that Harry's receptivity is *not* particularly high. What Harry is saying is: "I'm not really ready to proceed in the way *you* want."

ED. (Interestedly.) Which "stuff" . . . precisely . . . do you feel is irrelevant?

> Instead of losing his "Q4 cool," Ed responds with a probe. This is essential if he's going to spin up receptivity.

HARRY.   (Shifting ground slightly.) Irrelevant may be the wrong word. It's not that the form is irrelevant so much as it's *cumbersome*. We'll be here all morning going through this thing . . . and that's not necessary. As a matter of fact, Ed, I can summarize our whole situation . . . and my performance . . . in less than a minute.

> Notice how a probe can clarify a previous statement. Harry now says that he didn't really mean what he said a moment ago. "Irrelevant" has now become "cumbersome." Also notice the Q1 smugness: "I can summarize our whole situation in less than a minute."

ED.   (In a willing tone of voice.) Go ahead. Let's hear what you think . . . then we can talk about it.

> Ed continues to probe to learn what's on Harry's mind and to raise receptivity.

HARRY.   That's the whole point. There isn't really much to talk about. You know my feelings about performance appraisal . . . a guy's either doing the job he's supposed to do . . . or he's not. If he's doing the job, there's no need to drag out the appraisal. Just let him go back to work. If he's not doing the job, then he's got to be straightened out. Either way, there's no point in bureaucratizing what's really a very simple process.

> This is a standard Q1 response. According to Harry, everything is very simple. Someone's either doing good work or bad work. If he's doing bad work, the boss has to straighten him out. Any other approach is "bureaucratizing." Notice how Harry has put a negative label on the whole idea of performance appraisal.

ED.   (He asks the question in a low-key but interested way.) You consider our appraisal system "bureaucratic." Is that it?

> Ed responds with a summary statement, followed by a closed-end question.

HARRY.   (After pausing a few seconds to think.) Not exactly. Not at lower levels anyway. A lot of people in the organization need very careful structuring . . . and I think this system provides it. But . . . when it comes to you and me . . . I think we ought to dispense with this format and just have a good, brief, man-to-man talk.

> As often happens, a summary statement gets the other person to modify his flat assertions. Harry has now slightly backed off from his dogmatic position. But . . . in good, Q1 fashion . . . he insists that *he* doesn't need appraisal—only *other* people do. His receptivity is still not high.

ED.   Why *brief?*

Ed refuses to argue. He continues to probe and to let Harry speak his piece.

HARRY.   You're missing my point. I think we can have a brief talk because there's not really that much to talk about. We're meeting our major goals . . . both of us know that. We have some problems at a secondary level . . . nothing monumental . . . and we'll get them ironed out in time. But the *major* goal . . . the really significant goal . . . is well under control—and things are going extremely well. I'm not suggesting that we get cocky and start to rest on our laurels . . . but I *am* saying that we've got a six-month record we can be proud of. (He pauses a second, then smiles.) See . . . I told you I could appraise my performance in less than a minute.

This speech has all the earmarks of Q1 behavior. It's loaded with flat assertions; it puts the speaker in the best possible light; it plays down failure and talks up achievements; and it's arrogant.

ED.   Let me see if I've got this straight. You're saying . . . as I understand it . . . that *all* objectives are being achieved?

Summary statement.

HARRY.   No . . . that's not exactly what I said. I said our *major* objective is being achieved. And . . . let's face it . . . the major objective is what really counts.

ED.   I see. You're dividing your objectives into one major one and several minor ones . . . or into primary and secondary objectives. Right?

Summary statement followed by closed-end question.

HARRY.   Right. Exactly. And the primary one . . . to use your word . . . is being met very readily. That's why I think we've got every reason to be proud of our six-month record.

Notice how Ed has used several summary statements to get Harry to clarify his position.

ED.   Well . . . before we get into *that* . . . maybe we'd better define our terms. You're talking about major and minor goals . . . but, according to the way I analyzed things on *my* analysis form, I've listed five major goals that we agreed on in our last appraisal . . . and no minor ones. Why don't you explain which goal you consider major . . . and which ones minor.

Once again, Ed doesn't argue. Instead, he refers back to the record and then asks Harry where he disagrees. Not once has Ed done anything to threaten Harry's sense of esteem, which would only drive his receptivity down further.

HARRY.   (A bit impatiently; there's a hint of exasperation in his voice.) C'mon Ed . . . you know what I'm talking about as well as I do. *Sure* . . . we agreed on five goals at our last appraisal . . . but *one* of those five came *first*. The rest are subsidiary.

Harry is obviously feeling somewhat frustrated. When Q1 behavior is frustrated, it commonly becomes *more* Q1: more intense, more assertive, more insistent.

ED.   (Unperturbed.) Hang on, Harry. That's exactly what I'm trying to clarify. I've always considered all five of those goals *equal* in importance. In fact . . . as far as I can see . . . they're interrelated, and that's how I treated them on this preliminary analysis sheet. Maybe I'm wrong. If I am, I want to find out. That's why I'm trying to get you to spell out which of the goals you consider primary . . . and why.

Ed senses that Harry's receptivity has dropped; his mind seems more closed than ever. So he continues to probe, hoping thereby to spin the receptivity up. Probing rarely produces "instant" success.

HARRY.   (Somewhat mollified.) Okay . . . as far as I'm concerned . . . the number one goal is to increase new business. Right now, the other goals . . . all of which have to do with controls . . . come second. That doesn't mean they're not important . . . and I'm not saying that. It just means that they don't have the same priority . . . they're not as urgent. Our top priority . . . for the present . . . is to increase volume. Will you buy that?

Sensing Ed's persistent interest, Harry's receptivity rises a bit. He begins to explain his thinking in somewhat more moderate terms. He uses fewer flat assertions. And he even concludes with a question, indicating at least some willingness to have a dialogue about the matter.

ED.   No . . . at least not at the moment. Maybe I will after I've heard the rest of your analysis. But right now I still think you've got five equally significant . . . and urgent . . . goals.

Ed has made a mistake here. In responding to Harry's question, he is disagreeing with him. He should have responded with another probe, asking Harry why he *should* buy his thinking. Instead, Ed has voiced a dissent.

HARRY. (Obviously irritated.) For crying out loud! Are you gonna sit there and tell me that we ought to drop the ball on sales and start devoting our energies to budgeting? (His annoyance is very plainly showing.) You're dead wrong about that, Ed . . . dead wrong. That contradicts everything I've been trying to do for the last two years. Budgets don't mean a blasted thing unless volume is increasing. And I say (very agitatedly) we've got to keep on pushing for more volume . . . until this organization gets to the point where it eats, drinks, and breathes *new business*.

Ed is now paying for his mistake. He has diminished Harry's esteem, and driven his receptivity to a new low. Notice how Harry has begun to make flat assertions again. Ed has obviously provoked something he didn't want: an outburst of temper.

ED. (Unruffled.) You feel strongly about this . . . don't you, Harry.

This is the right response to use with someone who's displaying strong emotions: a reflective statement.

HARRY. (Vehemently.) Sure I feel strongly about it. I've staked my heart, soul, and guts on getting new business . . . and I've succeeded. Now I'm being told that I was wrong to invest so much of myself in upping our volume. Well . . . I think that's wrong . . . and it deliberately over-looks what I've done around here.

Harry is venting. Notice how his indignation seems to be building up to a peak.

ED. (In a low, but intensely interested, key.) As you see it, then, I'm telling you that your emphasis on new business is misplaced . . . is that it?

Ed's summary statement, like his previous reflective statement, is evidence of his strong interest in getting Harry's concerns out in the open.

HARRY. (Subsiding somewhat.) You haven't *said* that, Ed . . . but I think you're implying it. Or at least you're *going* to imply it before this appraisal is over. Right?

Harry is beginning to moderate his tone. Note his use of qualified statements instead of absolute statements, and his question at the end. All this is a sign that his bad feelings are dissipating and his receptivity is rising.

ED. Harry . . . that's exactly what we're here to determine. Right now, I'm not implying anything . . . and I'm not drawing any conclusions. I'm trying to create a situation where the two of us . . . together . . . can work our way toward a valid appraisal of your performance for the first half of the year. I've got some ideas of my own . . . sure. In fact, they're more than ideas . . . they're more like hypotheses . . . working assumptions. And, like every hypothesis, they've got to be checked out . . . tested out. That's for you and me to do *together*. What I'm trying to do is get your hypotheses . . . your tentative conclusions about your own performance . . . out in the open. And then . . . together . . . we can test them in light of the evidence and see which ones are right. Maybe we'll come to some *brand new* conclusions. I don't know yet. All I *do* know is that I haven't made up my mind irrevocably about anything. If I had, this whole business of asking for *your* thinking would be a charade . . . and you know I don't play charades around here. Right?

This is a good Q4 response. Instead of putting Harry down, or arguing with him, Ed makes it plain that his mind is open to Harry's ideas and that he's ready and willing to *learn* from Harry. And he makes it plain that he's being candid—that he's not playing games. All of this should help to raise Harry's receptivity even higher.

HARRY. (Sheepishly, but with conviction.) Right. I know you don't. I guess I just jumped the gun. Maybe I'm edgy about that meeting coming up with Lew. I don't know . . . forget what I said, Ed, and let's get on with the appraisal.

This is the point that Ed has been working toward. Harry's receptivity is now fairly high, and he's ready to proceed with a full-fledged appraisal.

ED. Okay . . . I'm with you. Look . . . let's not get into this business of primary and secondary goals right now. We'll come back to that later. Let's just take each of the five objectives . . . one at a time . . . and you tell me how you see your progress toward that objective. Just go down your analysis sheet and tell me how you size up the record. Okay?

Note that Ed isn't brushing off Harry's distinction between primary and secondary goals. Instead, he indicates that he's treating the matter seriously, and wants to get back to it later. And, once again, he asks for Harry's self-evaluation. All of this should help to keep Harry's esteem needs filled and his receptivity up.

HARRY. Okay . . . let's start with the goal I still consider (he smiles) number one: increasing new business.
ED. Fine. How do you see your progress?
HARRY. (Decisively.) Great . . . just great. That's how. Our objective is a 15% increase in sales by year's end. Here we are at the six-month

mark, and we're right at 15%. I expect to make . . . or beat . . . the goal by year's end. *Easily.*

This is typical Q1 self-inflation. Notice the self-assured, almost boastful, tone.

ED.   Okay . . . you expect to be at or beyond goal by year's end. Let's talk about that. Tell me: what's causing us to be on target as far as volume is concerned?

Ed responds with a summary statement, and then probes for further information. He asks an open-end question to find out *why* Harry thinks he's on target.

HARRY.   (A slight note of disbelief in his voice.) What's causing it? Hard-nosed management . . . that's what's causing it. It's taken a lot of pushing . . . a lot of head-knocking . . . and, if I have to say so my-self . . . a lot of guts. In the two years since I took this job, I've done something nobody ever had the courage . . . or the vision . . . to do. I've *demanded* that this become the toughest, scrappiest sales organi-zation in the industry. It may sound hokey, but the fact is that I've *inspired* this organization!

This is a common benchmark of Q1 behavior: taking full credit for an achievement. Harry's emphasis on "guts" and "courage" is typical Q1 behavior, as is his vigorous slapping of his own back.

ED.   Alright . . . in your estimation, tough-minded management has been a major factor. Right?

Notice the summary statement. This is a good way to check understanding.

HARRY.   Absolutely.

ED.   What other factors have contributed?

HARRY.   (Slightly peevish) There *are* no other factors. We've got our volume up 15% over last year . . . and the credit belongs to me and the people who've responded to my prodding. *We've* done it. You wouldn't argue with *that* . . . would you?

Expectedly, Harry doesn't want to give credit to *other* factors. He feels the credit belongs exclusively to him and, thanks to *his* prodding, to the people who work for him.

ED.   Well . . . let me answer that by telling you how I described the situ-ation on *my* analysis. I agree with you . . . completely . . . that we're on target. 15% is 15%. But . . . when it comes to possible causes . . . I divide the credit between you . . . and the situation.

This is the point at which Ed starts to offer his own evaluation. He begins by saying where he agrees with Harry, and then moves on to explain where he disagrees.

HARRY.   (Peevishly) The *situation?* What's the *situation* got to do with it? We've made our *own* situation.

Notice the Q1 tendency to listen impatiently and to argue.

ED.   Are there . . . perhaps . . . some elements in the situation that you *haven't* made?

Instead of counterarguing, Ed asks an open-end question. Obviously, instead of telling Harry what the situational factors are, he's trying to guide Harry toward discovering them for himself.

HARRY.   (Stubbornly.) Absolutely not. In my dictionary, "situation" is just another word for "luck." And there's nothing lucky about that 15% increase. That took hard work . . . not luck. Where do you get this "situation" stuff?

Harry's receptivity has dipped somewhat. Note his use of flat assertions. Obviously, his esteem needs are threatened at this point.

ED.   (Matter-of-factly) It's simple. The economy's been building up a terrific head of steam for the past six months. The whole industry's doing well. So I'd *expect* volume to be up. As I see it, your 15% increase is largely a reflection of business conditions. I'm pleased . . . naturally . . . but I don't really think you're outperforming the economy all that much. How do *you* see it?

Ed has just made another mistake. By saying "It's simple," he has belittled Harry, implying that Harry is dense. This may not have been Ed's intention, but that's surely the way it will come across to Harry. This whole speech is a deprecation of Harry's efforts. At the end, by asking "How do you see it?" Ed almost seems to be challenging Harry.

HARRY.   (Heatedly) I resent that. You're not giving credit where credit is due. You know perfectly well that an active economy doesn't guarantee a proportionate increase in volume.

Not surprisingly, Ed's last remarks have driven down Harry's receptivity. Instead of engaging in a cool, rational discussion with Ed, he is angry and defensive.

ED. Go on.

> This brief assertion is a good response. It indicates to Harry that Ed wants to hear his views.

HARRY. (In an earnest, reasoning tone.) Look, Ed . . . we've both been around a long time . . . and we've both seen situations where general business conditions are good, yet volume stays the same . . . or even goes down. There's no direct correlation between general business activity and sales.

> Ed's brief assertion has helped to calm Harry.

ED. (Imperturbably.) Well, then . . . what *do* you see as the relationship between the economy and new business?

> This open-end question is designed to get Harry to think through his own ideas and see where they lead. Once again, Ed is trying to stimulate self-discovery.

HARRY. (Cautiously.) Look . . . I'm not denying there's a relationship. Sure the economy is reflected in our figures . . . *but only up to a point.*

> Note how Harry is moderating his argument. This is a good sign of rising receptivity.

ED. Keep going.

> Aware that Harry's receptivity is on the up-swing, Ed is eager to keep it that way. This brief assertion should help.

HARRY. Even *with* an active economy, it took a terrific amount of *selling* to produce the 15% increase. And I think our sales effort deserves a big chunk of credit.

> Notice that Harry is no longer talking about "I" and "me." He's now talking about "sales effort." He's no longer hogging all the glory.

ED. So you're saying . . . in effect . . . that we're on target as far as one of our goals—increased new business—is concerned, and that there are two reasons: hard-nosed selling *and* very good business conditions. Right?

> Ed's summary statement is designed to get Harry to acknowledge that he's actually shifted his ground.

HARRY.   (Somewhat grudgingly.) Yeah . . . I guess that's right.

> This is the first time Harry has admitted that market conditions have influenced the amount of new business that's been brought in. He's not exactly jubilant about making the admission, but then people with strong esteem needs are rarely happy to admit that they've been wrong.

ED.   You sound unsure. Do you still have some reservations?

> This is a good Q4 tactic. Instead of ignoring Harry's lack of enthusiasm, Ed faces up to it. He wants to get *all* of Harry's feelings and ideas out in the open, so they can be dealt with.

HARRY.   (Thoughtfully.) No . . . no, I see your point. To an extent the figures do reflect the economy. In fact, I guess you could say that hard-nosed selling *and* general business conditions turned the trick. I'd buy that. I'm really not trying to be stubborn, Ed. It's just that I've been working so hard . . . so singlemindedly . . . to make this outfit *sales* conscious that maybe I've got a slight case of tunnel-vision. Your point about the economy is well-taken . . . let's go on.

> Ed's efforts have paid off. This response from Harry is really Q4—candid, reasonable, self-aware—not Q1.

ED.   Okay . . . how did you appraise the next goal on your analysis form?

> Another open-end question, designed to move the discussion to another topic.

HARRY.   Well . . . from here on out we're dealing with what I call *subsidiary* goals.

ED.   Well . . . setting the labels aside for a minute . . . tell me how you see your progress, and why.

> Notice that Ed refuses to argue about the word "subsidiary." Instead, he tries to get Harry to continue his self-evaluation.

HARRY.   (Stubbornly.) But the labels . . . as you call them . . . are important. This whole appraisal hinges on the fact that we're making our major goal . . . and that the only goals we're having any problems with are subsidiary . . . or secondary . . . goals.

> The matter of "major" and "subsidiary" goals is obviously important to Harry; he refuses to drop it.

ED. Harry . . . it would help me if you'd explain that . . . "This whole appraisal hinges" on the distinction between primary and secondary goals? I'm not sure I understand that.

Realizing that Harry *is* concerned about the major-subsidiary distinction, Ed wisely decides to deal with it. Notice the Q4 candor: Ed admits that he doesn't really understand what Harry means, and he asks for clarification. This is sure to appeal to Harry's esteem need.

HARRY. (Patiently.) Look . . . this is what I was getting to earlier. The next four goals all have to do with cost controls . . . and we both know we're having some problems in that area. There's no point in beating around the bush about it . . . after all, you see the same computer printouts that I see. But my contention is that the cost-control goals don't have the same priority . . . the same urgency . . . as the business-producing goal. Bringing in new business is absolutely basic . . . everything else comes second. It has to. If we don't agree on that, then I'm going to get zinged for something that's *not* of primary importance . . . and I'm not going to get the credit I should for what *is* of primary importance.

Harry's receptivity is high at this point. He's being reasonable, he's acknowledging the existence of problems, and he's defending his position in a calm, unheated manner.

ED. Let me see if I'm following you. You feel that the credit you deserve for increasing our volume overbalances any *lack* of credit for the goals that haven't been achieved. Is that right?

Ed uses a summary statement to confirm his understanding, and to see if Harry wants to add to what he's already said.

HARRY. (Warming to his subject.) Right. It's a matter of weighting. Goals shouldn't be assigned equal weight unless they're equally important. As far as I'm concerned . . . in *this* industry . . . new business outweighs other goals . . . and *that's* what we ought to focus on.

This is a clear, explicit statement of Harry's view. Ed now knows exactly what Harry's position is, and he can compare his own with it.

ED. I see. But you'd agree . . . wouldn't you . . . that these other goals still have to be examined?

This is a leading question, designed to get Harry to admit that the so-called "secondary" goals must be looked at.

HARRY.   Yeah . . . sure. And I'm prepared to do that. In fact . . . the very next goal I've listed on my form is: reduce sales cost by 5%.

> As expected, Ed's leading question produces agreement. Harry is now ready to proceed with an analysis of the next goal.

ED.·   Fine. Tell me how you've evaluated your progress on that one.

HARRY.   (A bit testily.) That's a loaded question. I'm not on target . . . we both know that . . . but that's true only in the technical sense.

> This is obviously a touchy area for Harry. People with strong esteem needs rarely feel comfortable talking about their failures. In fact, Harry is denying that his failure *is* a failure, except in the "technical sense."

ED.   (Puzzled.) The technical sense?

> This is actually a neutral question. What Ed really means is "Tell me *more* about what you mean by technical."

HARRY.   Yeah . . . *technically* we're behind target, but *actually* we're doing a heck of a job.

> Once again, we see a typical example of Q1 behavior: the attempt to transform failures into triumphs.

ED.   Go on.

HARRY.   (Earnestly.) Look . . . sales costs for the year are supposed to be reduced 5%. Right now, the reduction is only around 3%. Technically, that means we're behind target. *But* . . . let's put the matter in *context*. Last year we were only able to bring sales costs down by 2%. We're doing better than that this year . . . in spite of an increased rate of inflation. So if you look at what's *really* happening, you'll see that we're doing a heckuva fine job of controlling costs.

> This speech is a mixture of Q1 bombast and Q4 use of data. Harry isn't just sounding off; he *is* producing evidence to back up his position.

ED.   So . . . you're saying that reducing sales costs by 3% is really a performance achievement—not a performance discrepancy . . . even though the goal calls for 5%.

> Another summary statement.

HARRY. (He sounds a bit annoyed, as if he feels Ed is being unreasonably obtuse.) That all depends on how you use these performance analysis charts. If you want to be technical about it, we're faced with a discrepancy. But if you forget technicalities and use the charts to reflect reality, then we've got ourselves a real achievement. (He pauses a second, then continues with agitation.) Y'know . . . these goals don't mean much unless they're viewed in context. The point I'm trying to make is that 3% isn't bad . . . in fact, it's downright good . . . *if* you *interpret* it right. And you can't interpret any number unless you view it *historically*.

Here's an example of a summary statement *backfiring*. Ed was seeking more information; what he got was information *plus* a good deal of emotion. Any time a superior uses a probe, he runs the risk that the probe may generate heat as well as light. In the present case, Harry's agitated response shows how strongly he feels about the entire matter. From Ed's point of view, this is helpful; it makes him *aware* of Harry's feelings, so that he can deal with them.

ED. (He realizes Harry is upset. His voice is genuinely concerned.) You're really miffed, aren't you?

This reflective statement is the best way to vent Harry's feelings.

HARRY. (Still vehement.) You bet I am. You'd be, too . . . in my situation. (Calming somewhat.) Look, Ed . . . I don't enjoy blowing my top . . . and I've done that a couple of times today. But I don't intend to be trapped by the way the appraisal form is laid out, either. That's what I meant before when I referred to bureaucratization. What shows up on that form as a *deficit* may actually be an *accomplishment*.

Notice how the reflective statement has helped to defuse the situation, and gotten Harry to explain why he feels the way he does.

ED. I understand your point . . . and I share your concern. I don't want the form to become a straitjacket either. And I don't think it will . . . if we can just keep on analyzing performance without getting involved in these sparring matches. Any suggestions about how we might do that?

Here's an example of facing up to a "process hang-up." Ed candidly concedes that he's not sure what to do about the "sparring matches" which are hampering the appraisal. So he asks Harry for his ideas.

HARRY.   (Much calmer now. He sounds contrite.) Ed . . . the sparring matches are *my* fault. I'm touchy today . . . and defensive. (He smiles.) And I've got a grouchier temper than even Lew Emerson. I'll try to cool it. Let's get back to the subject.

Harry's esteem need has been filled by Ed's response and he's completely vented his indignation. His receptivity is up again.

ED.   Harry, let me ask you something about controlling sales costs.

HARRY.   Shoot.

ED.   Why do you consider a 3% reduction such an achievement? It seems to me that if sales costs declined 2% last year, they should have declined a lot more in the first six months of *this* year . . . because this year we've put in a much better system of controls. Where am I wrong . . . or am I?

Note that Ed is not saying that Harry is wrong. He's simply asking Harry to explain his position, and he's admitting that *he himself* could be wrong.

HARRY.   In a sense, Ed, you're *not* wrong. We *do* have a better system of controls this year. But we're still fighting inflation . . . and, even more important, we're handling a 15% increase in business. But in spite of that, we've managed to bring costs down 3%. I think that's pretty good.

This is a level-headed response. It shows that Harry's receptivity is high, and he's prepared for a rational discussion.

ED.   Tell me more.

A brief assertion, designed to bring out more information.

HARRY.   Well . . . there's not much more to tell. Increased volume almost always means increased costs. That's just the nature of the beast. There's no way you can increase new business by 15% and not have some increase in costs as well. That's why I'm so darned proud of the 3% drop.

Harry hasn't really produced more information, but he has clarified his point. This is a very explicit statement of his thinking.

ED.   I see. But tell me . . . what, . . . if anything . . . can you think of that might have reduced the costs even more? What . . . if anything . . . has been left *un*done?

Ed still wants to produce more self-discovery by Harry. So he asks open-end questions.

HARRY. (Puzzled.) I don't follow you. Give me an example.

It's obvious that Harry hasn't done any critical self-analysis.

ED. Well . . . like better budgeting. How do you evaluate your current budgeting procedures?

Note how Ed is now channeling the discussion.

HARRY. (Thoughtfully.) They're . . . well, they're adequate. Not great. Adequate.

This is a sign of fairly high receptivity. Instead of immediately springing to his own self-defense, as he was doing earlier, Harry now voices some slight dissatisfaction with his performance.

ED. How do you feel about that?

An open-end probe.

HARRY. How do I feel? Not too happy. I know our budgeting procedures ought to be tighter. (Determinedly.) And they *will* be . . . once I'm able to concentrate on something besides new business.

Harry is now doing some hard looking into his own performance.

ED. I see. Now . . . what else . . . as you see it . . . might reduce sales costs?

A neutral question, designed to elicit more information.

HARRY. (Slowly, as if thinking his way through the answer.) Well . . . there are some things that *ideally* should be done . . . once I get over the new-business hump.

Notice how Ed's probes are stimulating real thought on Harry's part.

ED. Like what?

HARRY. Well . . . like more systematic territory management . . . more discriminating placement of ads . . . better utilization of computer data . . . operating economies . . . all these things have to be done one of these days.

This is a remarkable change from Harry's earlier cockiness and unwillingness to admit any problems. Only skillful and persistent *probing* could have brought him to this point.

ED.   Harry . . . a little while ago, you referred to all this stuff as subsidiary. Tell me . . . as far as the *ultimate* consequences are concerned . . . and I'm stressing the word *ultimate* . . . what's the result of de-emphasizing cost controls and zeroing-in almost entirely on new business?

Ed is keeping his earlier promise to return to the question of major and subsidiary goals. Note that he is still not arguing with Harry; he continues to probe instead.

HARRY.   (Thoughtfully and good-naturedly.) I know what you're getting at, Ed. I may be a stupid salesman at heart . . . but even *I'm* savvy enough to get your message. Ultimately . . . we pay a penalty on the bottom line. I can't deny that . . . and I won't.

This is the so-called "aha" effect. The "light bulb" has gone on in Harry's head. Ed's Q4 strategy is really starting to pay off.

ED.   Okay . . . what do you think oughta be done about it?

Ed continues to guide Harry toward self-discovery.

HARRY.   (He is silent for a couple of seconds, then responds earnestly.) Y'know, Ed . . . I'm not the world's most introspective guy . . . but I do know my faults. Some of them, anyway. And one of my faults . . . or at least one of my problems . . . is that deep down—at heart—I'm a *salesman*. That's the part of this business I love . . . really love. Nothing turns me on like seeing volume go up . . . new accounts come in . . . revenues increase. I've been out of the field a long time now, but I still can't resist the lure of new business.

Harry is manifesting an impressive degree of insight. Ed has brought him from almost total refusal to confront his performance deficiencies to a candid acknowledgement of those deficiencies and, even better, an understanding of the *reasons* for those deficiencies.

ED.   So . . . marketing takes precedence over other things?
HARRY.   Yeah . . . I guess so. (Slowly) In fact, I *know* so. I've been in this job two years now . . . and the *emphasis* has gotten a little lopsided. I've been so strongly dedicated to upping volume . . . so intent on making everyone in this company as sales-minded as I am . . . that I've neglected some other things . . . or at least down-played them. And the point you're trying to get across is exactly right.
ED.   What point is that?
HARRY.   The point you haven't yet made . . . but are about to make . . . that *gross* is up and *net* is stagnating . . . and that the time has come to shift focus and zero-in on the bottom line. You don't have to hit

me over the head to make the light go on. In fact, I've been dimly aware of this situation for some time now, but I've put off acknowledging it. I've been having too much fun with marketing, I guess.

Harry's statement that he's been "dimly aware" of the situation is significant. Very often, people *are* "dimly aware" of the flaws in their performance, but, for all the reasons we explored in the book, they've never actually admitted or examined those flaws. Q4 appraisal is designed to bring matters out of "dim" awareness and into the *center* of the subordinate's consciousness. That's what self-discovery is all about.

ED.   Harry . . . let's summarize where we're at so far in our discussion. What's your view?

Note how Ed, in good Q4 fashion, is asking Harry to do the summary.

HARRY.   Hm-m-m. I'd say we've agreed on two points. One . . . sales are on target, mainly because we've had a very dynamic market. And two . . . sales costs are higher than they should be . . . probably because I've been so busy focusing on marketing that I haven't put my heart into cost control. End result: gross is up . . . but net isn't.

Harry is making exactly the point that Ed has been trying to get across from the start. But, because Harry discovered it for himself, he "buys" it. If Ed had *told* him instead of guided him, Harry wouldn't be nearly so committed.

ED.   That's the way I see it, too. Now . . . it seems to me that we'd both profit by digging a little deeper into why cost controls have been understressed. Let's go back to the appraisal charts and see if there are some problems we haven't considered yet. Maybe we'll find that *I'm* part of the problem. What do you say?

HARRY.   Makes sense to me. Y'know . . . in spite of my remarks a few minutes ago, I'm not knocking this appraisal system. It does make you look at things . . . *hard*. (He smiles.) The trouble is, some of the things you see are things you'd prefer not to see.

ED.   (Also smiling.) You're telling me.

It's worth noting two points in particular about this transcript:

1. It shows that receptivity can, and often does, fluctuate considerably. Never assume that high receptivity will stay high. As Ed saw, receptivity can be more erratic than the weather.
2. It shows that probing rarely produces miracle results. Probing is long, hard work, and anyone who stops probing too early is making a mistake. It takes patience and persistence.

Some Aids to Planning the Appraisal

In Chapter 13, "Planning the Appraisal," we set out a system for doing Q4 content planning (see Figure 15, page 210). The heart of the system is an analysis of *why* a given job goal was achieved or not achieved (or why you can't tell one way or the other). The boxes on the chart that help you do this analysis are 4a, 5a, and 6a of Figure 20.

Following are some points to be considered when doing this part of content planning. The list is not exhaustive. In fact, any one of the points we've listed may trigger several others that aren't on the list. The list, then, can be useful as a pump-primer—as a way to start you thinking about the four elements that explain why a goal was or wasn't met: the goal itself, the subordinate, you, and the situation.

POINTS TO CONSIDER ABOUT THE GOAL

1. *Unrealistic?*

Was the goal nothing more than a pleasant, but unrealizable fantasy? Was it a pipe dream, an indulgence in wishful thinking? Was it so implausible that it didn't deserve to be taken seriously? Were you kidding yourselves when you originally agreed to it?

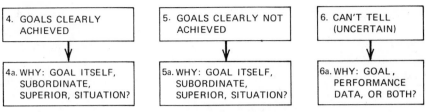

FIGURE 20

2. *Incomprehensible?*

Was it impossible for the subordinate to understand the goal? Did you phrase it in a jargon that only you understood? Did you word it so that it didn't make sense? Did you misuse words, so that you meant one thing while he thought you meant something else?

3. *Vague?*

Was the goal so general that any achievement might be considered as meeting it ("Do a good job," "Give it your best," "Don't let me down")? If so, is it possible that *you* think the goal hasn't been met ("I asked you to do your best and you didn't do it") while your *subordinate* thinks it has ("Oh yes I did")?

4. *Unfairly demanding?*

Did you ask your subordinate to do things that transgressed her moral or religious principles? Did the goal require behavior that she considered unethical or unscrupulous? Would carrying out the plan-of-action have violated her sense of integrity or code of honor?

POINTS TO CONSIDER ABOUT THE SUBORDINATE

You will want to look at at least seven major topics under this heading: (1) how well the subordinate plans, (2) organizes, (3) leads, (4) motivates, (5) controls, (6) his technical knowledge, and (7) his motivation.

1. *Planning*

At least five functions come under this heading:

- *Forecasting.* How effectively does the subordinate estimate and predict future conditions relating to his job? Is he future-oriented or does he take things "as they come"? Does he try to anticipate the consequences of his activities? Does he do this systematically, seeking out hard data and informed projections? Or does he rely mainly on guesswork and intuition?

- *Establishing objectives.* Does he set business job goals that are relevant to larger company goals? Are they specific, realistic, measurable? Does he set realistic behavioral job goals? Does he set job goals that challenge and motivate? Or "snap" goals that don't require exertion? Does he rely on vague hopes instead of exact objectives ("Let's all get out there and do a great job"; "Let's give it everything we've got")? Does he set goals that can't possibly be achieved, so that they either frustrate his people or get ignored?

- *Budgeting.* Does she effectively allocate capital and resources to get the job done? Does she stay within her allotted budget? Is she cost-conscious? Does she have a sense of priorities when it comes to allocating money, or does she squander funds on nonessentials and frills? Does she understand the company's budgeting system?

- *Action planning.* Does he develop sound programs for achieving his objectives? Does he have a systematic, step-by-step "map" for getting to his job goals? Or does he take each day as it comes? Does he move toward his job goals methodically, with each step building on the last, or is his work erratic and unpredictable?

- *Time management.* Does she budget time sensibly? Can she distinguish between more important and less important tasks, and does she allot most of her time to the more important ones? Does she have a sense of urgency? Can she move extra quickly and effectively when necessary? Does she waste large blocs of time socializing? Does she take deadlines seriously? Is she able to do her work in a reasonable amount of time, or does she spend so many hours on it that she's constantly fatigued and edgy? Do unfinished (or unstarted) tasks pile up on her desk? Does she seem to have too much time on her hands? Is she ever at a loss about what to do next? Does she try to do too much at one time, so that nothing gets done right? When the pressure's on, can she zero in on two or more tasks and do them all effectively?

2. *Organizing*

At least three functions fall under this heading:

- *Structuring.* Does the subordinate make all the pieces of his job *fit together*, so that everything he does moves him closer to his job goals? Does he see his job as a *unit*, as an integrated set of tasks, as an organic whole in which all the activities are related and affect one another? Or does he see his job as a loose group of activities that don't seem to have any single, overriding purpose? Does he treat his job as an entity, in which every task has a clear and significant function? Can he explain— at any time—*why* he's doing what he's doing, and how it relates to his job goals?

- *Delegating.* Does she do a good job of assigning responsibilities and accountability? Does she try to do everything herself, or is she willing to "let go" and get other people involved? Does she assign tasks intelligently, giving them to people who *should* be doing them, or does she assign them in a random, helter-skelter way? Does she use delegation as a *developmental* tool, sometimes assigning a task to an "unproven rookie"? Or does she delegate only to people she's sure can do the job? Does she *really* delegate, giving genuine responsibility with the assignment? Or does she keep all the decision-making power for herself?
- *Collaboration.* Does he work cooperatively with other people, inside and outside his own group? Can he function on a team, dovetailing his efforts with others in pursuit of a common goal? Or is he a loner, a maverick, a glory-hog, a disruptive force? Is he too easygoing, too quick to give in or acquiesce? Is he able to be candid without being hurtful? Can he share credit, and is he willing to acknowledge the contribution of others? Does he submerge his own immediate interests in favor of the organization's interests, both short and long-range?

3. *Leading*

This is a broad category, embracing at least eight functions:

- *Decision-making.* Does the subordinate make generally sound decisions, based on logic and relevant facts? Are her decisions easily understood? Do they command respect and commitment? Does she use a variety of decision-making techniques, and does she use them in the right situations (making some decisions alone, some after consulting with one or more other people, some after involving her entire group)? Are her decisions based on a thorough exploration of alternatives, or does she shoot from the hip? Is she decisive; can she make up her mind in a reasonable time? Or does she vacillate and put off decisions? Does she *really* make decisions, or does she look to you for signals and then decide whatever you seem to prefer? Does she frequently make decisions that are arbitrary, half-baked, or cop-outs? Or are most of her decisions deliberate and responsible? Is she able to make tough, unpopular decisions, or does she usually settle for the easy compromise?

- *Management by objectives.* Does he use job goals as a compass by which to guide the daily activities of his people? Does he relate everything that happens to *objectives*, so that the final criterion of performance is whether or not it brings the individual and the group closer to their goals? Does every member of the group work by a plan that's designed to achieve these goals? Or is there no discernible connection between daily activity and job goals?
- *Leadership style.* Does she get her people involved in matters relating to their job goals so that they make candid, open contributions? Does she utilize their ideas, opinions, and feelings, or does she ignore them? Do her people understand her decisions and directives? Are they committed to them because they've contributed to them? Or do they feel that the decisions have been imposed on them? Do they react resentfully, sullenly, apathetically?
- *Management by conflict.* Does he face up to disagreements and disputes, probe them, try to understand and resolve them? Or does he squelch them, bury them, pretend they don't exist, so that they go underground and continue to cause trouble? Is he afraid to acknowledge conflict? Is he eager for peace at any price? Does he "give away the store" in an effort to overcome conflict? Does he believe that conflict can be healthy, that it can provoke fresh thinking and creative ferment? Does he accept the fact that an optimal amount of conflict is essential to organizational health?
- *Communication.* Does she promote and encourage candid, open expression in all directions, up from her own subordinates, down from herself, and sideways to her peers? Is she receptive to new or unorthodox ideas, is she willing to permit venting, is she able to take bad news as well as good? Does she level with others and permit them to level with her? Do her people feel that, when she's around, certain subjects are taboo? Does she censor certain ideas, or twist them to serve her own purposes? Does she try to find out what's really going on, or does she prefer to live in a snug, make-believe world?
- *Staffing.* Does he select people on the basis of ability, potential, intellect, drive, and character? Is he thorough and analytic in his selections, or does he rely on hunches and gut feelings? Does he promote people on the basis of past performance and future potential, or does he play favorites and politics?
- *Initiative.* Does she initiate or react? Is she an innovator and self-starter, or does she usually hang back, waiting to see what others do first? Does she present her ideas with conviction? Is she willing to advocate an idea against powerful opposition? Or does she usually do the politically smart thing, speaking up when it's safe and keeping her mouth shut

when it isn't? Does she generally display drive, stamina, self-confidence? Do people look to her for guidance, or is she considered a dud who cannot and will not provide vigorous leadership?
- *Flexibility.* Is he adaptable? Does he readily accept intelligent change? Or is he dedicated to the status quo? Is he convinced that today's way of doing things is always the best, and does he resist new ideas? Is he willing to listen to other viewpoints and to consider other ways of operating? Or is he stubbornly sure that his way beats all others? Is he resilient? Does he bounce back easily from disappointment or defeat?

4. *Motivating*

At least five functions belong under this heading:

- *Gaining commitment.* Does the subordinate link job goals to her people's tangible and intangible needs so that they clearly see what they'll get out of achieving the goals? Does she make $J + N \rightarrow B \rightarrow P$ come to life? Does she connect job goals to needs so as to generate enthusiastic, vigorous, sustained performance?
- *Enthusiasm.* Does he convey excitement and zest, and does he stimulate these qualities in others? Does he turn people on, so that they work with gusto? Or is he apathetic, lackluster, a wet blanket who extinguishes sparks of fervor before they have a chance to ignite?
- *Feedback, coaching, appraisal.* Does she steadily supply her people with information about their performance so they can regularly evaluate their progress and improve their skills? Does she maintain an environment in which every experience becomes a *learning* experience? Does she give candid, objective information and advice? Or do her people stumble around in the dark, not knowing where they are, how they're doing, or how—if at all—they should change? Does she create the conditions for continuing, goal-directed growth, or for haphazard, accidental change?
- *Development.* Is he growth-oriented? Does he foster growth in his people? Or are most of them stuck in ruts that get deeper year by year? Is he afraid of being outshone by fast-growing subordinates? Does he feel most comfortable surrounded by mediocrities? Or does he do all he can to move people along, to help them realize their potential?
- *Climate.* Is the climate in her group characterized by strong emphasis on doing the job and getting results? By high morale and team spirit? Or do other factors, like one-upmanship, politicking, staying out of the line of fire, and being pals, get more attention than productivity and morale? Is the climate marked by cooperation or backbiting, manipu-

lation or respect, one-against-all or we're-all-in-this-together, game-playing or candor, pulling punches or telling it as it is, apathy or commitment? Does she stunt or foster growth and progress?

5. *Controlling*

This heading covers at least three functions:

- *Performance standards.* Has he set clear guidelines for evaluating work done in his group? Does everyone in the group understand these guidelines? Are they available to everyone, or are they a closely guarded secret? Are the criteria realistic, achievable, fair? Are the business job goals precise and quantified, or vague and hard to pin down? Do the people in his group have a system for knowing how they're doing, or is this mostly a mystery?
- *Performance measuring.* Has she developed methods for measuring results, for doing objective evaluations? Does she rely on adjectives (good, fair, nice, great, terrific, terrible, so-so) or does she rely on numbers (25%, $3000, first, second, third, etc.)?
- *Critique.* Does he have a system for telling his people how he thinks they're doing? Does he provide periodic critique? Does it follow an established format? Or does he do critique on a random, informal basis, following no schedule and no pattern?

6. *Technical knowledge*

Does she understand the technical aspects of her job? Is she "at home" with the content and the subject matter of her work? Has she mastered the essential information and theory? If not, where is she deficient?

7. *Subordinate's Motivation*

Seven functions should be considered under this heading:

- *Does not understand the job goal.* A subordinate may not be interested in a job goal because he doesn't understand what the goal *is.* He has a false perception of it, so he sees it as boring, trivial, stupid, demeaning, or what have you. The job goal (as *he* understands it) doesn't seem worth the effort.
- *Does not accept the job goal.* A subordinate may understand perfectly what her job goal is, but still reject it. She may resent the fact that, as she sees it, the goal was shoved down her throat. She may consider it beneath her dignity, or an affront on her integrity. She may consider it

silly or unethical. Or she may see it as endangering her relationships with other people ("That would require pushing some of my best friends, and I can't do *that*"). Whatever the reason, the subordinate would rather *fail* than achieve the goal.

- *Does not know how the job goal will benefit him.* Maybe the subordinate doesn't know what he'll get out of achieving the job goal. Maybe he doesn't understand how $J + N \rightarrow B \rightarrow P$ applies to him. He may understand J (the job goal), but he doesn't see how it ties in to N (*his* tangible and intangible needs). So, he has no way of knowing what B (the benefits) are, and an understanding of B is essential for P (committed performance).
- *Does not know consequences of not achieving job goal.* Maybe the subordinate doesn't know what will happen if she doesn't achieve the job goal, either to the organization or to herself. Maybe she doesn't realize that her failure will hurt the organization and herself, too.
- *Thinks reward for not achieving job goal is greater than for achieving it.* A subordinate may think he'll be *better off*—get a *bigger* benefit—if he *doesn't* reach a goal than if he does. This can happen in many situations. Here are two possibilities:

People with strong *security* (Q2) needs sometimes fear that by actively pursuing a job goal, they'll be *shown up* as incompetent. They're afraid of exposure, of drawing attention to their shortcomings. Lacking confidence, they figure that they'll be better off not pursuing the goal at all, or else pursuing it so half-heartedly that they're sure to fail. But aren't they afraid that this will put them in even *bigger* trouble? Not really. They usually rationalize their decision in one of several ways: "A year from now, the boss won't even remember having assigned that goal. So why risk falling on my face in pursuit of a goal that he'll forget about anyway?" "If the boss brings it up, I'll just tell him I didn't understand the goal, that I was confused. They can't shoot me for being confused, can they?" In other words, people with very strong security needs sometimes weigh one risk against another— the risk of actively pursuing a job goal and "looking bad" when they fail versus the risk of not bothering to pursue the job goal at all—and decide that pursuing it is the bigger risk.

People with strong *social* (Q3) needs may see more reward in *not* actively pursuing a job goal if the goal requires them to "toughen up," to "assert themselves," to "come on strong" with other people. They fear alienating or antagonizing friends, endangering social relationships, losing popularity, being seen as "bad guys." On the other hand, of course, if they *don't* pursue the goal, they may antagonize the *boss*. The subordinate with strong social needs may resolve this predicament by deciding: "To heck with the goal. I'm not about to start throwing my weight around and flexing my muscles . . . I just can't do that. If the boss brings the subject up, I can handle him. After all, we've got a good relationship between us." As so often happens, the subordinate with strong Q3 needs sees everything in terms of "good relationships."

- *Confidence.* Subordinates sometimes believe, rightly or wrongly, that they can't achieve a job goal, so why bother. In a way, this is sensible. If someone is *convinced* that she won't reach a goal no matter how hard she tries, it seems silly to try. In fact, some subordinates (especially those with very strong *security*—Q2—needs) are so short of self-confidence that they fear they'll make things *worse* by pursuing the goal. They are not only convinced they can't reach it, they are convinced they'll "mess things up" along the way. So, they sit on their hands, procrastinate, postpone, and never start *moving*.
- *Interest.* A lack of interest can be as deadly as a lack of confidence. If a goal seems dull and uninteresting, and if the work needed to reach it seems tedious or monotonous, the subordinate may yawn and shrug off the whole thing. Motivated performance depends upon the *benefit* to be gained, and not many people consider boredom a benefit.

POINTS TO CONSIDER ABOUT YOURSELF

Generally, your weakness, if any, will lie in one of five areas: Planning, organizing, leading, motivating, controlling.

1. *Planning*

At least six functions come under this heading:

- *Forecasting.* Did you give the subordinate inadequate or wrong information for estimating and predicting business conditions? Did you unintentionally mislead him so that his projections turned out wrong?
- *Setting objectives.* Did you let her set unrealistic or inadequate job goals? Did you give her the help and data she needed in setting them?
- *Budgeting.* Did you allot him sufficient resources (money, materials, people) to do the job? Did you withhold essential support?
- *Action-planning.* Did you emphasize the need for precise action plans to achieve the job goals? Did you review these plans? Did you conduct periodic meetings with her to determine if she was on target, and, if she wasn't, why?
- *Time management.* Did you give him the time he needed to achieve the goal? Did you impose unreasonable deadlines? Did you overload him with assignments?
- *Policies.* Did you consider the fact that organizational policies might interfere with achievement of the goal? Did you let him pursue a goal that violated or infringed policy?

2. *Organizing*

Three functions must be considered in this category:

- *Structuring*. Did you support his efforts to create a system for achieving the job goal? Did you delegate the power he needed to put together a workable strategy?
- *Delegating*. Did you set clear guidelines so that she knew exactly who was responsible for what? Were lines of authority and accountability clearly spelled out, or did you leave the whole matter uncertain and confused?
- *Collaboration*. Did you foster collaboration both inside and outside your group, so that he got the cooperation he needed? Or did you leave him to sink or swim?

3. *Leading*

This heading covers eight major functions:

- *Decision-making*. Did you make decisions on your own that should have involved him? Did you empower him to make necessary decisions on his own? Did you treat him like a puppet, holding the strings in your own hands?
- *Goal-setting*. Did you impose the job goal on him? Did you make him acquiesce in it even though he didn't fully understand or accept it? Or did you erroneously let him set his own job goals, without involvement on your part?
- *Management of conflict*. Did you let disagreements with the subordinate get in the way of job goal attainment? Did you explore these conflicts and try to resolve them? Did you deny their existence, shrug them off, or try to joke them away?
- *Communication*. Did you develop a climate in which you and she exchanged ideas freely and candidly? Were you available when she wanted to talk? Did you study the memos and other documents she sent you, or did you "file" them without really knowing what was in them?
- *Leadership style*. Did you inhibit his performance by your own arbitrary, autocratic practices? Or by copping out and letting him go his own way? Or by being too soft and easygoing?
- *Staffing*. Did you select people who were supposed to help her but who lacked skills, know-how, experience, character, or drive? Did you expect her to turn in a big-league performance with a minor-league team?

- *Initiative.* Did your own procrastination and indecision thwart him? Did you sit on the fence when he needed firm, vigorous guidance?
- *Flexibility.* Did you provide the adaptable leadership she needed to pursue her goals in the face of changed conditions? Were you willing to entertain new ideas and approaches, or did you turn thumbs down on any of her suggestions that were innovative or unusual?

4. *Motivating*

Five functions should be examined under this heading:

- *Gaining commitment.* Did you involve him in setting the job goals? Did you make both the J and the B in $J + N \rightarrow B \rightarrow P$ clear to him? Did you understand what his tangible and intangible needs were *before* you tried to link the job goals to them?
- *Inspiring.* Did you convey enthusiasm and encouragement to her? Did you sound as if you believe in the job goal? Did you make it plain that the goal is significant and urgent?
- *Feedback, coaching, and appraisal.* Did you give him periodic analysis of how he was doing, of what progress he was making toward the job goal? Did you provide systematic insight into his strengths and weaknesses? Did you help him to learn and improve as he went along?
- *Development.* Did you give her a chance to acquire the necessary skills, know-how, and experience? Or were you so authoritarian that she remained wholly dependent on you? Did you generate growth, or stunt it?
- *Climate.* Did you develop a serious, supportive, goal-directed climate that stressed high achievement and high morale? Or did you develop a climate in which anything goes, in which one standard is as good as another?

5. *Controlling*

At least four functions belong under this heading:

- *Performance standards.* Did you establish clear-cut criteria by which he could evaluate his work? Did you make sure he understood the difference between effective and ineffective performance?
- *Performance measures.* Did you develop methods by which she could get an exact, *numerical* assessment of her performance? Or did you let her rely on vague assessments like "Okay," "Not bad," "Pretty good"?

- *Critique*. Did you schedule and conduct regular analyses of his performance? Did you make sure he came out of these clearly understanding where he was at and what he had to do to reach his job goals?
- *Involvement*. Did you involve the subordinate to the point where she felt the goal was her goal? Or did it remain *somebody else's* goal—a goal she was stuck with, like it or not?

POINTS TO CONSIDER ABOUT THE SITUATION

On all the following items, be sure to ask: Is this a significant explanation for the failure to achieve the job goal? Granted that the situation exists, did it really hinder the achievement of *this* particular goal?

1. *Schedules*.

Did late shipments (from suppliers or the production department) prevent the subordinate from reaching his job goal?

2. *Economic conditions*.

Did recession or inflation hurt? Did changes in foreign currency exchange, the securities market, or fiscal or monetary policy block access to the job goal?

3. *Market conditions*.

Did the advent of new products or new competitors hurt? Was there a falling off of demand due to circumstances beyond his control?

4. *Customers*.

Did major customers move away or go out of business? Were they bought out by other companies, who then changed their buying practices?

5. *Labor problems*.

Did strikes, walkouts, slowdowns, or sabotage hinder movement toward the job goal?

6. *Budget.*

Did the subordinate have the money she needed to do the job? Was she strapped for funds?

7. *Competition.*

Did competition overwhelm him with a new or better product, a better advertising campaign, more salespeople, or more investment per sale? Did it slash prices or practice "giveaway" techniques?

8. *Legal.*

Did legal restrictions, threats of lawsuits, litigation or injunctions hamper him? Did state or federal regulatory agencies create insurmountable problems?

9. *Methods or systems.*

Was he thwarted by unworkable methods or obsolete systems? Was he slowed down by inefficient or overly complex procedures that he was powerless to change?

10. *Design.*

Was he hamstrung by a faulty or inefficient product or service? Was he given a second-rate product or service to sell or use?

11. *Compensation.*

Was he unable to hire the people he needed because of an inadequate compensation plan? Was he consistently outbid by competition?

12. *Material.*

Were the materials he needed unavailable? Did he encounter shortages that could not be overcome? Was he prevented from getting materials by strikes, war, or natural disasters?

13. *Facilities.*

Was he required to work with outmoded or inefficient facilities? Did this affect his ability to get the job done?

14. *Equipment.*

Was the equipment she needed available when she needed it? Was it adequate? Did she encounter frequent and damaging equipment breakdowns?

15. *People.*

Did he have qualified people to help him do the job? If not, was he permitted to go out and hire them? Was he allowed to provide suitable training?

16. *Transportation.*

Was she stymied by transportation strikes or by carriers who failed to deliver on time?

17. *Other departments.*

Did other departments lie down on the job—sabotage his efforts, refuse to cooperate, or unintentionally mess things up?

18. *Other.*

Was she frustrated by tornadoes, blizzards, thefts of industrial secrets, fires, deaths or illnesses of other people upon whom she depended? The number of "other" situations is infinite. Only *you* can fill in all the gaps.

Dimensional Appraisal Training

The final words of the final chapter of this book were "try it—and see for yourself." In the last analysis, there is no other way to become a Q4 appraiser. Books like this one provide insight and understanding, but, by themselves, insight and understanding won't make anyone proficient at raising receptivity or probing or using the Q4 format or applying $J + N \rightarrow B \rightarrow P$ or doing any of the other things we've talked about. Proficiency comes only with practice. In fact, if you "try it" just once, you still won't become proficient. What is needed is *steady* practice.

Many superiors, however, are understandably reluctant to try Q4 appraisal even once, much less repeatedly. There are two good reasons for this:

1. They feel too much is at risk; they don't like the idea of "experimenting" *on the job*. As one manager put it: "What if I mess things up? I'm not willing to fall flat on my face when the future of one of my subordinates is involved. If I make a botch of things, *he's* the one who will wind up getting hurt."
2. They don't have anybody to tell them how they are doing. As another superior put it: "Suppose I do try some of these techniques. And suppose I don't do as good a job as I should. How will I know?

It's like trying to teach yourself to play golf. How can you ever tell if what you're doing is right or wrong?"

To overcome both these problems, readers of this book may want to enroll in a Dimensional Appraisal Training (DAT) seminar. DAT seminars let managers practice Q4 appraisal skills in (1) a risk-free setting where (2) they get plenty of feedback on how they're doing so that they can keep on doing whatever they're doing right and improve whatever they're doing wrong. There is no more efficient way to start becoming a Q4 appraiser.

WHAT DOES DAT DO?

DAT teaches managers how to do Q4 appraisal. It helps them develop the necessary insights into human behavior, and the necessary skills. It does all this in a practical way by concentrating on the dozen "how-to's" we listed on page 289:

1. How to size up behavior—your own and each of your subordinates'.
2. How to motivate performance by tying job goals to the subordinate's tangible and intangible needs.
3. How to set job goals—business and behavioral—that get the subordinate to stretch.
4. How to size up receptivity, and how to spin it up if low.
5. How to probe.
6. How to listen.
7. How to generate dialogue.
8. How to make your ideas understandable and persuasive.
9. How to build trust.
10. How to plan the content and process of the appraisal.
11. How to use the basic Q4 appraisal format during the appraisal.
12. How to tailor the format to fit the behavior of each of your subordinates.

HOW DAT DOES IT

Psychological Associates, Inc. (with headquarters in St. Louis), the developers of DAT, offer two versions of the program, one lasting three days, the other five.

1. The three-day seminar is for managers who have completed Psychological Associates' Dimensional Management Training (DMT) or

Dimensional Sales Management (DSM) programs. Since these managers have already mastered many of the skills essential to DAT (for example: raising receptivity, probing, motivating), they're able to start working on Q4 appraisal skills more quickly than managers who have not been through DMT or DSM.

2. The five-day seminar is for managers who have not been through DMT or DSM. Following is an overview of what happens in this longer program.

There are two parts to DAT: the preseminar work and the seminar itself.

Preseminar Work

Before attending the seminar, participants are given approximately 30 hours of preparatory work to complete. They fill out questionnaires that ask them to evaluate and record their own appraisal strategies as they see them at the time. Then, after reading this book, they complete several tasks that test their understanding of the book and give them a chance to try out their behavior-analysis skills by listening to, and then analyzing, a recorded appraisal. Finally, they complete a questionnaire that will help them do "real-life" appraisal in the seminar.

The Purpose of the Preseminar Work

Because each participant has done this preparatory work, the DAT seminar begins at a fairly advanced level. There is no need to spend lots of seminar time on basic instruction; each participating manager is familiar with the textbook and with the fundamental Dimensional concepts before he gets to the seminar. Thus, after a brief period on the first day to clarify basic concepts, the seminar can move into the vital area of *skill-building*. By learning most of their theoretical underpinnings *before* they come to the seminar, participants can devote most of their seminar hours to learning Q4 *techniques* and how to apply them in real life.

THE DAT SEMINAR

The seminar starts early Monday morning and ends midafternoon Friday. The number of managers attending usually ranges from 10 to 30. Participants are assigned to teams of five. Teams normally finish their Monday, Tuesday, and Wednesday activities between 6 and 7 P.M. But, in spite of the long, intensive days (or maybe because of them) motivation usually runs so high that participants decide, on their own, to work late into the evening on Thursday. (Thursday evening is open-ended; teams either work late Thursday night or during the early hours of Friday morning.) The seminar wraps up on Friday in time for participants to make travel connections home.

The Purpose of Teamwork

The seminar group is divided into teams for two important reasons. One goal of DAT is to develop sizing-up skills, and this can be done more rapidly and thoroughly in small groups in which interaction is sustained and intensive. Small-group activity is especially important in helping a manager diagnose his *own* behavior; after being keenly observed by his teammates for four days, and after getting candid feedback from them, he gets a view of his appraisal strategy *as seen by others* that he couldn't easily get otherwise. Practically all DAT activities require teamwork. These activities, which are described below, are most effectively carried out in small groups marked by vigorous give-and-take and high candor.

MONDAY

Most of the time is spent clarifying Dimensional concepts, mainly those having to do with the models of appraisal behavior and with communication. Some of the clarification is done through lectures, some in team discussions. These discussions not only clarify and amplify the managers' understanding, but they serve as "icebreakers" for the team.

After an activity designed to reinforce Dimensional communication concepts, and a lecture on motivation, most of the afternoon is spent introducing the participants to a system of *analysis and feedback:* a technique for taking an appraisal apart, finding out what made it tick, and then feeding back the findings to the superior who did the appraisal. To acquaint participants with this system, the instructor shows them a videotaped appraisal; that appraisal is then analyzed, first by each manager and then by each team; finally, these analyses are compared with a videotaped analysis by several members of the Psychological Associates staff. On Monday evening, participants are given an assignment that prepares them for the role-played appraisals that will begin the next day, and in which they themselves will take part.

The Purpose of Lectures in DAT

Only about 15% of the seminar is taken up by lectures. These expand on the basic Dimensional concepts, clear up misconceptions, and give participants a chance to ask questions. But the lectures do *not* give the seminar its fundamental thrust; the basic impetus of DAT comes from the team activities. The lectures are important, but not as important as the *experience* that each participant gets from working his way through assigned tasks and seeing disembodied concepts become real and believable. Throughout, DAT emphasizes learning through *doing*.

The Purpose of Role Playing

Role playing, or simulated appraisal, does three things. (1) It lets each participant discover how other people view his appraisal behavior. (2) It lets each participant find out what his strengths and weaknesses as an appraiser are so that he can reinforce the strengths and overcome the weaknesses. (3) It lets each participant experiment with Q4 appraisal behavior in a supportive, risk-free environment. Role playing is *action learning*, which is basic to DAT.

Behavioral scientists have demonstrated repeatedly that people learn better in active rather than passive situations. Especially in training aimed at behavioral change, lectures are far less effective than was once thought. Managers learn more by doing than by merely listening; significant learning occurs when lectures are followed by action that implements the ideas in the lectures. A manager, for example, who hears a description of Q2 appraisal behavior learns a little, but a manager who tries to deal with Q2 behavior in a simulated situation learns a great deal.

Another behavioral-science principle used extensively in DAT is this: people learn best in supportive settings. If a manager is to improve his appraisal skills, he must experiment, and nobody can be expected to experiment willingly if he fears embarrassment, hostile criticism, or ridicule. In the open, supportive atmosphere of DAT, managers are encouraged to behave in new ways, to loosen up, to become more flexible. They know that their fellow team members, who share in the experimentation, will be open and candid with them, but not destructive. Equally important, they know they can afford to experiment since nothing is at risk. If a manager does a bad job in a role play, he loses nothing but he gains much from the analysis that follows. Few managers, of course, want to "take a chance" on new behavior when something's at stake. In the risk-free environment of DAT, learning flourishes as it seldom can in the real world.

The Purpose of Analysis and Feedback

A wealth of scientific data proves that people learn best when they know what their mistakes are, so they can take action to correct them. A manager who doesn't know he's doing something self-defeating will probably keep on doing it. This is why constant analysis and feedback are integral to DAT. They give managers clear insight into the impact of their behavior on others; with this insight, they can change their behavior with deliberate speed, before ineffective patterns harden.

The *system* of analysis and feedback used in DAT ties in to the Dimensional Model of Appraisal Behavior. Through this system, the model's relevance to real-life situations becomes crystal clear. By using the system repeatedly, the managers improve their observational skills; they learn to put an appraisal under an "interactional microscope," and they learn how to interpret what they see. Before long, they can apply the same system of analysis and feedback to their *own* behavior.

TUESDAY

After hearing a lecture on the Q4 appraisal strategy for Q1 subordinate behavior, each team does its first role-played appraisal, and its first analysis and feedback. The role play involves Q1 subordinate behavior; the "superior" is supposed to use Q4 appraisal skills. After the analysis and feedback, the group reassembles to watch a Q4-Q1 appraisal on TV. This TV scenario demonstrates the "right" way to handle Q1 subordinate behavior.

The same format is followed the rest of the day. Lectures on Q4 strategies (for Q2, then Q3, and finally Q4 subordinate behavior) are followed by role plays in which "superiors" attempt to use those strategies. Each role play is followed by systematic analysis and feedback. Then the whole group watches a demonstration, on TV, of how the Q4 strategy *should* be implemented. In each instance, participants see "models" of the Q4 strategies upon which they can pattern their own behavior.

An important aid in analysis and feedback is video tape. All role plays are taped. The tapes are reviewed by the team before the observers analyze the role play.

The Purpose of Video-Taping Role Plays

In DAT, closed-circuit TV is not a gimmick, but an important aid to learning. Taping simulated situations and then playing them back (using stop-tape and instant replay when needed) *speeds* the development of self-perception and the learning of communication skills. Video tape enhances *objectivity;* it helps people see their behavior as it appears to others. By giving them an "outsider's" view, it shatters misconceptions about themselves that many managers have carried for years. This is a salutary learning experience.

Video tape also improves the quality of analysis and feedback. By seeing each role play twice, once live and once on TV, the observers can check their initial impressions and modify them if necessary.

WEDNESDAY

After hearing a lecture on appraisal planning, the participants begin the Real-Life Appraisal Analysis. This is the point at which the seminar moves from the appraisal process *in general* to the appraisal process as the managers encounter it in their real jobs. In this activity, the team develops strategies for appraising real-life subordinates. The strategies are based on information that each manager recorded as part of his preparatory work for the seminar. After each "model" strategy is developed, it is implemented by the manager, who plays himself, and by another member of the team, who plays the real-life subordinate. Analysis and feedback are rendered by the observers after each presentation.

The Purpose of Real-Life Appraisal Analysis

If learning is to "take," it must be relevant to the learner; it must be significant to him. The Real-Life Appraisal Analysis provides significance. It helps each participant see how Dimensional principles can help him do a better job of appraising one of his people, how DAT concepts can be related to *his* work.

Why does this real-life activity come on the third day of the seminar? Why are the role plays on the first two days fictitious? The reason is that each manager must understand the *interpersonal processes* of appraisal. In order to get managers to think in terms of *process*, DAT begins with fictitious role plays in which the managers aren't much concerned about the factual details (content) of the jobs being appraised. If these early role plays involved a manager's *own* situation, he'd probably get so wrapped up in questions about pricing, quality, production, competition, and so forth that he'd ignore the interpersonal processes. By the third day, participants are almost always ready to focus on *both* process and content.

THURSDAY

The Real-Life Appraisal Analysis continues. After each manager on each team has role-played his model strategy and received feedback on his appraisal behavior, each team begins the culminating activity of the seminar.

Summary Feedback

In the team rooms, each member of each team receives a "summary" description of his behavior from the rest of the team. In Summary Feedback, all of the behavioral impressions that the team has gathered about him during the seminar are fed back to him. Improvement goals designed to sharpen appraisal skills are recommended to each manager by the team, and a plan-of-action for achieving each goal is discussed with him.

The Purpose of Summary Feedback

Summary Feedback gives each participant an overall view of his appraisal behavior *as other people see it*, and an understanding of its impact on others. It makes each manager aware of the strengths and weaknesses he exhibited during the week, and of the changes he needs to make in his appraisal behavior. All of the feedback is about behavior that affects appraisal performance; none is just about personal characteristics not related to appraisal effectiveness. Thus, Summary Feedback gives each manager information he can *use* and *profit* from.

Summary Feedback is based on the premise that self-development occurs most rapidly in people who are self-aware, alert to their strengths, and conscious of their weaknesses. Self-awareness is the springboard to growth. A manager who gets candid and constructive Summary Feedback can, it has been estimated, learn as much about himself as he would ordinarily learn in years of everyday experience.

FRIDAY

The participants finish up Summary Feedback. Then, once again, they fill out the questionnaires they filled out before coming to the seminar, and the two sets of responses (preseminar and postseminar) are compared so that shifts in their attitudes or in their perception of their appraisal behavior resulting from the seminar can be spotted. Only group shifts, not individual shifts, are reported to the group. The questionnaires almost always show that attitudes about how appraisal should be done have shifted toward the Q4 quadrant, and that appraisal behavior is now viewed more objectively and realistically; participants typically leave the seminar not only with *greater* belief in the value of Q4 appraisal behavior, but also with the realization that their own appraisal behavior is *less* Q4 than they had earlier believed.

The last hours of DAT are devoted to goal-setting. Each manager sets goals—to be achieved on the job—that will require using the Q4 skills he has acquired in the program. The emphasis is on setting Q4 goals—goals that meet the criteria set forth in this book. These goals are reviewed by his team, which may suggest modifications. The idea is to build a bridge between the seminar and the real world by making it necessary for the manager to *use* what he's learned.

The Purpose of the Questionnaires

Generally, questionnaires filled out *before* the seminar reveal that managers are somewhat skeptical of the practical worth of Q4 appraisal behavior, but that they nevertheless see themselves largely as Q4 appraisers. Or, put another way, they have an idealized view of themselves but aren't sure that the idealized behavior they attribute to themselves is very useful in appraisals. The same questionnaires filled out at the *conclusion* of the seminar generally reveal that the participants are considerably *more* convinced that Q4 behavior "pays," and they're considerably *less* certain that their own behavior is Q4. In other words, their attitudes about appraisal have changed and, as a result of the intensive feedback they've received, so have their evaluations of themselves. Their idealized self-image has been at least partly replaced by a truer self-image; they now see themselves more as others see them. With their increased acceptance of Q4 attitudes and their more realistic self-perception, they're ready to *continue* improving their appraisal behavior.

The Purpose of Goal-Setting

DAT isn't a mere interlude between two periods of work. It's a prelude to more effective work. By setting goals that can only be achieved on the job, and that can best be achieved by the exercise of Q4 skills, each manager knows that he'll get to utilize what he's learned in the seminar, and that he can look forward to a *payoff* where it really matters: on the job.

THE PRAGMATIC APPROACH

DAT exemplifies what Psychological Associates calls "the pragmatic approach to training." The pragmatic approach says, very simply, that a training program can *only* be justified if it produces *results on the job*. To make sure this happens, a training program should follow a 10-step format. We'll list the 10 steps, then explain how each of them is carried out in DAT:

1. Spell out the appraisal training goals.
2. Provide "cognitive maps" of superior and subordinate behavior.
3. Develop sizing-up skills so superiors can "position" themselves and their subordinates on the cognitive maps.
4. Teach appraisal techniques tailored to the positions observed on the maps.
5. Build in plenty of opportunity to practice the techniques.
6. Give superiors feedback on how they did in the practice session.
7. Set individual goals based on these in-depth analyses.
8. Develop plans of action to achieve these individual goals.
9. Review the results of the plans of action.
10. Do research on the results.

This system is pragmatic in the root sense: it's concerned with results (steps 9 and 10) and with what to do to get those results (steps 1–8). Figure 21 shows how the 10 steps fit together.

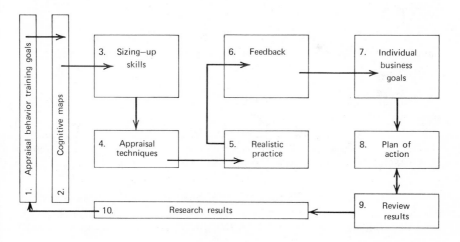

FIGURE 21. The Dimensional System of Appraisal Training.

Let's look closer at each of the ten steps:

Step 1. *Spell out the appraisal training goals*

Starting a training seminar with vague goals is like starting out on a trip to "somewhere in the Middlewest": you'll burn up a lot of fuel and energy going nowhere in particular. The goal of Dimensional Appraisal Training is clear and precise: to help managers develop into Q4 appraisers by mastering the twelve skills listed earlier.

Step 2.   *Provide cognitive maps*

Imagine taking a course on "Discovering Buried Treasure." The first day, the instructor teaches you how to use a compass; the second day, how to use a divining rod; and, the third day, how to use a shovel. Then he pats you on the back and says: "Get out there and put your skills to use." After stumbling around for a few hours, you realize that what you need before anything else is neither a compass nor a divining rod nor a shovel; it's a map! Before you can get started, you need to know what's "out there." What general area is the treasure believed buried in? What's the terrain like? Where are the danger spots—the swamps and ravines and so on? Without an *organized* idea—a map—you have no way of knowing what it's like "out there" or what direction to go in—and you'll probably give up in confusion long before you get near the treasure.

Some training is like that. It teaches skills, techniques, methods. But it never provides a map—a *cognitive map*—an organized, understandable description of the behavioral terrain through which superiors must move.

This situation is easily corrected. In recent years, behavioral scientists have drawn a number of excellent cognitive maps that give managers a realistic picture of the "psychological topography" in which they have to work. And, like all good mapmakers, the behavioral cartographers have charted the "danger spots" that lie in wait, like quicksand, to trap the unsuspecting.

DAT uses four cognitive maps, all of which we've discussed in this book: (1) the Dimensional Model of Superior Appraisal Behavior; (2) the Dimensional Model of Subordinate Appraisal Behavior; (3) the Pyramid of Intangible Needs; and (4) the Self-Discovery Continuum.

To sum up: managers, like searchers for buried treasure, can most readily get from here to there, from where they are to where they want to be, if they know what's between here and there. That's what maps, including cognitive maps, are for. Cognitive maps are a vital part of any training program that's intended to change appraisal behavior.

Step 3.   *Develop sizing-up skills*

Cognitive maps are worthless unless they're used. If they're going to produce results, the information on the maps must be applied—put to work. Superiors must use the concepts to size up themselves, their subordinates, and the relationships between them. A pragmatic training program must teach superiors to answer three related sets of questions: (1) What is my appraisal behavior usually like? What patterns can I discern in the way I appraise performance? (2) What kind of behavior does each of my subordinates usually display in an appraisal? What patterns can I detect in the way they respond to me? (3) Taking each of my subordinates one by one, how do we typically interact? What patterns can I discover in my relationship with each of them? What can I learn from these patterns that will help me get better appraisal results?

These questions "pay off." They're pragmatic. They're concerned with results. Without the sizing-up skills that make it possible to answer these questions, the payoff from appraisal training will probably be low.

DAT doesn't preach the virtues of using cognitive maps to develop sizing-up skills; it lets each manager discover for himself how sizing-up skills can help him. It does this through activities in which managers repeatedly diagnose appraisal behavior. They learn the value of diagnosis by diagnosing. As they do, they acquire new insights into themselves, their subordinates, and the whole business of performance appraisal.

Step 4. *Teach appraisal techniques*

If you are going to become a better appraiser, you need more than sizing-up skills. You need specific appraisal skills that incorporate your diagnosis and then enable you to do something with it. Imagine, for example, that you become very proficient in diagnosis and, putting your proficiency to work, you develop two behavioral portraits, one of your own appraisal behavior and the other of one of your subordinate's appraisal behavior.

SELF-PORTRAIT. I display a lot of Q3 behavior. I put being liked ahead of everything else . . . I waste a lot of time on chit-chat . . . I seldom make a negative evaluation, even if it's deserved . . . I back away from tough subjects . . . I make alibis for my people . . . I'm too quick to agree with them . . . I set easy goals . . . I don't challenge my people to optimal performance. . . . etc.

PORTRAIT OF SUBORDINATE. He displays a lot of Q1 behavior. He considers me a pushover . . . grabs control of every appraisal . . . and tries to keep me off balance. He's quick to pat himself on the back . . . never gives credit to anyone else . . . and refuses to budge from his positions. He uses the appraisal as an opportunity to advertise his own virtues. He's not really interested in acquiring self-insight.

These are examples of sizing-up. But so what? What difference will these portraits make in your future interaction? What impact will they have upon results? The answer is that the portraits won't make *any* difference unless they're coupled with action—the use of *skills*—to improve the interaction. It isn't enough to know why you're not doing a good job of appraising. You must also know what to *do* in order to do a better job.

So, in DAT, many of the activities used to develop sizing-up skills are also used to develop appraisal skills—skills in raising receptivity, demonstrating benefits, generating involvement, gathering information, enhancing understanding, breaking through resistances, handling negative emotions, and so on. We'll see how this is done in Step 5.

Step 5.   *Practice the techniques*

As we've said, people best learn how to do things by doing them. So DAT provides plenty of opportunities for *using* Dimensional skills—for practicing, implementing, applying, experimenting. In DAT, the real teacher is *experience*.

Much of this experience is acquired in role plays. Most of these deal with real-life situations. The role plays have two major purposes.

1.   In each role play, the manager who plays the "superior's" role must size up, on the spot, both his own and his "subordinate's" behavior, and then adapt his own behavior to fit the situation. This gives him a chance to try out new ways of behaving, to experiment with new appraisal techniques. He finds out, for example, maybe for the first time in his life, what it feels like to probe, patiently and tenaciously, until a tight-lipped subordinate "opens up" and starts to communicate. Because most of the role plays are based on real on-the-job situations, the superior does all this in an environment that resembles the real world. This increases the impact of the activity.

2.   Simultaneously, other managers observe the role play and, when it's done, analyze it. Ordinarily, DAT role playing occurs in five-person teams. Two people play the roles while the other three observe. The observers, using the structured Analysis and Feedback format, dissect the appraisal. They take it apart and examine it part by part to see what made it tick. Then they feed back their findings to the "superior." As they do, they not only help the "superior," they sharpen their own sizing-up skills and their understanding of the dynamics of appraisal.

Step 6.   *Give feedback*

We've just described how the observers give feedback to the "superiors" in the role plays. We'll add only one important point: developing feedback in small groups has a *synergistic* effect. It would be possible, of course, to set managers in front of a TV set, by themselves, show them a series of appraisals in which they played roles, and have them analyze their own behavior. But it's doubtful that they'd achieve much insight that way. They'd probably "judge themselves by their intentions" rather than by their actions as seen by others.

In small groups, however, each team member gets the benefits of the others' thinking. Insights rub against one another, viewpoints are weighed against other viewpoints, one interpretation triggers others. The team as a whole is more productive than the sum of its parts, and each manager emerges with broadened perspective and understanding.

More than this, in small-group feedback a superior learns that his way of looking at things isn't the only way, or even the best way. A long-winded superior who starts each appraisal with three or four anecdotes and then observes another superior doing exactly the same thing in a role play may evaluate this as "a great way to begin an appraisal." He will then be startled to hear teammates evaluate it as a "real waste of time." For the first time, he may realize that there are other and better ways to start an appraisal, a realization that might never have dawned without synergistic, small-group feedback.

Step 7. *Set individual goals*

Ultimately, each manager must ask himself: What do I do with all the insight I've acquired in the program? How do I bridge the gulf between the snug world of the appraisal seminar and the rough, demanding world outside? The answer is: set goals to be attained in the real organizational world—goals that require using the skills I've acquired in the program. Here's how DAT helps managers build this bridge:

1. Each manager works up a Real-Life Appraisal Strategy, a set of plans for appraising a real-life subordinate. Using a structured format, he evaluates everything he knows about the subordinate and works out a set of tactics for deploying Q4 skills in an authentic situation. These "model" strategies are role-played in the seminar. All of them are intended to be used—successfully—in the real situation.

2. Toward the end of the program, each team gives each of its members *Summary Feedback*, a complete, candid view of each manager's appraisal strengths and weaknesses as observed during the seminar. This gives each manager a frank, rounded view of his appraisal behavior as seen by a group of fellow managers who have had plenty of opportunities to observe him at close range.

3. In addition to Summary Feedback, the team gives each member recommendations for improving his appraisal effectiveness. Each manager gets to "see himself as others see him." The question now becomes: What is he going to do about it?

4. The answer: He's going to set some hard-headed improvement goals—goals he can achieve only by changing his appraisal behavior. Thus, each manager will leave the seminar with clear-cut improvement objectives, and clear-cut plans of action for achieving them.

Step 8. *Develop action plans*

We've already described how DAT does this, but we haven't talked about how important it is. The point cannot be overstressed: goals, *by themselves*, aren't worth much. All of us set many goals (New Year's resolutions are a good example) that we never achieve—not because there's anything wrong with the goals, but because we don't have a plan for achieving them. A good appraisal training program should culminate not merely in goal-setting, but in action-planning. Without concrete procedures for attaining the goals, goal-setting doesn't make much sense.

Step 9. *Review*

Plans of action should never be carved in stone. A plan of action is tentative, subject to revision in the light of subsequent experience. A good plan of action is like a good hypothesis in science; it represents your best current thinking, designed to be tested out. In appraisal, as in science, the empirical approach, the willingness to be guided by practical experience, pays off.

So, in Dimensional Appraisal Training, the plan of action may be changed or improved as experience dictates. This is pragmatic: it recognizes that means and ends are inseparable, but that, in the last analysis, the ends govern the means. It's the final payoff that counts.

Step 10. *Do research*

Since the final payoff is what counts, it's critically important to know what the final payoff is. If pragmatism is both a concern for results and a concern for the process by which the results are achieved, then pragmatism demands that the results of appraisal training be studied so that improvements in the training process can be made. Psychological Associates helps those organizations that want to verify the results of DAT to set up post-seminar monitoring systems by which the impact of DAT can be measured.

Bibliography

Readers who want to know more about the behavioral science concepts on which Dimensional Appraisal Training is based will find the following books and articles well worth their while:

Allen, Louis A., *The Management Profession*, New York: McGraw-Hill, 1964.

Argyris, C., *Personality and Organization*, New York: Harper & Row, 1957.

Bales, R. F., *Personality and Interpersonal Behavior*, New York: Holt, Rinehardt, & Winston, 1970.

Barnard, C., *Functions of the Executive*, Cambridge, Mass.: Harvard University Press, 1968.

Bennis, W., *Changing Organizations*, New York: McGraw-Hill, 1966.

Drucker, P., *Managing for Results*, New York: Harper & Row, 1964.

Etzioni, Amitai, *Modern Organizations*, Englewood Cliffs, N.J.: Prentice-Hall, 1964.

Festinger, L., *A Theory of Cognitive Dissonance*, Palo Alto, Calif.: Stanford University Press, 1957.

Haire, M., *Psychology in Management*, New York: McGraw-Hill, 1964.

Herzberg, F., B. Mausner, and B. Snydeman, *The Motivation to Work*, New York: John Wiley, 1959.

Hughes, Charles L., *Goal Setting*, New York: American Management Association, 1965.

Keefe, William F., *Listen, Management*, New York: McGraw-Hill, 1971.

Leary, T., *Interpersonal Diagnosis of Personality*, New York: Ronald Press, 1957.

Leavitt, H. J., *Managerial Psychology*, Chicago: University of Chicago Press, 1958.

Likert, R., *New Patterns of Management*, New York: McGraw-Hill, 1961.

Likert, R., *The Human Organization*, New York: McGraw-Hill, 1970.

Mager, Robert F., and P. Pipe, *Analyzing Performance Problems*, Belmont, Calif.: Lear Siegler/Fearon, 1970.

Maslow, A. H., *Motivation and Personality*, New York: Harper & Row, 1954.

Maslow, A. H., *Eupsychian Management*, Homewood, Ill.: Dorsey Press, 1965.

McClelland, D. C., J. W. Atkinson, R. A. Clark, E. L. Lowell, *The Achievement Motive*, New York: Appleton-Century-Crofts, 1953.

McClelland, D. C., J. W. Atkinson, R. A. Clark, and E. L. Lowell, *The Achieving Society*, Princeton, N.J.: Van Nostrand, 1961.

344   Effective Motivation Through Performance Appraisal

McGregor, D., *The Human Side of Enterprise*, New York: McGraw-Hill, 1960.
McGregor, D., *The Professional Manager*, New York: McGraw-Hill, 1967.
Morrisey, George L., *Appraisal and Development Through Objectives and Results*, Reading, Mass.: Addison-Wesley, 1972.
Murray, Henry, *Exploration in Personality*, New York: Oxford Press, 1938.
Odiorne, George S., *Management by Objectives*, New York: Pitman Publishing, 1965.
Schien, E. H., *Organizational Psychology*, Englewood Cliffs, N.J.: Prentice-Hall, 1965.
Tannenbaum, R., I. R. Weschler, and F. Massorik, *Leadership and Organization: A Behavioral Science Approach*, New York: McGraw-Hill, 1961.
Whyte, W., *Money and Motivation*, New York: Harper, Hayser and Row, 1955.
Whyte, W. H., *The Organization Man*, New York: Simon and Schuster, 1956.
Zaleznik, A. and D. Moment, *The Dynamics of Interpersonal Behavior*, New York: John Wiley, 1964.

Index